THOMAS H. COOK, a native of Fort Payne, Alabama, has won extensive critical acclaim for his eight novels, including two Edgar Award nominations for *Blood Innocents* and *Sacrificial Ground*. He lives in New York.

W9-AAD-070

EARLY GRAVES

GRAVES

The Shocking True-Crime Story of
the Youngest Woman Ever Sentenced
to Death Row

Thomas H. Cook

AN ONYX BOOK

ONYX
Published by the Penguin Group
Penguin Books USA Inc., 375 Hudson Street,
New York, New York 10014, U.S.A.
Penguin Books Ltd, 27 Wrights Lane,
London W8 5TZ, England
Penguin Books Australia Ltd, Ringwood,
Victoria, Australia
Penguin Books Canada Ltd, 10 Alcorn Avenue,
Toronto, Ontario, Canada M4V 3B2
Penguin Books (N.Z.) Ltd, 182–190 Wairau Road,
Auckland 10, New Zealand

Penguin Books Ltd, Registered Offices:
Harmondsworth, Middlesex, England

Published by Onyx, an imprint of New American Library,
a division of Penguin Books USA Inc. Originally published in a Dutton edition.

First Signet Printing, June, 1992
10 9 8 7 6 5 4 3 2 1

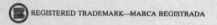

Printed in the United States of America

AUTHOR'S NOTE:
In the interest of protecting the privacy of the individuals whose identities are
not central to the true story told here, certain names and other descriptive
details have been altered in several instances.

For Timothy Seldes and Miriam Altshuler
Love, Honor, and Obey

and for

Kenneth Kines, and his son, Seth

Acknowledgments

Early Graves could not have been written without the generous cooperation of a great number of people. At the very beginning of my research, John Siler, Cathy Drake, and Brown Keyes were instrumental in setting up my interviews with Alvin Neelley. But they were only the first of a large number of public officials who selflessly gave of their time. I would particularly like to thank Kenneth Kines, who devoted many hours to assisting me, but also David Burkhalter, Elaine Snow, Mike Jones, Mike Ragland, Lonnie Adcock, and Ralph Bishop, of the Rome Police Department, Jim Carver and Sam House of the Georgia Bureau of Investigation, Linda Adair and Ken Dooley of the Rome Youth Development Center, Craig Fowler of the Georgia Department of Family and Children's Services, Sue Hitchcock of the Open Door Home, District Attorney Ralph Van Pelt and Investigator John Bass of the Chattooga County District Attorney's Office, Linda Allen of the Macon Youth Development Center, Harold Richards, Gary Wright, Cecil Reed, Jackie Tanner, and Charles Houston of the Dekalb County Sheriff's Department, District Attorney Richard Igou, Assistant District Attorney Michael O'Dell, and Investigators Danny Smith and Darrell Collins of the Dekalb County District Attorney's Office, Court Bailiff Mary MacPherson, and Jimmy Lindsey and the staff of the Dekalb County Clerk's Office, Judge Randall Cole and his assistant, Lisa Hall, John Kilbourn and Rodger Morisson of the Alabama Crime Laboratory, and Joe Blackwell and Wade Hill of the Fort Payne Fire Department.

In addition to these public officials, many private citizens assisted me in my investigation. Of particular importance were John and Donna Hancock, Debbie Kines, Fay Freeman, Dennis Benefield, Claire and Dallas Dougherty, Lillian Ritter, Virgil Cook, Dr. Jean Jones and Dr. John Steiner of the Ethel Harpst Home, Britt Miller, Ben Farrington, and George Westmoreland.

Two other people deserve special mention. Mickie Strickland gave invaluable assistance both as a research assistant and as a sounding board for ideas about the case. Hers was a steadily helpful presence in the writing of this book. I cannot thank her enough. And last, it should be noted that my mother, Mickie Cook, continued over a period of many years to remind me of the case. Once I began to work on it, she assisted me in a number of critical ways. This book could not have been written without her care and attention, and for that I offer her my most profound appreciation.

A Note on the Book

During the many months of research into the lives and crimes of Alvin and Judith Neelley, I had occasion to interview scores of individuals. Differing accounts of certain events inevitably emerged. When accounts have been in conflict, I have presented the ones that seemed to me the most plausible from my own knowledge of the people and events connected to the case. In addition, police summations of lengthy and often repetitious interrogations are notoriously condensed, hours of testimony reduced to a few short pages. In recounting such interrogations, I have tried to use the actual language of the participants on those occasions when it has been available to me, as in tape recordings, for example. Otherwise, I have attempted to recreate the actual nature of the interrogation as it has been described to me by people who were actually present. In other cases, I have combined numerous interrogations into one so as to avoid repetition and for the benefit of the narrative form. Courtroom testimony rivals police interrogations for repetitiousness and the accumulation of irrelevant detail. Wherever possible, I have edited courtroom presentations, whether as witness testimony or attorney arguments, in such a way as to preserve both the trial's relevant information and its undeniably dramatic tone.

The Convergence
of the Twain

HE WAS BORN on July 15, 1953, in Trion, Georgia, a small village in the mountainous northwestern corner of the state, a region of pine forests and green wooded slopes that seem to swirl one around the other. He was the youngest of three children, and there was something so cute about him that his older brother and sister petted him continually, laughing and joking with him as they played games in the yard of their small, white-shingled house. From the very beginning, charm was his forte. He was a jokester, a prankster. All his life, he had a smiling face.

She was born on June 7, 1964, in Murfreesboro, Tennessee, a dingy little town of seedy trailer parks and honky-tonks about ninety miles south of Nashville, just near enough to give off a sense of drying up and turning brown under the heady lights of the Country Music Capital. Local iconography consisted of Jesus nailed to the cross or Elvis painted on velvet. There were plenty of twanging guitars, but they were played by country-music has-beens or never-weres in the steamy red-neck bars. It was an easy town to make jokes about, and as she would later discover, he had a million of them.

*   *   *

Everyone thought he was great, particularly his mother. It was that smile of his. When he flashed it, his whole face lit up. There was just something about him, the watery blue eyes and pink, roly-poly body, that made everyone grin.

All the kids in the neighborhood loved to play with him. One day they even played a little golf when the kids next door brought out their father's putters and knocked the balls around. There were hills to climb and swimming holes and creeks to swim in. It was a great childhood, filled with days of hunting and fishing and hanging out with the other Boy Scouts in Troop 101. He learned to say the Pledge of Allegiance, to honor God and country, to build a fire, to tie knots. His childhood was a festival of joy. He would never complain about a single day of it.

Her mother worked as a housewife, her father as a construction worker and carpenter. She saw her mother all the time, but her father was often busy, so that she did not see him as often as she would have liked.

She had a sister, Dottie, and a brother, James, whom everyone called Jimbo. They were both older than she. And then there were Bill and Davey, her two younger brothers.

They lived in the section of Murfreesboro known as Walter Hill. They had a garden and trees to climb. They were not rich, but they were not poor either, and none of the children ever lacked for food and clothing. It was not a bad childhood. She would never claim that she had been deprived.

His first school was Fort McHenry Elementary, and from the very beginning he was the class clown. He loved to tell jokes and rib the teachers. And once, when one of them asked him a question he couldn't answer, he broke the other kids up when he told her that if he'd already known the answer, he wouldn't have been in school in the first place.

It was the girls he liked to rib the most, and often, during recess, he'd go down to the pond and bring back a few baby frogs to scare them with. They'd scream wildly when he came up suddenly and stuck one of the frogs in their faces. It made him laugh and laugh.

Like all the other children in her neighborhood, she attended the Walter Hill School from 8:30 to 2:45, then played throughout the remainder of the afternoon. It might have gone on like that forever. It was even getting better for a while. Her father had started his own construction company in 1973. He was making good money, between two hundred fifty and three hundred dollars a week. Sometimes he drank a little, and most of the time he seemed far away, but he never said harsh things or lifted his hand against her. The drinking didn't really matter, she loved him anyway.

When he was in the fifth grade, one of the teachers slapped his behind for hanging out the window and he went tumbling to the ground. The kids laughed hysterically, and he played it to the hilt. A few weeks later, feeling his oats, he talked back to the principal, which landed him in trouble, but only for a while.

The Christmas of 1973 was the one she would always remember. Her sister Dottie got a little pink Cinderella watch. Bill got an orange bicycle and Jimbo got a little Honda motorcycle.

As for her, she sat quietly and watched the other children tear open their presents. Then her father came over, sat down on the floor with her, and helped her open her presents. One was a little blond-headed doll with a pink polka-dot body. The doll talked when the string behind its head was pulled. The box said its name was Drowsey. She never changed the name. She also got a "Tote-a-Tune," a little red keyboard with a strap around it. It used batteries and came with a book of songs. It made her laugh when her father showed her how to play it because his hands were too big and his fingers wouldn't fit the keys.

As the years passed, these two toys became her most precious possessions, the only things she ever owned with which she would not part.

In seventh grade, he started picking up girls and taking them to the pool. Other people had a tendency to show up, too, once they heard that he was there. It got so the pool owner would let him in free just so the other people would show up and pay the entrance charge. A funny guy, a prankster, someone with a great sense of humor, always attracted a large, admiring crowd.

One Saturday night in March of 1974, when she was nine years old, her father mounted a motorcycle and headed down the road. He'd been drinking, and he made a mistake, perhaps no more than a tiny miscalculation, but enough to slam him into the highway guardrail. He rode it for a hundred feet before it spun into the air and hurled him to the pavement. When they told her he was dead, she could hardly believe it. She had always been the quiet one, but for a long time after that, she seemed to turn to stone.

PART

ONE

UNKNOWN
VOICES

CHAPTER
1

City of Seven Hills

YEARS LATER, REMEMBERING it all again, Ken Dooley would find it hard to believe that so much horror could begin so mundanely, with no more dramatic fanfare than the ringing of his phone.

He answered it immediately, glanced at the clock, and unconsciously recorded the time: 7:00 P.M.

"Hello."

The voice at the other end did not alarm him. It was a female voice, calm, precise, without a hint of nervousness, nothing to make him in the least suspicious.

"Is this Ken Dooley's house?"

"Yes, it is."

"My name's Susan. I'm a friend of Cherie, your wife. From way back. When she lived in Kentucky."

Dooley nodded dully, glanced about the dining room, his mind more on finishing the dinner he'd just made for himself than on the voice still holding him on the line.

"I'm going to be passing through Rome," the woman said, "and I wanted to stop by and see Cherie."

"Okay, that's fine," Dooley said.

"How do you get to your house?"

Dooley gave precise directions. "Well, once you get to Rome, get on Maple Street and come to Lindale, to

3

the Daither Park Diner and take a right. After you take a right, we're the third brick house on the left."

Dooley waited for the woman to answer, and when she didn't, he decided to make absolutely sure that she couldn't miss his house. "There'll be a red Volkswagen in the driveway," he told her matter-of-factly. "And a green and white Buick, too."

The woman seemed satisfied that he had told her enough. "Okay," she said. "Well, you tell Cherie that I'll see her when we get to Rome."

"Okay," Dooley answered. Then he hung up, finished his dinner, and stretched out in the den.

For the next few hours Dooley remained home alone. His wife and son were at the Rome Little Theater where Robby had been scheduled to audition for a part in one of the theater's upcoming productions. But the solitude didn't bother him. He needed the rest and relaxation. It had been a long day at the YDC, Rome's Youth Development Center, where he taught the female juvenile offenders who'd been placed there. He liked some of them, joked with and counseled them. But there were others he didn't care for at all. They were hard, cold, calculating, with as many different personalities as they needed to survive. He'd been around long enough to understand how important it was to know who you were dealing with at the YDC, because the one thing all the girls had in common was that in the end they'd be on the streets again, free to do the good or evil that was already in their hearts.

Cherie and Robby returned home at around nine in the evening. Robby was tired from the long day's activities and trudged directly down the hallway to his room. Cherie sat down on the sofa in the den, and Ken stirred himself enough to ask how Robby had done at the audition. Outside he could hear the early-September winds as they rustled through the trees and shrubbery that formed a ragged, easily penetrable wall between his house and the street.

4

"By the way," he said after a moment, "you got a call tonight."

"Who from?"

Ken glanced outside. It was very dark except for the small area of grayish light that swam out from the den's large, well-lighted window. "Some friend of yours from Kentucky," he said. "She said she was coming through Rome and she wanted to stop and visit."

"What was her name?"

"Susan."

Cherie Dooley looked at her husband quizzically. "Susan?"

"Yeah."

"That's strange."

Ken's eyes drifted toward his wife. "What is?"

Cherie shrugged lightly. "What she told you."

"What's strange about it?"

His wife's answer was not enough to nudge Ken Dooley from the night's deepening peacefulness. "I don't have a friend from Kentucky named Susan," she said.

In the South, as in the rest of America, September is a busy month. With the summer at an end, schools reopen, and the resulting shift in schedules inevitably throws the general pace of life into a higher gear. In Rome, football season had already begun, and on Friday nights, the rural roads of the surrounding counties were dotted with bright yellow school buses on their way to and from the scores of regional intramural games. On the night of September 10, Ken Dooley traveled to Bremen, Georgia, with the team he coached and Robby managed. For the next few hours he rooted loudly from the rickety wooden stands while his team fought for every inch of the one-hundred-yard field. At the end of the game he was exhausted, and the long bus ride home, with the team shouting and laughing behind him, hardly served to ease the strain that had been steadily accumulating all day. It was a plea-

sure finally to reach his own house, and he smiled at
the prospect of a hot shower followed by a long, deep
sleep.

Cherie met him at the door. "You got a call tonight," she said.

"Who from?" Dooley asked as he walked past her
and made his way into the den, where he slouched
down on the sofa by the window.

Cherie stood at the entrance to the den, her shoulder against its wooden frame. "I don't know who it
was," she told him.

Dooley drew in a long, weary breath. "They didn't
say?"

"It was a girl, that's all I know."

Dooley thought of the YDC, the many girls he
knew there. It was not uncommon for one of them to
call him. "Well, what'd she want?" he asked.

"Just to know if you were home."

Dooley's eyes shifted over to his wife, suddenly
struck by the oddity of the question. "To know if I
was home?" he asked. "When was this?"

"Around nine," Cherie said. "I told her you weren't
here but that you'd be in later. I think it was probably
one of the people from the Center."

Dooley nodded. "Could be."

"Anyway, she said she'd call you back."

Dooley looked at his watch. It was nearly eleven.
"And she called just that one time?"

Cherie nodded.

"Okay," Dooley said with a shrug. For a time he
remained on the sofa, then he got up and headed
down the hallway to his bedroom to prepare for bed.
Far away, in the distant bedroom, he could hear the
phone as it rang suddenly, then his wife's voice as she
answered it.

"It's for you," she called to him.

Dooley headed for the dining room.

"It's that girl again," his wife whispered as she
handed him the receiver.

6

Dooley took the phone. "Hello."

There was a moment of silence, then, to his surprise, he heard a male rather than a female voice.

"You've screwed the last girl you're going to screw," the man told him coldly. "And you're going to pay."

Dooley was thunderstruck. He had never heard a voice so threatening. "Who the hell is this?" he demanded.

The man hung up immediately, leaving Dooley standing motionlessly in his dining room, half-dazed by the threat.

"Who was it?" his wife asked as she came back into the room.

"I don't know," Dooley told her. He returned the phone to its cradle, then headed back to the bedroom.

As he prepared for bed, Dooley continued to think about the voice, how hard it was, how threatening. He talked about it to his wife, then decided to get it off his mind by checking his closet to see if there was anything he might want to add to the various items Cherie had gathered together for the yard sale she was having the next day. On the way to the bedroom he looked in on his children. Both eleven-year-old Robby and three-year-old Carrie were sleeping soundly. Everything seemed normal, so he walked on down the hall to the bedroom and opened the closet.

The sounds came quickly, four of them, loud pops that at first seemed like nothing more than a flurry of backfiring from the street. Then he heard his wife screaming to him that someone was shooting into the house.

He plunged down the corridor, through the dining room at the far end of the house, where he met Cherie, who was running toward him. He scrambled past her, hurled through the den and out the far end of the house. The front yard was completely silent. He glanced right and left, trying to make out any movement in the chilly darkness. Finally, he looked toward the road. Far down the street, he could see the red taillights of a speeding car. For an instant he thought of following it, but the car disappeared almost immediately. There was nothing to do but return to the house and call the police.

After making the call, Dooley walked through the house to check for damage. In the den he could see where two bullets had entered the house. One had come through the wall and hit the tan wicker shade of the swag lamp that hung above the sofa. A second shot had also come through the wall, then veered left and slammed into the bottom of the door. Two others had hit the roof above the window of the den, and later, as he stood outside, staring back toward the house, he realized that the gunman had been deadly serious, that he'd fired at the only lighted window in the house.

Patrolman Ray Logan of the Floyd County Police Department arrived a few minutes later. He gathered what evidence he could, then wrote up complaint number 82-09-00381.

"I'm sorry this happened to you," he told Dooley before leaving. "And I wish we had more to go on." But there were no witnesses, no identification of the car or its drivers, only two voices and a pair of taillights that had flickered briefly, then disappeared. "If I were you," Logan added darkly, "I wouldn't sleep at home tonight."

But Dooley did remain at home that night. His children were still sleeping soundly, as they had through all of the events of the evening, and he decided not to wake them. Instead he simply returned to his bedroom and lay down, aware, as he remained all through the night, of the loaded pistol that rested on his closet shelf only a few feet away. It seemed like his best friend.

The next morning at the Rome YDC, Dooley told his supervisor about the incident. The supervisor listened carefully, then asked him to keep the whole matter under wraps, since such an event might frighten other people at the Center. Dooley did as he was asked. Throughout the day, he didn't tell any of his students, or any of the staff, even the assistant director of the Youth Development Center itself, a tall blond woman whose name was Linda Adair.

CHAPTER
2

Fire in the Night

ON SATURDAY, SEPTEMBER 11, 1982, the day following the shooting at Ken Dooley's house, Linda Adair returned home after shopping and dinner with her husband. Her daughter was to be married the following week, and she and her husband Gary, an investigator for the Floyd County fire marshal, had dinner at the Country Gentleman, a steak house on north U.S. Highway 27, and then, at around seven in the evening, headed for the Riverbend Mall, still gathering the necessary paraphernalia for the upcoming wedding.

They returned home at around ten in the evening, and Adair noticed that Brent, her neighbor's enormous Saint Bernard, was still curled up on her back steps. For the last three days the dog had remained more or less in place, looking very somber and refusing to go home. Normally Brent would greet Linda as she came home, barking and leaping about the carport enthusiastically until she got inside. Then he would invariably head back across the backyard to his owner's house next door. Lately, however, he'd refused even to get up as she approached. She'd even had to step over him to get inside her house. It was very odd for him, and she'd been wondering if the dog was all right. She bent down and petted him gently.

"How you doing, Brent?"

The dog did not move, and after a moment she stepped over him and went inside.

Once inside the house, Linda took a bath and put on a nightgown and housecoat.

Her husband was still fully dressed, watching television in the den, when she came into the room and stretched out on the part of the sectional sofa that she thought of as hers.

Gary was about to take his usual place on the other side of the sofa when the phone in the kitchen suddenly rang. He looked at her, but Linda was already too comfortable. She waved her hand. "No, you get it," she said. "I'm all stretched out here. I don't want to get up."

The phone rang again and Gary walked into the kitchen to answer it.

From the den, her eyes closed wearily, Linda could hear him in the other room.

"Hello."

"Sure. Hold on just a minute."

Linda continued to lie on the sofa as her husband, tugging the long cord behind him, brought the receiver to her.

"It's for you," he said.

"Who is it?"

Gary shook his head and Linda took the phone.

"Hello," she said.

There was a slight pause. She could hear other sounds coming through the line, slightly metallic, like a television playing in the background.

"Hello," she repeated. "Hello."

Silence.

Gary still remained over her. "Who is it?"

She handed him back the phone. "I don't know," she said. She looked at him quizzically. "No one said anything?"

Gary shook his head. "Just asked if you were home."

"Was it a man or a woman?"

"It sounded like a young girl," Gary told her.

Linda shrugged. "Well, I guess they didn't want to talk," she said as her husband headed back toward the kitchen.

A few minutes later, at around 11:30, Linda got up from the sofa and headed for the kitchen. She could hear the shower running in the bathroom where Gary was preparing for bed. Tomorrow was Sunday, and she needed to put a roast on for their dinner. She prepared the meat, then turned off the kitchen light and headed through the den toward her bedroom. She'd almost reached the hallway at the other side of the den when the phone rang again. She turned and started back toward the kitchen. The phone rang again, and as it did she could also hear something beating frantically at her back door. For an instant she seemed suspended between those two urgently demanding sounds, and in that instant her eyes shot toward the dining-room window and she saw a high wall of yellow flame enveloping the front of her carport. Her eyes swept toward the back door, and through its dark glass she could see the face of a young boy, still beating at the door. The phone rang again and automatically, in a kind of disbelieving daze, she answered it. A woman was screaming at her, "Linda! What's happening! Somebody just threw a bomb at your house!"

It was Susan, her next-door neighbor, and Linda instantly looked back at the fire. She could hear Brent snarling angrily somewhere beyond the flames, along with the sound of the boy at the door and the steady hiss of Gary's shower. She rushed to the corridor and yelled to him, "Gary! Gary! Get out of the house! Somebody's trying to burn it down!"

Clutching at his robe, Gary rushed from the bathroom, then the two of them ran back through the house and out into the yard. For a moment they simply stood together, Linda, Gary, the next-door neighbor who'd rushed over to help, the young boy who'd beaten wildly at her back door . . . and Brent, who,

Linda noticed, had begun to huddle very closely at her feet.

The police arrived immediately and began their investigation. Susan told them that she'd heard Brent snarling loudly and had then looked out her window in time to see a car hurriedly backing out of the Adairs' driveway.

"Brent was following the car," she told the officers. "He was jumping up on it and biting at it." It had backed out to the left, she added, then someone had hurled the bomb.

The young boy had been driving home from having dropped off his date for that Saturday night. He'd seen the bomb explode just as a car whizzed past him, speeding in the opposite direction. It was a brown car, with white or silver stripes that ran from the rear end to the front and which he thought might be an early-seventies Dodge Demon. There'd been two people inside, a man and a woman. He had been able to get a brief glimpse of them in the instant the two cars had met. The man had been in the passenger seat. The woman was behind the wheel. As his lights had swept over her, he'd been able to see that she was white and that she had long, reddish hair.

While the questioning continued on the front lawn, other officers processed the scene, working the physical evidence. It was obvious from the beginning that the bomb itself was a crude contraption, as simple as they came, consisting of a Nu Grape soda bottle, gasoline, and what appeared to be, in its smoldering remnants, a bathroom cloth of some kind. It had landed a few feet from the carport and to the right of Gary Adair's official state car, far enough from both to explode, burn a moment, then gutter out without setting fire to anything else.

As the night wore on, Linda and Gary were both interrogated. Several of the officers knew that Gary was an arson inspector for the fire marshal. They asked him about any ongoing investigations. Gary told them he had been working on a case in Cave Springs, a small town only a few miles from Rome. A motel had been set afire, and on the day he'd arrived to investigate for arson, an informant had told him the motel itself was being used as a house of prostitution. According to the informant, that was the reason someone had tried to burn it down. The owner of the motel, Gary remembered now, was a woman.

The police then turned their attention to Linda as she stood in her bathrobe, shivering in the chilly fall air. She told them she had no idea who might have done such a thing. She was not aware of having any enemies either in her private or professional lives. She had not recently had any kind of argument with anyone, and as far as she knew she was well liked by the people with whom she worked at the YDC.

The investigators asked about anything she might have seen during the last few days that seemed suspicious. She was unable to think of anything that might have alarmed her. There were no suspicious phone calls, no suspicious cars or pedestrians. She had not noticed anyone following her. She had not received any threatening mail.

She was still answering their questions when the phone rang again inside her house. She went in to answer it.

"Hello?"

"Linda?"

It was a female voice, but Linda didn't recognize it. "Yes, this is Linda," she said.

"I'm calling about the shooting at Ken Dooley's house last night and—"

"What shooting?" Linda asked. She had seen Ken Dooley several times during the day, but he hadn't mentioned anything about a shooting. "What are you talking about?"

The woman did not seem to hear her. She simply

went on without pausing in a voice that struck Linda
as very calm, strangely cold.

"—the attempted firebombing of your house tonight
and—"

Linda Adair felt her whole body stiffen as the woman's voice suddenly quickened, as if the caller had
suddenly gotten a burst of energy, something that sent
her rushing ahead, the words coming very rapidly like
shots from an automatic.

"—and you both will die before the night's over."

Linda stood motionlessly in her kitchen, utterly
stunned. Then suddenly she felt her body begin to
shake and heard her voice blurt out a desperate demand. "Who is this?" she cried. "Who is this?"

The woman hung up immediately, but for an instant
Linda continued to press her lips toward the receiver.
"Who is this?"

There was no answer, and so she dropped the phone
and ran back into the yard, trembling uncontrollably
as she spoke to the investigators.

"That call just now," she said, barely believing it
herself. "That was a threat on my life!"

The men looked at her in disbelief. "A threat?" one
of them said. "From who?"

"It was a woman," Linda said.

The men pressed in toward her, firing questions.
"What did she say?"

For the next few minutes Linda struggled to recall
the exact words the caller had used. Then the long line
of questions began again: Where do you work? What
do you do there? How long have you worked there?
Have you fired anyone recently? Do you know of any
disgruntled employees? Has anyone left the Center
recently who might have hated you? Do you know of
anyone who might want you dead? Who do you fear?
Who do you think might try to kill you?

After a moment the questioning abruptly took another turn. "What do you know about Ken Dooley?"

"He works at the Center," Linda answered. "What happened to him last night?"

"Somebody shot into his house," one of the officers told her. "Four times."

Linda walked back into the house and phoned Dooley immediately. "They say somebody shot into your house last night," she said.

Dooley, standing once again in his dining room, his eyes moving reflexively toward the den where the bullets had slammed through the wall and into the swag light and the door, could not imagine how Linda had found out. "That's right," he told her. "I wasn't supposed to tell anybody. They were afraid it would get people upset at the Center."

"Well, somebody firebombed my house tonight."

Dooley could hardly believe his ears. "Firebombed?"

"Just a few minutes ago," Linda said. "And somebody called here. They asked me about the shooting at your house, and . . . and that we were both going to die. That we might die tonight!"

Dooley shook his head uncomprehendingly. "Linda, what could this be about? Who could these people be?"

"I don't know," Linda said weakly. "I just don't know."

They talked a moment longer, then Linda returned to the front lawn as another police car pulled into her driveway. Two officers got out; one of them was carrying a tape recorder.

"We got something we want you to listen to," he said to her. "It's a call that just came into the county police department. Officer Brock took it at 1:41 A.M."

Then he played it.

OPERATOR BROCK: County Police, Brock.

CALLER: Ah, yes, I'm calling in reference to the . . . uh, uh . . . shooting at Ken Dooley's house on Old Lindale Road last night.

BROCK: Uh-huh.

16

CALLER: And the firebombing of Linda Adair's house tonight.

BROCK: Yes.

CALLER: Uh, for the sex abuse that I went through in the YDC.

BROCK: Okay, what kind of abuse did you take?

CALLER: Sex abuse. And for the abuse I took, they are both going to die. And who knows? It might be tonight.

BROCK: Who is this calling?

At that point the caller hung up.

Linda listened carefully to the tape, first once, then again. "It sounds a lot like the woman who called me," she said.

"All right," one of the officers told her. "I'd like for you and Dooley to come down to police headquarters tomorrow morning at 9:00 A.M. Both of you need to listen to this."

Linda nodded. "Okay," she said.

Within a few minutes the officers were gone. As the last one left, Linda noticed Brent resting calmly on the front lawn. He'd always been a somewhat excitable animal, but she realized that during all the past few hours, while various investigators had come and gone, he had remained entirely calm, as if he'd been able to sense that they'd been called to do her good.

CHAPTER
3

Boney and Claude

THEY WERE ON the road again, this time headed south, toward Macon. It had been a wild few days. Several months before, someone had called them Bonnie and Clyde, but they'd agreed that they were more like a comedy version of that infamous couple. Later, they'd even come up with a new name for themselves, "Boney and Claude." But now, after all they'd done in Rome, they were coming close to the real thing. Shootings, firebombings. That was one way to show people you weren't joking anymore.

But there were other ways, too, and on the way to Macon they hatched a few new plans. In prison he'd been told that if you gave people certain kinds of shots, the cops wouldn't be able to tell they'd been murdered, so they stopped at a drugstore and picked up a few diabetic needles and a bottle of Liquid Drano and Liquid Plumr.

Once on the road again, he kept his eyes on her brown Dodge as it cruised along in front of him. He liked his own car best, a red Ford Granada that he kept nice and neat. That was one of the differences between them. She was sloppy and unkempt, and her car always looked that way. That was one of the reasons he didn't want to drive with her anymore. The other was the way she acted, nice at times, then cold, mean. It was as if she would say things just to tick him off. Then the air would suddenly get sharp, and the whole world would start to ache. Traveling separately, and yet together, was one way to keep the pain at bay. It was better to have two cars and just talk to each other over the Cobra CB radios they had installed in each of them.

Once in Macon, they stayed in another crummy little motel, the kind that smelled dank, as if there were pools of stagnant water under the floor. There were times when they hated it, but when that happened, they just moved on. That seemed to help a little, as if the movement, the endless heading down endless roads, was the only thing that relieved the tension that grew around them when they stopped. The road cut them some slack, but only for a while, only until they stopped again at the next motel, another one that looked the same, felt the same, had the same crummy furniture and dank wet smell.

During their first couple of days in Macon, they came up with lots of great ideas, but finally agreed on just one to start with. He sat on the bed next to her when she dialed the phone. When Mrs. Allen answered, she told her that her husband was beating her up and that she needed help. Then she asked Mrs. Allen if she would meet her at her motel. Mrs. Allen said she would drop by the next day at around 5:30. The couple laughed together about how easy it was going to be.

But Mrs. Allen was just the beginning, so the next day they rode around Macon looking for John Brownlee's house, one of the security people from the Macon YDC. There was a plan to deal with him, too, but that would come later, after they'd finished with Mrs. Allen.

Then, suddenly, there was a hitch. At around five in the afternoon, someone from the YDC called to say that Mrs. Allen had had to go out of town and would not be able to come to the motel.

They suspected Mrs. Allen had lied, and so the next day they drove out to the YDC office and spotted Allen's car. She'd not been called out of town at all. They shook their heads at what liars other people were.

Since Mrs. Allen had slipped by, they decided to go after Brownlee instead. They drove and drove, chattering incessantly on the CB until they found Brownlee's house. Then they drove back to the motel and she called Brownlee up. She'd always known he had an eye for her, and so she spoke to him flirtatiously, using her hot-little-country-girl act. She wanted to meet him, she said, then she reminded him he'd once told her that if she were ever in town, he wanted to see her.

But Brownlee couldn't meet her because he'd gotten married only a few months before. Maybe some other time, he told her, if he could bring along his wife.

After she hung up, they discussed a plan to drop her off at Brownlee's house when no one was at home. She could go through the window and let her husband in. Together they could wait for the Brownlees to get home, then he could knock Brownlee out, wait until he came to, and rape his wife in front of him. He could do that to all the wives of the men at the YDC. Every one of them who had done bad things to his wife. Now he could do bad things to their wives. Rape and kill them. That would show them it was really payback time.

It was a good idea, they agreed, but in the end it never got off the ground, so they started riding around again, talking, talking, talking. They looked for Mrs. Green and Mrs. Shoemaker and other YDC employees, but they couldn't find any of them.

After a few days it was clear that things weren't panning out in Macon. Everything was going wrong.

The other people kept slipping away from them just when they had them in their grasp. They'd had better luck in Rome. Maybe it was time to go back.

It was now late September 1982, and on the way to Rome, the feeling of being together came back over them. They talked on the CB and laughed again. She sang her version of the lyrics in the telephone-company commercial they'd seen on television. They loved to sing it together. It made them laugh to hear the words coming over the CB as they barreled down the road. The laughter reminded them of what it had once been like between them, so they sang the lyrics with a terrible desperation: "Reach out and snatch someone."

CHAPTER
4

"Where Is Lisa Ann?"

SHE WAS A small, frail-looking little girl with long dark hair and she'd just left the Magic Market, a small convenience store that served the neighborhood. She was only a few blocks away from it when she saw a large woman approach her.

"Are you Phyllis?" the woman asked.

The little girl shook her head.

"How old are you?"

"I'm thirteen."

"Do you want to go for a ride?"

"No."

"I could take you anywhere."

The little girl shook her head again. "No, I'm just on my way home."

The woman said nothing else, and the little girl from the Magic Market walked safely home.

A short time later a young blond-haired girl made her way toward the Red Diamond Food Store in west Rome. To her right, she could see the line of dingy motels that fronted both sides of Martha Berry Boulevard in that part of the city, bleak, one-night-stand affairs that usually had pickup trucks or late-model cars standing in their parking lots. One of them was the Oak Hurst, and even its tall vertical sign looked as if it needed to be washed.

She walked steadily until she reached the newspaper vending machine at the front of the store. She carefully put in the required amount of change, then took out the newspaper and headed back across the parking lot.

"Are you Phyllis?"

The girl glanced over and saw a woman approaching her. She was dressed in a white T-shirt with a Confederate battle flag stenciled over it and the word "Forever" written across the flag.

"Are you Phyllis?"

"No, that's not my name."

"What is your name?"

"Dorothy."

For a moment they silently faced each other, then the blond-haired girl excused herself and hurried away.

That same afternoon two cars pulled onto Martha Berry Boulevard from the rough, gravel parking area of the Oak Hurst Motel. They made their way north, then swung onto Shorter Avenue, where they continued to cruise northward until the long stretch of squat brick malls and fast-food joints dwindled away at the far end of the city. At that point they turned around and headed south again, down Shorter Avenue, past the Alto Shopping Center on the left and the Thornwood School on the right, to where Shorter turned into Turner-McCall Boulevard as it continued into the more affluent section of west Rome and its central shopping center, the Riverbend Mall.

By the fall of 1982, the Riverbend Mall had already been the major shopping area of west Rome for ten years. It faced Turner-McCall Boulevard, one of the city's busiest streets, and had a Belks Department Store, a J. C. Penney's, and a Morrison's Cafeteria, along with a scattering of less well known enterprises such as the King and Queen Styling Salon and, next to it, at the glass-enclosed front entrance to the mall itself, a video arcade whose bright red, illuminated sign read ALADDIN'S CASTLE.

The arcade had been opened the same day as the mall. It was a large, rectangular room that held between forty and forty-five video games and pinball machines. The floor was covered with a low-pile yellow carpet that seemed even brighter under the glaring ceiling lights. The noise at times was deafening, but that never seemed to bother the scores of young children and teenagers who hung around the arcade, especially on a Saturday afternoon.

On that particular Saturday afternoon, Suzanne Clonts had already been at the mall for several hours. She was nineteen years old and had been married for three months. She'd come to the mall with her husband to do some shopping. They'd finished by around five in the afternoon and had stopped at the arcade for a few games before leaving. David, Suzanne's husband, liked to play Tron, and for a time she'd stood and watched him play, growing increasingly bored as the minutes passed. As her eyes began to wander from the screen, she could see another couple only a few feet away. The man was playing Frogger while the woman stood by, watching. For a few seconds her eyes lingered on the other couple, then, suddenly, the other woman's eyes swept over to her, held a moment, then returned to the game.

David Clonts continued to play at Aladdin's, but after a while Suzanne got tired of watching him. She wasn't very good at video games, and still had one unused token in her hand when she decided to step away from her husband and out into the center of the game room. Even from that position, she was still overwhelmed by the loud clattering of the machines, but at least she could look out into the mall itself. It was busy that afternoon, and for a few minutes she

idly watched as the crowds moved in and out of its
large glass doors.

For a time her mind wandered to the activities of
the last month. It had been very busy. Her husband
had just had his birthday on September 14, and she
would have her own, her twentieth, on the twenty-
eighth. For a few minutes she thought of her in-laws.
They'd just returned from a trip to the Bahamas, and
Suzanne and her husband planned to visit them as
soon as they left the mall.

As the minutes passed, she continued to stand alone,
then suddenly she heard a voice that seemed to be
directed toward her.

"Are you Kim?"

Suzanne turned and saw a woman staring at her. It
was the same one she'd seen a moment before. She
was dressed in a white T-shirt with a large Confederate flag emblazoned on the front and a pair of faded
blue jeans. She looked dirty and unkempt, as if she
hadn't bathed in a long time. She didn't have on any
makeup, not even a faint blush or a line of lipstick to
brighten the washed-out pallor of her face. Her long
reddish brown hair hung in tangles to her shoulders,
and Suzanne noticed immediately that she wasn't wearing a bra. She looked like the kind of girl who could
often be seen walking along the grimy streets of Lindale
and Clemondsville, the kind that came from the wrong
side of the tracks.

"Are you Kim?" the woman asked.

Suzanne shook her head. "No, my name's Suzanne."

"I thought you were Kim."

"No."

"Are you from around here?"

"I'm from Armuchee."

"Really?" the woman said. "I live in Armuchee,
too."

"You do? Where?"

The woman looked puzzled.

"Well, Armuchee's a very small place," Suzanne reminded her.

The woman said nothing.

Suzanne tried to help her. "Do you live anywhere around Max's Trailer Park?"

"No," the woman said, as if she'd never heard of it. Then she changed the subject quickly. "Are you alone?" she asked.

"No. I'm with my husband."

"I was just passing through and I called a friend of mine to meet me here at the mall, but she hasn't come by yet."

Suzanne did not reply and the woman stared at her silently for a moment, the conversation simply fizzling out.

Then suddenly the woman blurted, "Well, I guess I'll let you go on and play a game."

Suzanne nodded, then watched as the woman walked back into the arcade. She could see the same large, heavyset man she'd seen before. He was dressed in a white T-shirt, too, but he kept his back to her, and she couldn't tell whether it also bore the same stars and bars across its front. She expected the woman to return to him, but she didn't, and so he remained alone, still playing his game. He was very large, even bigger than the football players she saw on television. He stood in the far left-hand corner of the room, in a wedge of darkness that seemed to creep away from the overall brightness of the room. The only thing she could tell for sure about him was that he was still playing Frogger, a high-speed video game in which the player tries to get an animated frog to the top of the screen without letting it get crushed by a speeding car.

David finished playing his last game of Tron a few minutes later and he and Suzanne went to their car. She felt strange, eerie, and she knew that it was the woman who'd made her feel that way. She'd looked so odd that Suzanne, a born-again Christian, had felt that she should have "witnessed" to her before they parted, told her about her own experience with Jesus Christ. As they drove toward David's parents' house, the large sign of the Riverbend Mall growing small in the distance, she told him about the woman and about what she'd sensed about her. She felt guilty for not having followed her sudden religious impulse, she said, maybe she could have helped. David didn't think so. He soothed her, told her not to worry, assured her that everything would be all right.

Suzanne hoped that he was right, but something continued to trouble her, something about the woman. She didn't look beaten up or abused in any way, but neither did she look like an ordinary, healthy human being, and as she continued to think about it, she realized that during all their conversation, despite the friendliness in the woman's voice, she had never smiled.

At approximately 6:00 P.M., a van arrived in the parking area of the mall. It had come from the Ethel Harpst Home, a facility for neglected girls located about twenty miles away in the village of Cedartown. Six girls piled out of the van, along with their substitute house parent, Gail Henderson, and proceeded into the mall. Once inside, Henderson took the youngest of the girls with her, then told the other five to stay together while shopping. They were to regroup an hour later in front of the Radio Shack.

At the end of that hour one of the girls failed to return. Her name was Lisa Ann Millican.

Henderson asked the girls about her and they answered that Lisa had gotten separated from them. They'd tried to find her, but hadn't been able to. The group waited for Lisa awhile longer, then Henderson ordered them to divide into teams of two and look for her throughout the mall. Twenty minutes later the teams drifted back to the front of the Radio Shack, and as each one came down the wide corridor, Henderson's eyes searched frantically for Lisa. When all the girls had returned without her, she called mall security. Several officers searched the mall once again, but without success.

"I think you'd better call the police," one of them told Henderson.

She did, and within a few minutes Rome police officers made a third search of the mall. When they couldn't find Lisa, they told Henderson to call the Harpst Home and ask if perhaps she'd returned there. Henderson called and was told that Lisa had not returned. She was also told to return to the home with the other girls and to leave the rest to the police.

Rome police then began to extend their search beyond the narrow confines of the Riverbend Mall. An official missing persons' bulletin was dispatched to all officers. They were to be on the lookout for a thirteen-year-old girl named Lisa Ann Millican, a white female, dressed in blue jeans and a white checkered blouse. She was approximately five feet five inches tall, with brown hair cut in a shag.

Along the rural byways south of Rome, two cars moved steadily farther from the city. There was still enough light in the early-autumn sky to glint off the two chrome CB radio antennas that swung lazily as each car glided by.

By nightfall they had reached Franklin, Georgia. It was a Saturday night, and the entire town was gearing up for the Franklin Country Music Park, a weekly spectacular that drew the biggest names in country music—Alabama, the Oak Ridge Boys, and other headliners. It had become a major attraction in the area, drawing people from several neighboring counties, along with large numbers from Atlanta. They were lucky to find a place that still had its vacancy sign shining in the dark.

In the office of the Chattahoochee Motel, Claire Dougherty continued with her work. It would be a busy night, and she didn't expect to close the office until nearly midnight. Several people had already checked in, and the people in Room 3 needed towels and soap. She gathered them together and headed down the walkway toward the far end of the motel. She could see a large man as he stood at the back of the car. He was one of the ones who'd checked in earlier, along with a woman and a young girl. As she came closer, she saw him lift an enormous cooler from the back of the car. He was a big man, very big, and there was something about him that made her feel strange.

As night deepened over the streets of the city, Rome patrolmen continued to glance from their patrol cars in the hope of glimpsing a thirteen-year-old girl, a white female with short dark hair, dressed in blue jeans and a checkered blouse. From long experience, they knew that she might appear to be lost, but that on approach, she might try to avoid them. They knew that if questioned, she might say that she was simply on her way home, but that she would stumble when asked where that home was. They knew that she might give a false name, a false birthday, that for the first few moments of their encounter, everything she told them might well be a lie.

At the Chattahoochee Motel, Claire continued to work with her husband, Dallas. As they worked, they could see the man in Room 3 come out again, as he had been doing periodically for the last few hours. He headed down the long line of rooms to the Coke and snack machines at the opposite end of the walkway, only a few feet from the office. He was naked to the waist, his large belly hanging in a round ball over the top of his jeans. The Doughertys had been in the motel business for a long time, and they knew people well. This one struck them as the "shack-up" type, the sort who only dropped by for a quick screw and would probably be gone before morning. The man definitely had that look, they agreed, as they watched him amble slowly down the cement walkway and finally disappear into the small snack room. They could hear him going at the machines again.

"He ought to stay off those snacks," Claire said. "He's big enough already."

Her husband nodded, his eyes on the man again as he slowly made his way back to the room. Definitely the shack-up type, he thought. He'd seen that kind before, and this one fit the profile exactly. The only thing that didn't fit was the little girl.

Several hours later, at around eleven in the evening, Claire Dougherty saw a woman and girl come out of Room 3. They walked across the parking lot to the motel office. The girl walked beside the woman, slowly, relaxed. The woman reminded Claire of someone she'd known in South Carolina. "She looks just like Cindy," she told her husband, who remained in their living quarters just next to the office.

"We want to get something to eat," the woman told Claire after she came into the office. "Is there any place open?"

"Open?" Claire asked. "At eleven at night? Not in Franklin, Georgia."

"Well, where could we get something?"

"I don't know of any place you could get food except out of the machines we have here at the motel."

The woman seemed satisfied. She started to leave.

"We're about to close," Claire told her. "Are you going to need anything else?"

The woman turned toward her. "No, ma'am," she said. Then she turned and left the office, the little girl walking close at her side.

As they walked away, Claire Dougherty got the strange feeling again. Dallas had gotten it earlier, too. It was nothing he could put his finger on, just a strange feeling that he sometimes had about people, that there was something wrong with them. These people had certainly given it to him, though, and he'd even found that he'd felt somewhat relieved when he realized that it was the night of the Franklin Music Park. That would mean that the motel would be full, and because of that, if anything weird began to happen in Room 3, he would be sure to hear about it.

But Dallas Dougherty did not hear anything at all during that night, and by the following morning the people in Room 3 were gone. At around 10:00 A.M. he went to the room with the maid so that it could be made ready for the next customer. When he opened the door, he found the floor and tables and chest of drawers littered with candy wrappers and soda cans. That was not unusual, of course. But one thing was. There'd been three of them in the room the whole night, but only one bed needed to be made up. The other one hadn't been used at all. Dallas Dougherty turned to the maid. "Well, that guy must have had a good time last night," he said. Then he thought again, this time of the little girl.

Two days later, on the morning of September 28, 1982, Passotam Patel, owner of the Five Points Motel in Scottsboro, Alabama, opened Room 12. For the last forty-eight hours, it had been occupied by a large man, a woman, a girl, and two small children, a boy and a girl who looked about two years old. The room was filled with empty soda cans, food bags, and boxes from nearby fast-food joints along with an assortment of candy and cookie wrappers. There were two beds in the room. But only one of them had been used.

CHAPTER
5

"Where I Left Her"

WATCH COMMANDER LONNIE Adcock had just walked past the communications center at the Rome police headquarters when he saw Sergeant Wilson motioning to him frantically.

"Can you watch the radio for me," Wilson said. "I need to go to the bathroom."

Adcock hesitated. "Oh, I don't know, buddy. Every time I take your place at that radio, I get into trouble."

"Oh, come on," Wilson pleaded. "I'll be right back."

Adcock smiled, then motioned Wilson out of his chair. "Okay," he said.

Wilson headed quickly down the short corridor that led to the bathroom, and Adcock dropped into the seat in front of the radio. A call came in immediately, then another and another.

Adcock glanced at the clock. It was 12:56 P.M., Tuesday, September 28, 1982.

The phone rang and Adcock answered it with the usual response.

"Adcock, City Police."

The voice at the other end was female.

"Uh, yes, y'all looking for Lisa Ann Millican on run from the Harpst Home?"

The voice was soft, and Adcock had trouble hearing it. "Lisa Ann who?"

"Millican," the woman answered, a little sharply. "I can tell you where she is."

Adcock listened carefully. "Where's she at?"

The woman answered him calmly, giving her directions with a matter-of-fact precision.

"Go up to Little River Canyon in Alabama," she said. "Just as you cross the Little River Canyon Bridge, turn to the left, go up into the national park. You'll see on the left some, uh, picnic tables, and a big rock parking area, and look off the side of the canyon—where there is a . . . uh . . . power line going across it, and look straight down the canyon, and you'll find her where I left her."

Adcock started to ask another question, but the woman immediately hung up.

For a moment he sat at his desk, rethinking the call. He had received hundreds of crank calls since joining the Rome PD in 1959, and this didn't sound like one. He replayed the tape that was automatically made of all incoming calls, listened carefully, then played it again. There was something about the call that seemed serious. He turned to Betty Minshew, another radio operator in the room.

"You know, Betty," he said, "this just doesn't sound like a crank to me." Then he glanced out the large glass window of the communications room and saw Captain Mike Ragland as he made his way down the corridor. He called to him immediately and Ragland joined him in the room.

"I want you to listen to something," Adcock told him. "This just came in a minute ago."

Ragland listened carefully as Adcock played the tape.

"It sounds real to me," Adcock repeated.

Ragland nodded. "It could be some runaway trying to get some attention." He listened to the tape again. "You hear all that noise in the background?" he asked.

"Lots of traffic. You can even hear big trucks passing by."

"Yeah," Adcock said. "She must have been calling from a booth that's pretty near the street."

"A pretty busy street, too," Ragland said. Rome had relatively few such streets, and he decided that with a little luck and some fast action, they might actually be able to find her. "Come with me," he said to Adcock.

The two men walked out to the police parking area behind headquarters and got into a patrol car. They turned left on the road that fronted headquarters, then right onto North Second Street. At Shorter Avenue, the city's busiest thoroughfare, Ragland swung left again, heading north toward the foothills of Alabama.

They had been driving down Shorter only two or three minutes when they spotted a young girl as she stood talking on an outdoor phone near the street just in front of the Alto Shopping Center. She was wearing a pink shirt, blue jeans, and dirty tennis shoes.

"Well, look at that," Ragland said.

He guided the patrol car up to the telephone and the two men got out.

The girl was still talking when they reached her. They waited until she'd hung up.

"Where were you calling?" Ragland asked.

"Alabama."

"Is your name Lisa?"

"Yeah."

Ragland could hardly believe it. "Lisa Millican?"

The girl shook her head. "No, Lisa Miller."

"Lisa Miller," Ragland repeated doubtfully. "You're not Lisa Ann Millican?"

"No."

"Did you call Rome police a few minutes ago?"

"No."

Ragland didn't believe her. "I think you'd better come on down to headquarters with us," he said. "We need to find out for sure who you are."

The girl went with them willingly, riding silently in the backseat.

Once back at headquarters, Ragland contacted Cathy Fortner. Fortner told him that Lisa Ann Millican had been placed at the Open Door Home on Leon Street for the thirty days before she was finally sent to the Harpst Home in Cedartown. Debra Ann Medaris, the director of the Open Door, would be able to tell him if the girl he'd picked up on Shorter Avenue was Lisa Ann.

Within a few minutes Ragland, Fortner, and the unidentified girl were on their way down Shorter Avenue once again, heading north toward Leon Street.

As he drove, Ragland continued to question the young girl who still sat silently in the backseat.

"How come you're not in school?" he asked.

The girl shrugged and said nothing.

"What were you doing at the phone booth then?"

"I was waiting for my aunt," the girl said.

"What for?"

"I was waiting for her to pick me up."

"You live with your aunt?"

"No, but that's what I want to do."

"Where does your aunt live?"

"Monroe."

The questioning continued as the patrol car once again passed the Alto Shopping Center.

"Why didn't you register to go to school in Rome?" Ragland asked.

Once again the girl shrugged. "I just didn't."

"What grade are you in?"

"Eighth."

"Where'd you go to school?"

"Last time I went, it was to Garden Lakes."

"Who were you talking to when I came over to the phone booth?"

"Marty."

"Who's that?"

"Just a boy," the girl replied.

Once they arrived at the Open Door, Ragland got out, leaving Fortner and the girl in the car.

Fortner glanced toward the backseat and noticed that the girl had become nervous, that she was biting fiercely at her nails.

"Do you know Lisa Millican?" she asked.

The girl shook her head.

Fortner turned back toward the Open Door. A black woman was standing next to Ragland now, both of them staring toward the little girl in the patrol car.

A minute or so later, Ragland came back to the car.

"There's nobody here who can identify Lisa Millican," he said. Then he turned back to the girl. "Does your mother live in Rome?"

The girl nodded. "On Jones Street," she said.

After verifying that Lisa Miller did in fact live with her mother on Jones Street, Ragland and Fortner returned to headquarters. Ragland asked Fortner to copy the original call on a cassette, then he called authorities in Walker County to see if the other Lisa, Lisa Millican, had turned up. She hadn't. He called the Harpst Home and asked the same question. Lisa, authorities at the home told him, was still missing.

Once the cassette tape had been made, Ragland listened to it again. He still suspected that it was a runaway who wanted to draw some attention to herself, but he could not be sure. He listened to the tape again, then again. Still, he could not be sure. He decided that it had to be checked out, that there might really be a little girl lying somewhere at the bottom of Little River Canyon.

Eddie Wright of the Dekalb County Sheriff's Department was on the third floor of the County Courthouse in Fort Payne, Alabama, when he was notified that a call had come in from the Rome Police Department. The caller was a woman, they'd said, and she'd told the Rome police that a girl's body could be found at a particular place along Little River Canyon.

It was not the first such call in Wright's experience. Most of them turned up as cranks, but all of them had to be checked out. He decided to take Alabama State Trooper Gerald Taylor with him, since few people ever liked going to the canyon alone.

The road that leads up the mountainside from the valley town of Fort Payne and finally intersects with Little River Canyon is a steep, winding, and treacherous one, which skirts for several miles along the sheer precipice of the mountainside. Here and there along the route, the metal guardrail has been bent or broken through by cars that have slammed into it during the road's long and deadly history. For decades it has functioned as a daredevil alleyway for local high-school boys, one with sudden dips and turns that only the steadiest of drivers can negotiate at high speeds. At the bottom, a concrete wall four feet thick has been constructed to stop the huge trucks that periodically barrel down the road, their brakes sheared away by the downward momentum, until the wall rises to stop them with a terrible finality. To the locals, the wall has long been humorously referred to as Joe's Truck Stop.

But all lightheartedness dies away as the canyon approaches. It is a deep, granite gorge that moves like a gigantic scar across the plateau of Lookout Mountain. Even in bright sunlight, the canyon floor is often shrouded in deep shadows. Its immense gray walls tower over a narrow stretch of falls and white-water rapids whose currents have long been regarded with a kind of mystical ominousness by the few people who have managed to reach its whirling banks. The canyon has generated many diabolical tales. It is said to be a favorite haunt of satanists who carry out their demonic rites on the canyon floor, of murderers hiding the evidence of their crimes, of solitary lunatics and hermits who periodically stumble onto the paths of those few isolated campers, hikers, and spelunkers who are either unaware of the canyon's local reputation or remain courageous enough to ignore it.

Eddie Wright had never ventured into the canyon, and never intended to. He was mildly acrophobic, and as he drove up the mountain road he talked quietly to Taylor about the mundane details of law enforcement, his mind far away from the canyon edges he had no wish to approach.

At the top of the mountain the two men continued along Highway 35 until they neared the bridge that crossed the canyon itself. Then they made a hard right, according to the directions that had been given to them by the Rome police, and headed down the road until they came to a spot where a series of power lines cut through the surrounding landscape and crossed the road at a place known locally as Rocky Glade.

Wright pulled the car off the road. He could see a small picnic area between the road and the edge of the canyon, and he and Taylor moved toward it slowly.

"That canyon's deep at this spot," Wright said as they came nearer to the edge.

Taylor nodded. "Sure is."

"Got to be careful not to fall off this thing," Wright added, almost to himself.

The two men slowed even more as they came toward the edge of the dark, granite outcrop that stretched out beyond the canyon wall. Neither intended to go too close to the very rim of the wall. Instead they walked as close to the edge as they could, then leaned backward and peered down toward where the distant river ran in a slender, white-speckled ribbon along the canyon bottom.

"You see anything?" Wright asked after a moment.

Taylor shook his head.

They looked out again, but saw nothing but the shadowy depths of the canyon itself and the bare gray limbs of the trees that covered its dark floor.

At almost the same time Danny Smith, an investigator for the local district attorney's office was heading along the Adamsburg Road. His job at the moment was to take Bert Latham, the district attorney from neighboring Cherokee County, home. While the two men talked, they listened to the police radio in Smith's car. They could hear the activity that had suddenly resulted from the call from Rome.

They listened closely for a moment, growing more and more interested. Finally Latham spoke. "Maybe we ought to go by and take a look at this, Danny."

Smith nodded. "Fine with me," he said.

Smith continued down Adamsburg Road until he reached Canyon Rim Road. As he drove he tried to remember the directions he'd heard in the original dispatch. According to them, he would need to go to Little River Canyon, then move around the canyon to where a group of power lines crossed the road.

After a while, still moving along Canyon Rim Road, they found a place that seemed to fit the description. There were power lines and there were picnic tables.

Smith pulled the car over and he and Latham walked to the edge of the canyon and peered out. Only a short distance away Wright and Taylor were doing exactly the same thing, and with the same result.

"Just a crank, I guess," Smith said as they returned to the car and headed once again toward Cherokee County.

Moments later, Dekalb County officials called the Rome Police Department. They had good news. There was no body in the canyon.

Rome was glad to hear it, although it meant that a problem yet remained for them. Lisa Millican was still missing, and that was bad enough. But now the problem had been compounded. Someone had given them a false clue.

A second clue arrived almost immediately. But this time it did not come to the police.

Jenny West, News Director of WRGA Radio in Rome, was working at her desk when the phone rang.

The woman who spoke to her was direct and to the point.

"I have a news tip for you," she said. "Lisa Millican, that girl that ran away from the Harpst Home on Friday? She's been killed and the Rome police are covering it up."

The woman was speaking rapidly, and West scribbled frantically across a piece of paper in order to get it all down.

"Harps Home?" she asked. "Is that spelled H-A-R-P-S?"

"Yeah," the woman answered crisply, "Harpst Home in Rome. She was killed by a female juvenile officer. She's in Little River Canyon."

West continued to write frantically as she listened. "Where's Little River Canyon?"

"In Alabama," the woman answered. Then she started to reel off the directions, but she was speaking too quickly for West to get them down.

"Whoa! Whoa! Whoa!" West blurted. "How was she killed?"

"Shot," the woman said. "She was shot by a female juvenile officer from the Harpst Home this morning. She was at the Little River Canyon and she's still there."

"What's your name?" West asked quickly.

"I'm not going to tell you," the woman replied.

West quickly glanced at the clock. It was 1:25 P.M. She went over her scrawled notes, studying the details carefully. A few words stood out. "Killed" was one of them. The others were "covering it up." It seemed like a tip worth checking out.

West arrived at Rome police headquarters a few minutes later. She walked into the dayroom, a large open area crowded with metal desks. She was well known to the detectives who were scattered about the room, and none of them thought it particularly unusual for her to be there.

"Hey, guys," she said, "I just got this call over at

the station. Somebody said the Rome PD is trying to cover up a murder."

Mike Ragland was the first to respond. "What are you talking about, Jenny?" he demanded.

West produced the notes she'd taken during the call and showed them to the detectives.

They were not impressed. They told her that they'd gotten the same information, and that they'd already relayed it to the authorities in Dekalb County. Officers in Alabama had been dispatched to the location given in the caller's directions, but nothing had been found.

West pursued the point, one question at a time. Was anyone missing from the Harpst Home?

Yes, the detectives told her. A girl named Lisa Ann Millican had disappeared Saturday afternoon while on an outing to the Riverbend Mall. But they'd checked out the people at the home, and the girl herself was considered a likely candidate for running away. She hadn't been happy there, had wanted to return to her family in Lafayette. She was most likely on her way there now, although she had not made it back yet or been seen by anyone since her disappearance.

"So there's no murder?" West asked finally. "Nothing to cover up?"

The detectives shook their heads. Absolutely not.

But just to put the matter to rest, they told West that they'd telephone the Dekalb County Sheriff's Department once again, tell the authorities there that a second call had been made, this one to a Rome radio station, and that the caller had accused the police of knowingly concealing the whereabouts of a murdered girl.

That should get them going in Alabama, the detectives reasoned, all but laughing to themselves as they made the call.

It was almost twenty-four hours before the laughter stopped. Then, suddenly, on Wednesday, September

29, at around 5:30 P.M., Jackie Tanner, a dispatcher for the Dekalb County Sheriff's Office in Fort Payne, Alabama, answered an incoming call.

"Sheriff's Office."

The voice he heard at the other end was a woman's.

"Have ya'll found a body in the canyon?"

"No," Tanner said, "I haven't gotten a report on it."

Instantly she hung up.

Tanner called to the night chief and asked if anyone had found a body in the canyon. No one had, and Tanner resumed his duties, routinely taking calls and dispatching officers.

At around 6:15 P.M. the woman called again. Tanner listened carefully as she spoke to him.

"If you'll go out to the canyon to where the power lines go across and look off," she said, "you'll find a body with a bullet in it."

Again, before Tanner could ask another question, she hung up.

Tanner called to James Mays, a deputy with the Dekalb County Sheriff's Department, and as he was describing the call, the telephone rang a third time. Mays decided to take the call himself.

"Sheriff's Department."

The voice at the other end was female.

"If you want to know where a young girl's body is at," the woman said, "I'll tell you."

"Where's it at?" Mays asked.

The woman then responded by giving Mays a series of very precise directions. But Mays had trouble getting them all and asked her to repeat them.

She obliged, speaking very calmly as she repeated the directions. "If you'll go to Leesburg," she told him, "go up the mountain on 35. When you get to Little River Canyon, to County Road 176, turn left. Go approximately a mile. Under the power lines down there, you'll find a young girl's body where I left her at."

Then she hung up.

Mays turned to the other men in the room. There were several of them, a varied group of men who'd gathered from across the county to have a meeting of the County Lawmen ball team that evening.

"Somebody says there's a body in the canyon," Mays said. "It's already getting dark. If we're going to check on it, we better do it now."

Then Mays headed for a car. Three other men went with him, Chief Newman Slaton from the Ider Police Department, Robert Trottman from the Henagar Police Department, and Chuck Nelson, another Dekalb deputy, all members of the County Lawmen softball team, and only one of them, Nelson, in uniform.

All together in one car, the four men made their way toward the canyon. On the way up, Mays could hear nearby radio transmissions from State Trooper Tommy Brock. Mays radioed him a 10-20, requesting that he join the other men at the designated area.

As Mays's car turned left onto Highway 35, Brock fell in behind them in his own patrol car, and within a few minutes both cars pulled into the unpaved parking area of Rocky Glade.

It was after seven in the evening by then and already growing dark. For a few minutes the five men searched about the area along the lip of the canyon. Then they decided to look off into it as well. For a time they stood as near the edge as possible, staring off into the canyon as Wright and Taylor had done the day before.

The floor of the canyon was growing dark, and after a moment the men got down on their stomachs, dragged themselves to the very edge of the canyon, then dropped their heads forward to stare directly down upon the canyon floor. Seeing was difficult in the growing twilight, so Brock retrieved a flashlight from his patrol car, the only light the five men had.

Once again on his stomach, Brock, his head in midair out over the granite ledge of the canyon wall,

aimed his flashlight down toward the canyon floor.
The air beneath him had taken on a hazy, milky blue
tint. It was hard to see through it, so he moved the
flashlight delicately, allowing its dull, yellowish beam
to cut through the canyon's steadily darkening air. It
passed over a pair of jeans hanging from a limb, then
down toward the canyon floor itself, across its loose
scattering of dead limbs and brown autumn leaves.
Slowly it filtered through the nearly leafless bramble
until it drifted onto a tiny square of cloth that looked
like the soiled remnants of a white checkered blouse.
For a time the men on the canyon rim thought it might
be a department-store mannequin that someone had
thrown over the cliff, but as they lingered at the edge
of the canyon, staring at the motionless figure that lay
facedown some eighty feet below them on the canyon
floor, they could see a dark red stain that swam up
from just above the top of the blue jeans and spread
out over the back of the blouse. "Then we knew," one
of them would say many years later, "that it was a
human being."

CHAPTER
6

"To Feel Like a Father"

ONCE THE BODY was discovered, one of the officers walked back to the radio car and called for assistance.

Eddie Wright had already picked up radio transmissions about a "cargo" in the canyon, and he arrived at Rocky Glade almost immediately. He was followed by other officers from the Fort Payne Police Department, the Dekalb County Sheriff's Department, along with Danny Smith and Darrell Collins from the district attorney's office. Working together, the men began stringing floodlights and roping off the area, securing the crime scene so that it could be carefully processed the next day.

It was now 7:30 P.M. and there were approximately ten to fifteen men on the brow of the canyon, staring off into it while they worked, their eyes sometimes drifting over toward the single shaft of yellow light that continued to connect them to the body down below.

Within minutes, Eddie Freeman and Glenn Leath, members of the Fort Payne Fire Department's rappeling team, also arrived on the scene. Wright gave them careful instructions. First, they were to check the body immediately in the faint hope that it might still be alive. If not, they were to return to the top of the cliff.

45

They were to touch absolutely nothing, neither the dead body itself, beyond what was necessary to make that determination, nor anything in the area around it.

Once Wright had finished his instructions, the two men tied a rope to a pine tree approximately thirty feet from the edge of the canyon, got into their rappeling gear, and dropped over the rim of the canyon wall, literally disappearing into the engulfing darkness as they swung beneath its granite edge.

Once he reached the bottom of the canyon, Freeman unfastened the rappeling gear and headed toward the body. It had come to rest over a fallen tree and appeared almost broken in half by it. The face was pressed into the ground, the back slightly hunched over the trunk of the tree, the arms dangling from the sides. For a moment Freeman couldn't tell if the body was male or female. Then he noticed that the fingernails had been painted. He stooped down, felt for a pulse, then alerted the people waiting on the canyon rim that there would be no need to send down emergency medical equipment, that the body was that of a little girl, and that she was dead.

By the time the two firemen had made their way out of the canyon, night had fallen over the Appalachian foothills of northern Alabama. In the canyon, the darkness was nearly impenetrable, and so it was decided that the body could not be brought up or the area around it processed as a crime scene until the following morning. A few minutes later a light connected to a portable generator on the canyon rim was lowered into the canyon. It would shine all night, illuminating the body and the area immediately surrounding it.

At approximately 9:30 P.M., Dennis Weaver, a seventeen-month recruit with the Dekalb County Sheriff's Department, was given the unenviable assignment of remaining with the body itself, alone on the canyon floor. Throughout the night he stood his station while other officers kept watch from the granite cliffs above.

The light shone brightly in the area around the body, but after a time the eeriness of the nightbound canyon, all its odd, indecipherable sounds, began to wear on Weaver's nerves. One in particular bothered him, the sound of something large moving through the brush. He listened carefully, but was unable to determine what it was. After a while he alerted the men above him that something or someone perhaps as big as himself was stalking through the darkness around the murder scene. Then he asked that one additional item be lowered down to him. None of the officers who remained at the top of the canyon hesitated to send Weaver what he needed to complete his vigil: an AR-15 fully automatic rifle.

By eight o'clock the following morning, September 30, 1982, the area of Rocky Glade bustled with activity. Official cars lined the narrow roadway while as many as thirty people spread out along the brow of the canyon. Police officials from Fort Payne, Dekalb County, and Rome, Georgia, mingled with a mixed bag of firemen, Alabama state troopers, agents from the Alabama Bureau of Investigation, and investigators from the local district attorney's office. The atmosphere was very tense. Many of the officers suspected that all the preceding events might be setup—a murder, followed by a determined series of phone calls—that seemed perfectly designed to lure large numbers of law enforcement agents to a single location. The apprehension among some of the officers was so great that when Fort Payne Water Commissioner Pete Little pulled up to the scene, his car backfiring, he got out to find himself staring at scores of grim-faced police officers, their hands already reaching for their guns.

The tension had not noticeably eased approximately an hour later when officials from Alabama's Department of Forensic Science arrived from Huntsville. Firemen had already strung a rope handrail down a nearby slope, and they used it as they made their way along the tricky, circuitous route that descended into the canyon.

Danny Smith was there by then, processing the scene for the district attorney's office. While the people from forensics concentrated on the body, he paced around it in ever-widening circles, looking for anything that might prove valuable to the investigation. It was not easy to sort things out, because the canyon was routinely used as a makeshift dump site, its bottom slopes often littered with debris. Still, even under those conditions, a few things stood out, and he gave them his particular attention.

High in the air, he saw a pair of blue jeans hanging from a slender limb. They hung almost at their full length, the right leg slung over the limb at a point near the knee. For a moment his eyes concentrated on the jeans, moving up them slowly until he reached the place where they doubled over the limb. At that point, it seemed to him, he could make out a faint red stain. He carefully aimed his camera, photographed them, and moved on. Not far away from the jeans, and perhaps fifty feet from the body, he found a white towel, folded over. It looked very white, very clean, as if it had only recently been hurled over the canyon edge. He photographed it, then opened it up slowly, carefully, so that nothing would spill out. Inside, he found two plastic insulin syringes. They looked as if they'd recently been used, the residue of a cloudy liquid still visible inside. Once again, he photographed them as possible items of evidence and moved on.

A few feet from the towel, he came upon a third syringe, lying pristinely on a bed of scattered leaves and twigs. It also appeared to have been recently used, and once again he could see small drops of the same milky liquid inside.

By the time Smith had finished walking the scene, the initial forsenic investigation had been completed. In the distance he could see the body, still lying face-down, but slightly suspended, the chest folded over the rounded trunk of the fallen tree. He had already photographed her from every angle, noting the small, nearly perfectly round hole that had been torn into the back of her blouse and the dark red stain that surrounded it. He wouldn't need an autopsy report to tell him that the girl had been shot in the back and that the bullet had been a "wad cutter," a type of ammunition that was generally used for target practice, designed to tear into paper rather than into flesh, and to leave behind a precise indication of the bullet's point of entry.

For a time Smith paced the area once again, carefully studying one square of ground at a time. He was still doing that when a curious silence suddenly fell over the canyon, and as he glanced once again in the direction of the body, he realized the canyon had suddenly gone completely still. Several yards away, he could see long gray ropes stretching down from the overhanging cliffs, and he knew that the forensic experts had finished their work at the scene and that the body was now being brought up. Like all the others in and around the canyon, he stood silently as the orange fiberglass rescue basket with the body inside was slowly drawn along the granite face of the canyon, scraping gently against the wall. As it rose through the surrounding stillness, the firemen sounded cadence, tugging gently as each number was called: One. Two. Three. With each call the stokes lifted higher and higher until it disappeared over the high jagged precipice. Then, as if on a signal from somewhere far away, the men on the canyon floor began to work again.

Once the stokes reached the top of the canyon, the plastic body bag was unzipped and forensic experts made a few additional observations.

While they worked, others gathered around the stokes. They could see the girl's face for the first time. Her dark hair was littered with leaves, and there were scrapes and cuts along her cheeks and chin and forehead. Small reddish welts dotted her skin. Her eyes were half-open, which gave her a drowsy look.

One of the people who stood beside the stokes, staring down at the lifeless face, was Debra Ann Medaris, the director of the Open Door Home on Leon Street. She had been brought to the scene by the Rome Police Department to make a positive identification. After a moment she nodded to the detective beside her. "That's Lisa Ann Millican," she said.

The bag was then closed, lifted onto a stretcher, and placed in the back of the white station wagon that had come from Huntsville. It pulled away immediately, moving along the rim of the canyon, then north toward Huntsville, where a full forensic examination was to be performed.

A wide variety of officials remained on the canyon after the station wagon's departure. They paced the area again, or simply stared out over the canyon as if looking for the killer within its treeless folds. Pete Little, a member of the Fort Payne Rescue Squad who remained on the canyon rim that day, thought he knew why they could not leave. "She was just a little girl," he recalled later, "about twelve or thirteen years old. And a lot of the men had little girls about that same age. Seeing her like that, in that body bag, it was the sort of thing that really caused you to remember your own kids, to feel like a father."

For a long time after the body had been taken from the canyon, Danny Smith and Darrell Collins continued to work the scene, Smith at the bottom of the canyon, Collins, his partner in the district attorney's office, some sixty feet above. Smith carefully bagged everything he'd found in the immediate area of the body: the towel, the few syringes, and the pair of jeans. They would be sent to John Kilbourn at the crime lab, but Smith really couldn't say that he was expecting them to reveal very much. Especially the syringes. One member of the forensic team had already told him they were probably just the worthless leftovers of some drug freak in the canyon.

Once Smith had finished with his work on the canyon floor, he returned to the top of the canyon and joined Collins and other officers as they talked about the case. By then they knew that Lisa Millican had been from Lafayette, Georgia, and to Smith and Collins this was simply another indication that the crime had Georgia rather than Alabama connections. By late afternoon he, Collins, and several other officers decided that the place to begin the next stage of their investigation had to be Rome.

One of the men who agreed with them was David Burkhalter, a detective from the Rome Police Department. He'd first come over the night before, then returned the following morning, so that by late evening he'd been working in and around the canyon for nearly twenty-four hours. He was tired and aching, and he wanted to get home. But before returning directly to Rome, he telephoned Mike Ragland and confirmed the information he'd relayed earlier. The girl was definitely Lisa Ann Millican, he said, and she'd been shot in the back with what looked like a .38-caliber wad cutter. It was a "through-and-through" wound, he added, the bullet having exited just above her left breast. The scene had been processed thoroughly and several items had been sealed in evidence bags and taken to Huntsville by the Alabama Crime Lab. That was all he had for now, he said. Then he hung up.

At Rome police headquarters Ragland called one of his detective sergeants into his office. "It's a killing," he told him. "I'm throwing it to you."

The detective sergeant nodded. He was a rough-skinned, red-haired man who smoked incessantly, the tips of his fingers growing yellow with the years. He was tireless and driven and hard-bitten, his blunt street language softened with a native Southern drawl. His name was Kenneth Kines.

PART
TWO
ROMAN CENTURION

CHAPTER
7

Roman Centurion

ROME, GEORGIA, RESTS deep in the heart of a South
dotted with place names that, in a bizarre kind of
mimicry, recall cities greater than themselves: Sparta
in Mississippi, Athens in Georgia, Memphis in Tennessee. It began as a Cherokee post office conve-
niently situated in the Appalachian foothills at the
point where the Etowah and Oostanaula rivers converge to become what residents still insist on calling
the "mighty Coosa," although it is a relatively small
waterway, which then meanders out of Rome to cut
narrowly through western Georgia and Alabama in a
jagged green line.

According to legend, Spanish explorers under Her-
nando de Soto summered in the small river valley in
the early 1500's, some six hundred men who were, in
the words of a local brochure, "the first civilized
men to pause and feel the lure of the lush and fertile
land."

After the departure of the Spanish, the small river
valley returned to its Cherokee origins, and the original post office grew into a village that the Indians
named Chihaha. Here they created an agricultural and
commercial society that was fully developed by the
1830's when a phantom "gold rush" ended in their

lands being parceled off to whites through a lottery system.

Early in the summer of 1834, two lawyers and a cotton planter met by chance at the site of the old Cherokee post office. The physical surroundings impressed them, and a few months later the three men, now joined by two others, met to confirm their plans and to name the site. They fell into a dispute over the name and finally brought the matter to a close by writing down each man's choice, then drawing one of the small slips of paper from a hat. The choices were Hillsboro, Hamburg, Warsaw, Pittsburg, and Rome, the name chosen by Colonel Daniel R. Mitchell because the converging rivers wound around seven distinctly visible hills.

For nearly thirty years after that, Rome continued to thrive as the cultural and economic center of northwestern Georgia. While cotton remained king, its rivers and railways served as a vital commercial outlet, and the city became the regional hub for trade and manufacturing. During the Civil War, it also became a target, and in 1864, invading Union troops burned it to the ground.

Rome was rebuilt after the war, once again emerging as the central city of the region, so that by 1982 it had grown into a town of approximately thirty thousand people, the central city within the so-called "golden triangle" whose three connecting points were Atlanta, Birmingham, and Chattanooga—a position that made it, according to one local publication, "an executive's dream come true."

But there was another Rome, one that existed almost entirely apart from the city's Orchestra and Little Theater, its Chihaha Harvest Festival and Heritage Holidays, its eight golf courses and forty-nine tennis courts. This was a Rome composed of the dark, drug-infested streets of the eastern projects, the delapidated shanties of Clemondsville and south Rome, the pitted streets of Armour Duck, and the long line of sleazy motels that stretched for miles along Martha Berry Boulevard. This was the Rome of red-neck bars and greasy automobile shops, of used-car lots and discount clothing stores, the raw, low-rent districts that exist on the other side of Division Street in every town on earth, the dark and mythical City of Dreadful Night.

No one ever knew that part of Rome better than Detective Sergeant Kenneth Kines. He was not a large man, but there was something about the tangled wisps of red hair, the rough pale face, the jagged, fiercely neglected teeth, and small, penetrating eyes that gave him an appearance of physical force well beyond his size. Seeing him come toward you was like hearing someone rack a shell into a shotgun; the gravity of the moment could not be underestimated.

He was born in Rome on July 25, 1945, the son of a warm, affectionate woman who cared for her children as fervently as she supported local Fundamentalist preachers, and a hard-working father who'd joined the Teamsters at a time when trade unionism was barely a whisper in the winds of Southern labor.

All his life, the city was his beat. As a child, he played in its wide, shaded streets, roamed its alleys and playgrounds, toured the bases of its many ballfields. He eventually rose through every baseball league, finally trying out for the Baltimore Orioles, where his baseball career ended because he was too small.

As a boy, he was good-humored, likable, and self-confident, popular with both boys and girls. Outwardly he was sociable and his life was dotted with romantic episodes. But at bottom he remained strangely solitary, with a restlessness at his core that showed itself in the way his eyes darted about or in the nervous twitch of his upper lip, an odd, almost silent tumultuousness that trembled continually on the surface and was, more than anything else, the visible manifestation of a curious, inexpressible hunger. He could never remember a time when he had not felt it.

Once out of high school, this restlessness drove him

from job to job until he finally ended up as the collection manager for a local finance company. It was the first job that had ever appealed to him, although at first he hardly understood why. Then, after leaving it for the higher pay of working the loading docks of Carolina Freight, he realized that what the old job had offered him was the sense of discovering things that others tried to hide, of finding people who did not want to be found, and of bringing them back to pay their lawful debts. At the finance company, it had been only a matter of money, and that had not been enough to motivate him. Now it struck him that other debts were more critical, the kinds that had to do with retribution, vengeance, justice.

In 1967, at the age of twenty-two, Kines took the test for employment at the Rome Police Department. It was a written test followed by an oral interview, and after passing both, he was hired. "If I had been a millionaire," he was to say many years later, "I would have been a cop. It was the only thing I ever felt good doing."

After a short time as a foot patrolman, he joined twenty others for a three-week period of instruction at the Federal Bureau of Investigation's Police Academy in Atlanta. While there he learned various investigative procedures, everything from patrol techniques to the intricacies of homicide investigation.

As the years passed, he moved into various undercover operations where he worked for both the Vice and Narcotics divisions. Still, in his mind, the ultimate crime was murder, and his eyes remained fixed on a place in the Detective Division, Homicide.

But Kines's curiosity propelled more than his career as a policeman. He also became a ceaselessly driven reader, devouring scores of books each year. It had started by accident, when a schoolmate mentioned that a writer by the name of Mickey Spillane had written a book with another guy named Kines in it. Kines read the book immediately, found that he enjoyed it, then read others, concentrating on mysteries until his growing familiarity with police work and the underside of life made them seem unreal. By then, however, he had developed a real love for reading. He went on to the writings of Freud, Maslow, Adler, and Pavlov in psychology, to Eldridge Cleaver, Huey Newton, Stokeley Carmichael, and Martin Luther King in race relations, to Albert Seaman, Frank Serpico, and the works of the Knapp Commission in urban police studies, and then into a vast array of biographies and memoirs that stretched from Julius Caesar to Elvis Presley, and to histories from ancient to modern times, the books accumulating by the hundreds as the years passed, stacked in boxes in his closets, piled beside his bed, feeding his dream of building a special room for them one day, a library of his own.

Still, it was the puzzle of investigation that remained the steady, driving force in his life. It was this he saw as the ultimate riddle. Early on he had come to realize that he did not have a tendency to sentimentalize his cases. Ultimately isolated, and aloof, afflicted with that peculiar male loneliness that Southern literature has always associated with a wind in the pines, Kines worked at a carefully maintained emotional distance. There were times when the human condition as a whole struck him as cruel and absurd, but he assiduously maintained his distance in specific cases of cruelty or absurdity. He did not moan for the victims who passed his way any more than he raged against those who victimized them. For Kines, police work was essentially an intellectual pursuit, a challenge to the mind rather than the heart. It was the riddle within each case that kept him awake at night, walking the floors of his large rambling home off Kingston Road, which whispered incessantly in his brain even while he played with his son Seth or talked to his wife Debbie. For Kines, the greatest challenge was the one to his intellect, and privately he dreamed of a mythical case that would force him to use all his intellectual skills in finding its solution. For fifteen years he had been looking for such a case while he prowled the streets in his patrol car or sat sleeplessly in the all-night diners, smoking one cigarette after another, his eyes trained on his own reflection in the window. There were times when he could almost feel it waiting for him, like a wolf in the shadows.

Then, suddenly, on the evening of Thursday, September 30, 1982, when he was thirty-seven years old, Mike Ragland summoned him into his office. "It's a killing," Ragland said, "I'm throwing it to you."

"I don't know why," Kines would say quietly many years later, "but there was just something about it. I knew it had come, the case I'd been waiting for all my life."

CHAPTER
8

Who Was Lisa Ann?

ONLY A FEW minutes after the white station wagon bearing Lisa's body left the canyon, a caravan of cars moved out of the crowded grounds of Rocky Glade. They turned right on Highway 35 and wound their way down the southern slopes of Lookout Mountain toward Rome.

Approximately a half hour later Danny Smith, Darrell Collins, and other Dekalb County investigators walked into the large detective squad room at the rear of police headquarters in Rome.

Detective headquarters was located just to the left of the rear entrance. It was a large, matter-of-fact room with bare, flat walls. Nothing had been done to make it look comfortable. Instead form and function had united in a Spartan display of scattered desks and chairs, but with nothing else. It was the sort of room Kines liked, one that minimized distractions.

Kines, along with Detective Burkhalter and Chief of Detectives Ragland, was already waiting for the Alabama officers, and after brief introductions, Jackie Tanner and James Mays, the dispatcher and deputy sheriff who'd taken the woman's call at the sheriff's department in Fort Payne, were seated at an adjoining desk, where they listened as Kines played the tape of the woman's call to the Rome Police Department.

"Well, was that the woman you heard?" Kines asked each of them at the end of the tape.

Tanner and Mays nodded. Yes, it was the same woman who'd called the Dekalb County Sheriff's Department the day before. Both of them were sure of it.

"All right," Kines said. "At least we know we're only looking for one woman."

"And she's probably from Rome," Smith told him, "because that's where Lisa was picked up, and she called Rome police headquarters before she called the sheriff's department in Dekalb County."

"She called a Rome radio station, too," Collins added.

Kines nodded. "Yeah," he agreed. "I think we all know that the whole case should be worked out of this office." Then he assured Smith, Collins, and the other Alabama officers that they could have free run of the Rome headquarters—desks, phones, anything they needed.

"What do we know about the dead girl?" Smith asked.

"She could have been a runaway," Kines told him, "but we don't know that for sure. It may have been a kidnapping, too." He displayed a stack of incident reports, the forms that are filled out for all criminal occurrences other than such common offenses as traffic violations and public intoxication. "We looked through these reports. They're all from the vicinity of the Riverbend Mall. We didn't come up with anything. No abduction attempts that we know of." He shrugged. "So we're pretty much stuck with a woman's voice." He played the tape again. "Hear that?" he asked at a certain point. "She's got sort of a slur. A speech impediment, maybe. The way she says 'Abama,' without pronouncing the 'l.' "

"There's something else, too," Smith added immediately. "She calls Little River Canyon a national park.

It's not a national park. Nobody from around Fort Payne would call it that."

"Unless they were trying to throw us off," Collins added.

Other officers speculated that the caller might have known Lisa before her abduction.

"That's possible," Kines agreed. "I think we need to learn a lot more about Lisa Millican."

They started out immediately, three carloads of investigators, all of them on their way to the last place Lisa had lived before her death, the Ethel Harpst Home in Cedartown.

While Kines and the other officers were en route to Cedartown, a separate phase of the investigation began at the Alabama Crime Lab in Huntsville.

Early that same morning criminalist John Kilbourn had received the jeans that Smith had seen dangling from a slender limb only fifty feet from Lisa's body. He noticed the same red stains that Smith had earlier observed, and sent them to Rodger Morrison for serological analysis.

Now he could begin work on the drug and microchemical analysis of the disposable syringes that Smith and others had also noticed on the canyon floor.

As a first step, he delivered one of the syringe barrels to Martha Odam, a criminalist and drug chemist who worked at the laboratory. She was to examine it for the presence of drugs, particularly those classified by the state as drugs of abuse.

Odam completed the tests promptly and they came out negative. There was no evidence of drugs on the syringe barrel.

Kilbourn then examined the two additional syringes himself, putting each of them through the process of microanalysis, a type of analysis that is necessary in the examination of minute amounts of material, some so small as to be invisible without magnification.

Kilbourn had noticed a slight film on the syringes,

and he wanted to know its chemical composition. From the look of it, he suspected there might be some type of crystalline material in the two syringes. Using various chemical tests conducted under a microscope, he might be able to derive some conclusive findings from the syringes.

For the rest of the afternoon, Kilbourn continued to work on the syringes. The further the analysis took him, the odder it became.

He found that all three syringes contained a very alkaline substance, one with an extremely high basic pH. Chemicals that are acidic in nature, such as sulfuric or hydrochloric acid, invariably have a lower pH such as one or two. The higher the pH above seven, up to fourteen, the more alkaline the substance. On analysis, the film inside the syringes had an extremely high pH which indicated a very strong alkaline content.

Once Kilbourn had determined that he was dealing with an alkali, he ran additional chemical tests to determine exactly what kind it was. These tests showed the presence of sodium and hydroxide.

This caused Kilbourn to suspect that the chemical residue he'd found in the syringes might be a simple sodium hydroxide, a very strong substance. But he had also identified hypochlorite. Whatever the film was, then, it had to be composed of sodium hydroxide and hypochlorite ions, the general chemical constituents, Kilbourn realized immediately, of such common commercial products as Liquid Drano and Liquid Plumr.

When combined with the earlier autopsy findings of six needle punctures, each surrounded by an area of liquefied fatty tissue, the final conclusion of the analysis could hardly have been more obvious. At some point before her death, Lisa Ann Millican had been subjected to a form of chemical torture. She had been injected with some form of caustic drain cleaner, and at the point of injection it had boiled the fatty tissue beneath her skin, finally reducing it to an odd liquid which resembled burnt cooking grease.

Just down the hall from Kilbourn's lab, Rodger Morrison, a thirty-two-year-old criminalist whose speciality was serology, was working on the vaginal swabs that had been taken during Lisa's autopsy. He removed them from their plain manila envelope, then took a few fibers from several of the swabs and placed them in a white ceramic plate for analysis. Then, using an eyedropper, he deposited first a few drops of alpha naphthol onto the fibers, then another few drops of fast blue B, a dye. A dark purple precipitate formed immediately, indicating a high level of phosphatase on the swab fibers, a circumstance highly indicative of the presence of seminal fluid. Next, Morrison tested for the presence of choline, another chemical compound that usually exists in high concentrations in seminal fluid. He used two different reagents, and the fibers turned pink, again a positive finding. Last, Morrison tested for the presence of zinc. The reagent immediately turned a bright reddish orange, again indicating the presence of seminal fluid. Finally, Morrison obtained an extract from one of the swabs, spun it in the centrifuge, and obtained a small quantity of cells. He then stained the cells, and the bright red heads and green tails of numerous spermatozoa immediately appeared on the slide. This was conclusive evidence that shortly before her death, Lisa Ann Millican had had sexual intercourse. Because she was only thirteen years old, this amounted to a finding of statutory rape.

Kines and the other officers arrived at the Harpst Home before noon. It was run by the United Methodist Church and had been named for Ethel Harpst, a woman whom the Women's Home Missionary Society had sent to Cedartown in 1914. Her task had been to take charge of the McCarty Settlement House there. At that time the settlement house had operated both as a public school and a church mission, but upon arrival in Cedartown, Harpst had perceived the community's needs as already considerably greater than could be met by the McCarty Settlement House as it was currently constituted. Over the next few years she expanded its work to include the actual housing of neglected, abandoned, or homeless children, and in March of 1924 she acquired a rambling, seven-room house on a rolling hill overlooking Cedartown. During the following years the home had grown steadily, so that by 1981, when Lisa arrived from Walker County, Georgia, her few belongings bundled in her arms, there was a large main house that served primarily as an office building, a church, a recreation room, a swimming pool, and several separate cottages for the children who lived on the grounds. Most of the cottages had been named for people who had supported the home in some manner—Boykin Cottage, for example, or Pfeiffer. Lisa's cottage had been built by a family named Black, however, and as home officials pointed out, given the racial climate of the surrounding area, it had been decided to call it "Family" instead.

Once at the home, Kines, Smith, Collins, and the others were ushered into a room within the main house that struck Kines as quite homey with its comfortable brocade sofas and chairs. It had a determined, reassuring middle-class air, as if it had been designed by the people who built the sets for the same family-oriented shows the girls were encouraged to watch on television, but which Kines thought must have powerfully conflicted with the economic and family relationships of the girls themselves. "They'd had it pretty rough," he remembered many years later, "and here they were now in these pretty little rooms with the fancy wallpaper. I always wondered how they felt about it."

After a few brief introductions, the questioning began with Gail Henderson, the substitute house parent who had taken Lisa and the other girls to the Riverbend Mall that Saturday evening. Henderson told Kines and the other men that the trip itself had been Lisa's idea.

She had talked it up with the other girls, and together they had all persuaded Henderson to take them.

"Do you think Lisa was planning to run away?" Kines asked.

Henderson didn't know. She said, however, that she had decided to go along with the idea partly because Lisa had wanted it so much. She had taken a lot of initiative, and Henderson said that she had finally decided that it would be a good chance for Lisa to mingle casually with the other girls.

"She hadn't been doing that already?" Kines asked.

"She was a little distant," Henderson said. "She hadn't adjusted very well."

"Why not?"

Henderson told Kines that although she had not known Lisa very well, she had gotten the feeling that she was not terribly popular with the other girls.

"She was a loner?" Kines asked.

Yes, Henderson told him, and she hadn't been able to come out of her shell.

Kines thought he knew what Henderson was saying. "She was a streetwise kid?"

"Yes."

"A little rough," Kines said, already feeling a certain affection for her because he now had a line on what she must have been like, abandoned, cast aside, like hundreds he'd seen in Rome, children reared by parents who were themselves children, or worse, people who, in his severe estimation, should never have been born in the first place. "Tossed around a little," he added.

"That's right."

He could see Lisa Millican well now, a little cold, with a certain distance and edginess, tough with a tender center that was hardening a little every day and would end up solid rock.

"What happened when you got to the mall?" he asked.

Henderson answered that five of the girls had gone

in one group while she had taken the sixth girl, who was only twelve years old, with her. They had all agreed to meet an hour later in front of the Radio Shack. Lisa had never shown up.

"Did Lisa act in any unusual way during the trip?"

"No," Henderson said. "All the girls had been told the rules before we left. They knew it was going to be a short trip, and they knew what they were supposed to do once they got to the mall."

"Which was?"

"Window-shop," Henderson said. "Somebody had mentioned looking at some What-Me-Not candles."

"What happened when you got to the mall?"

"Lisa wanted to go to the bathroom."

"Right away?"

"As soon as we got there," Henderson said. "So the rest of us waited for about ten minutes while she did that."

"She was in the bathroom for ten minutes?"

"Yes."

"What happened when she came out?"

"She wanted the girls to split up," Henderson said. "She didn't want them all to go shopping together as a group."

"Did you agree to that?"

"No. The five had to stay together."

"And Lisa didn't like that?"

"No, she didn't," Henderson said. "But she had to go along with it. I wouldn't let the girls split up."

"So they left as a group," Kines said. "And that was the last time you saw Lisa?"

The last time, Henderson said, then went on to describe what had happened after Lisa had failed to return with the other girls. They'd searched the mall for her, then notified mall security and finally the Rome Police Department.

"Was the mall ever sealed off," Smith asked, "once you'd talked to the security people?"

As far as she knew, Henderson answered, the mall had never been sealed.

As the interview progressed, Henderson continued to maintain what she had thought from the beginning, that Lisa had planned the trip as the first stage of her escape. She'd felt so strongly about it, she told them, that before returning to Cedartown, she'd even driven by the Open Door after Lisa had disappeared to see if she'd gone back there.

As Kines listened, Henderson's idea did not strike him as farfetched. If it were true, he thought, if Lisa had planned to run away from the Harpst Home on that Saturday afternoon, then it was possible that the woman on the tape had been enlisted by her as a part of her plan, that she was the second stage of her escape.

From Program Director Jean Jones, Kines learned that Lisa Millican had been even harder than he imagined. She had been referred to the home by Melba Davis, a Family and Children Services worker in Walker County. Before that, she'd spent thirty days at the Open Door in Rome. She was the oldest of four Millican children, all of whom had been placed in foster care. She had previously run away from no fewer than two foster homes and been asked to leave two others.

"Why was she asked to leave?"

"Trouble controlling her," Jones told him. As a result of her difficulties, she added, Lisa had finally been placed in the Open Door Home on July 13, 1982. On August 13 of the same year, a more permanent placement had been found for her at the Harpst Home. At the time of her death she had been a seventh-grader at Cedartown Middle School.

As the day progressed, still other staff members went into somewhat darker areas of Lisa's past and character. She had been taken from her home in Lafayette after her father had been charged with sexual abuse. But though her own home had clearly been unfit, she had not adjusted well to any of her placements. Like many of the girls in her situation, she could be difficult. She was somewhat withdrawn. She'd written to her mother regularly and wanted to return to her in Lafayette. It didn't matter how bad her home was, the investigators were told, Lisa had wanted to go back to it.

Kines and the others persisted in their questioning. They wanted details. Exactly what was the home in Lafayette like?

They were told that Melba Davis would know more about that.

Did Lisa have any enemies at the home?

She'd been in the usual scrapes, but nothing beyond that.

Had she been visited by another woman lately?

No.

What about her sex life? Did she have a boyfriend with whom she might run away?

Not that anyone knew.

A girlfriend then? A woman friend, maybe?

Or just the opposite, perhaps. A woman who might want her dead?

The answers came back clipped and short: No. No. No.

While Kines and the other investigators continued their interviews, Chief of Detectives Ragland set up shop in what had been Lisa's room at the Harpst Home. It was a small, but not uncomfortable room, with a bed, a desk, and a chest of drawers that Lisa had arranged the way she wanted.

For the next two hours Ragland searched the room, all the drawers and shelves, every pocket of every shirt or pair of pants. He uncovered a number of letters, and after he'd gathered them together, he began reading them closely, searching for any hint from someone she'd written to or someone who had written to her that might give him a clue either to her intentions on the afternoon of September 25 or to what had happened to her during the next three days.

At the end of the process, however, he'd found nothing. "Just what she brought with her," he would remember later, "and those letters that were just little-girl letters with nothing in them that could help us." On his way out Ragland glanced back into her room. "And I guess that was the time when I really felt for Lisa," he said long after the case had been completed. "From then on we just thought about her killer."

After the interviews with the home's staff had been completed, the investigation moved on to the other girls in the Family Cottage.

Kines began by informing them that Lisa was, indeed, dead, that she had been murdered at some point after disappearing from the mall, and that her body had been found some thirty-five miles from Rome, in a canyon in Dekalb County, Alabama.

All the girls had been looking directly at him when he spoke, and he noticed that when he'd finished, one of them had smiled.

He looked at her intently. "Why'd you smile?" he asked.

The girl shrugged, but didn't answer.

"There must have been a reason."

The girl did not reply.

"Well, what was going through your mind?"

"Nothing."

"Then why'd you smile?"

"I just didn't like her."

"You didn't? Why not?"

The girl shrugged again. "I don't know."

Kines realized that he was getting nowhere, and so he decided to go on to the other girls. Most of them felt sorry for Lisa, they said, she'd had a rough life, but basically she was a "sweet kid." She could be rough, and there'd been one particular girl whom she'd really hated.

Which one?

The girl's name was Patty Chester.

Was she at the Harpst Home?

No, she'd gone somewhere else. Some of the girls thought that she'd been sent to the Open Door, a placement that would have put her only a short distance from the Riverbend Mall.

Kines motioned for Burkhalter. "I want you to get somebody over to the Open Door and find out about this Patty Chester," he said.

Burkhalter headed for a phone, and Kines returned his attention to the girls. He couldn't keep from noticing that a few of them did not seem in the least concerned about Lisa's death. They hadn't smiled, but they hadn't greeted the news with any real sadness either. He questioned a few of them further about how they felt about Lisa. Lisa was all right, they said, but they hadn't really liked her very much. She was a "street kid," they added, and could be smart, sharp, hard to get along with. She wasn't always very nice. She liked boys a lot, they said, and she could be a flirt.

As the girls explored this particular aspect of Lisa's life, Kines realized that a couple of them had been jealous of her, that they'd resented the fact that she was pretty, that some of the boys at the home had had an eye for her. More and more as he continued to listen, it seemed to him that the Family Cottage was "family" in name only.

CHAPTER
9

"2 Good 2 Be 4 Gotten"

BEFORE LEAVING FOR Cedartown earlier that morning, David Burkhalter had telephoned John Bass of the Lafayette Police Department. He informed him of Lisa Millican's murder in Alabama and asked him to assist in a background investigation of Lisa herself, as well as her family, friends, and local associates.

Bass had had considerable contact with the Millican family before Burkhalter's call. He knew exactly where they lived and much about the conditions they lived in. He immediately headed down West Main Street, past Cedar and Magnolia until he came to Pine Street, where he could see the Millican house only a few yards down the block. It was a short run-down street, hardly longer than a football field, but one of the worst in the city, a squat row of ragtag structures, some barely standing, their drooping porches laden with rotting furniture. The yards were dusty and grassless, often used as makeshift junkyards for gutted cars, refrigerators, and rusting auto parts. Windows were cracked, with cardboard tacked over them to keep out the winter wind, and in the backyards, hand-me-down clothes hung limply from sagging lines or on the low-slung limbs of trees. It was the kind of street the local police in any small community always knew a good deal better than any other, and for the local Lafayette police, a call to Pine Street was always a call to be particularly careful. Bass himself had been on Pine Street many times, and on more than a few occasions to the house of Fred and Frankie Millican, Lisa's parents.

Bass parked at the upper end of Pine Street, then began walking slowly down it, talking to anyone he saw on the way. It was a raw, fall day and he turned his collar up as he walked. Only a few feet from his car he ran into a Mrs. Ruth Atkins. She told him that she knew Lisa well, but that she'd not seen her since she'd been taken to Cedartown. She had heard that Lisa had run away, but nothing more.

Bass walked on, talking to other people, knocking on their front doors if he found no one in the yard or on the porch. The Pine Street neighborhood was tightly knit in its own peculiar way, and most of the people on its blocks knew Lisa. One of them, Bill Davis, had even dated her.

"Would she have contacted you if she thought she was in trouble?" Bass asked.

"No," Davis told him. "But she would probably contact the Burtons." Davis added that the Burtons had a phone and he immediately gave Bass their number. Bass wrote it down and then moved on, talking quietly to whomever he met, spreading the word that Lisa was dead and that the police were looking for her killer.

Toward late afternoon Bass returned wearily to police headquarters. By then he'd talked to everyone he'd been able to find in and around Pine Street. He knew that the whole neighborhood would be buzzing with the news of Lisa's murder. His years with the police had taught him that it was a myth that neighbors or convicts or family members never betrayed each other. As a matter of fact, it seemed to him, they did it all the time, and as he settled in behind his desk late in the afternoon he was confident that hands and voices would soon be rising from Pine Street, pointing fingers, naming names.

He did not have to wait very long. The first accusations rose in a raspy duet even sooner than Bass had expected, on Friday, October 1, 1982.

Lisa's father, Fred Millican, and his brother turned up at Lafayette police headquarters with plenty to say—all of it about Fred's wife, Frankie. The Millican brothers told Bass that Frankie had been dating a man named Slick Harris. He was just out of prison, they added, and he was no good. When Frankie wasn't around, he chased after Lisa. He wanted them both, mother and daughter.

Bass thanked the Millican brothers and promised them he'd check Harris out.

A few minutes later another report came in. A second detective working Pine Street that morning had talked to Mr. George Pitts, one of Lisa's neighbors. He'd gotten a strange telephone call, he said, from a boy whose voice he hadn't been able to recognize. When Pitts had asked him what he wanted, the boy had blurted, "I want to know who hurt Lisa," then hung up immediately.

Bass thanked the detective, then headed out to Pine Street himself. He wanted to talk to the Burtons, the people Davis had claimed Lisa would call if she were in trouble. He found Bob and Mable Burton at home. They told him they were close with Lisa, but that they hadn't heard from her in a long time. Bass asked when that time was, and the Burtons said that it was on September 21, four days before her disappearance at the Riverbend Mall. The call had come in late at night, but there'd been nothing strange about that. Bass asked how Lisa had sounded. The Burtons told him that she'd sounded as she always did, that nothing had alerted them to any trouble.

Back at the station, Bass got another telephone tip. There had been a party on Pine Street, the caller told him. It had taken place on September 24. The caller had noticed that almost everyone at the party was a friend of Lisa's. Then, suddenly, a dark blue car had driven by the house, blown its horn, and left.

At approximately 12:30 the same day, Bass talked to Charlotte Prince. Charlotte told him that Lisa had recently visited her mother. During the visit Lisa had told her that there were lesbians in the Harpst Home. Lisa went on to say that she had told her caseworker at the Walker County Department of Family and Children Services that some of the women at the home were mean to her, and that she did not like them.

As his investigation continued, Bass gathered other information, street talk, rumors. He heard that Lisa was sexually precocious, that she drank 4D Cough Syrup to get high, that she was bisexual. He recorded these unsubstantiated gleanings from Pine Street in his notebook and moved on to the next interview.

It was with a woman named Phyllis Sheridan, who suddenly came forward and, in a long interview, gave Bass the most penetrating look he had received so far of Lisa's life on Pine Street.

Lisa had lived with Sheridan for nearly a year and during that time had told the older woman many things.

Once, during the summer of 1981, she had picked Lisa up on Pine Street. Lisa had been hysterical and had begun to talk in a kind of frenzied way about her father putting his "greasy hands" up her vagina. She said that he had even given her an infection there, and added that she had also been made to wipe the same grease from her father's crotch.

Sheridan had called the Walker County Department of Family and Children Services (DFACS) immediately, and one of their representatives had met Lisa at the Tri-County Hospital, where Lisa told the DFACS worker about her father. He had forced both herself and her mother to go to bed with him, she told the worker, and on those occasions, she and her mother would both get undressed and lie naked beside Fred

Millican. Millican would then pull and suck at the women's breasts. He would also put his penis near her vagina and rectum, Lisa said, but he had never entered her.

Lisa added that after these episodes, Frankie Millican would tell Lisa to say nothing, to forget them entirely, since, no matter what, her father would always "be too drunk to screw you."

According to Sheridan, the DFACS representative had then confronted Lisa's mother. At first she had denied everything, but later she had confessed, and the sexual abuse was turned over to the district attorney's office.

After that, Frankie had become very angry with Lisa and had even thrown her out of the house for a time.

In the meantime, Sheridan said, Frankie had fallen in love with Slick Harris. Before his release she had written to him in prison and had even told Lisa to write to him as well. Lisa had done so, and later, after his release, Harris had taken an interest in both Frankie and Lisa. He had kissed and fondled Lisa, Sheridan said, but had had sexual intercourse only with her mother.

According to Sheridan, Harris's sexual interest in Lisa had caused Frankie to "fuss" with her daughter. They had fought like schoolgirls over the same boyfriend, Sheridan said, and she believed that this fighting might easily have turned violent.

"If you ask me," she told Bass confidently, "if you want to find out who killed Lisa, you ought to take a real close look at her mother and Slick Harris."

"When was the last time you talked to Lisa?" Bass asked.

"It was about a week before she died," Sheridan replied. "On the tenth or the eleventh of September."

"What'd she say?"

"That she didn't like the Harpst Home much," Sheridan said. "She told me she wanted to come home."

"Did she mention any plans for running away?"

"No."

"Did she mention any woman who might help her?"

"She didn't mention no woman," Sheridan said. "The only woman you ought to be checking out is Frankie Millican."

Bass assured her that lots of people would be doing just that.

Later that day, Bass transmitted the substance of his interviews to the Georgia and Alabama authorities when they arrived in Lafayette, sleepless and exhausted after having completed two full days of interviews in Cedartown. He also gave them the only physical evidence he had been able to collect on Lisa, the last letters she had written to people in Lafayette—one to her mother, one to Slick Harris, and the last to a boy she'd known at school.

Kines and other officers read them carefully that same afternoon. Although they were of no investigative importance, they were crucial in that they were all that still remained of Lisa Millican's character and voice. The young girl who rose from the ungrammatical lines was playful and teasing, with a toughness that seemed more a pose made necessary by tough surroundings than her natural personality, "a little girl who'd never quite found herself," as Kines put it later, "and who never would."

9-16-82

Dear Mother,

What's up? Not much here. How is Calvin & the boys. I'm o.k. except a pulled musel in my leg where I got in a fight over my boyfriend. I've tried to call you seven times but Willie wouldn't take the calls. Did you keep the white card with flowers? If you did you got the wrong one. the brown one is yours. Have any luck on a job? I hope you like it. I do it costed enough. Here is some letters of mine. I got to ask you something. I can't understand why all these lovers keep throwing it away they not even trying to keep it alive. What's the glory of living? It don't make sense. I found me a real nice boy friend. I'm going to the fair tonight. I don't have much to say so I'll let you go by Love you,

Love
Lisa

Hey Slick

What's up? Not much here. How's life treating you? I'm fine except I got into a fight and got my head cut in 3 different places. I hate it down here. Have you found you a job? You better not be mad at my mommy. Just wait till say something out of the way. Me & Myra will get you ourselfs. Just joking. I don't have much to say so I'll let you go.

Love
Lisa

9-16-82

Dear Bobby

What's up? Not much here. Boy I miss you alot. I'm going with a boy that all the girls at school want to go with. I've got in 3 fights over him. The first one was broken up. the 2 fight I lost. But the last one I WON [underlined]. I have a pulled musel However you spell it. But I'm o.k. They put me in the 7th, I'm doing o.k. so far. In gym I did 34 situps in 1 min. 19 push ups in 30 seconds. And stood on my head for 4 min. & 5 seconds. I don't

have much to write so I'll let you go o.k. by love
you.
P.S. Sissy and that sorry boy?

Love
Lisa

Sorry
Sloppy 2 good
        2 be
        4 gotten

Once in Lafayette, Rome investigators began to pur-
sue their part of the investigation. One of them, Mike
Jones, went directly to the Walker County Department of Family and Children Services, hoping to find
a caseworker there who might know something about
Lisa's past and her associates.

Michael Craig Fowler had been working in the department for only a few months, and during that time
he'd had relatively little experience with the Millicans.
Still, he did know a few things. He told Jones that Lisa
had made several calls on the Saturday she disappeared, including a couple to the Open Door Home in
Rome.

That was all he knew for sure. There were other
things he had ideas about, however, and he gave those
ideas to Jones, too. He noted that the woman had
called WRGA, a radio station in Rome, rather than
WLAF, a radio station in Lafayette. He pointed out
that she had also called the police in Rome rather than
the police in Lafayette. The police, he believed, were
looking for Lisa's killer in the wrong place.

At the end of the interview, Jones played the Rome
PD tape. Fowler listened carefully, but could not identify the voice. Before joining the Department of Family and Children Services, Fowler had worked as a
policeman for many years, and there was something
about the tape he noticed immediately, an expression

that was not in common usage among the general population. It was a phrase the woman had used, the way she'd said that Lisa was "on run" from the Harpst Home. Only a woman who'd been in the juvenile system would use that phrase, he told Jones. Everyone else would say that Lisa had "run away," or other words to that effect. "On run" was part of the private vocabulary of people who'd been in the system, Fowler said. Whoever the woman on the phone was, she probably had a juvenile record.

Almost an hour later, Danny Smith, Darrell Collins, and other officers from Dekalb County, Alabama, also entered Lafayette. Thus, by late afternoon, three separate sets of investigators from three different jurisdictions were busily questioning the friends, relatives, and acquaintances of Lisa Millican.

One friend told them that Lisa had hung around with Paul and Carol Hart. They were an odd couple, the informer went on. For one thing, they had matching guns. Both of them carried them all the time. Worst of all, Lisa had dated Paul while Carol was dating him.

Another informant singled out a man named Dale Bottomly as a likely suspect.

A neighbor of Lisa's said that her brother sometimes received letters from Lisa, and that in one of them she had enclosed the photograph of an unknown girl.

The Dekalb County investigators had brought a tape of the call that had been made to the Rome Police Department which they played at the end of each interview. Most of the people they interviewed did not recognize the woman's voice, but a few of them thought they did.

Bill Davis said that it sounded like the voice of a woman Lisa had met at one of her foster homes. He'd never met the woman, he said, but he knew that her name was Norma.

His sister, Louise, couldn't identify the voice, but

said that she'd first heard of Lisa's death at around noon on September 30. The person who'd told her about it was a local girl named Mary Ann Stover.

Mrs. Davis then listened to the tape and said that the voice she heard sounded a lot like Mary Ann Stover.

Another informant stated that not long before being taken from Lafayette, Lisa had kicked a pregnant girl in the stomach. As a result, the girl had lost the baby. The girl who'd miscarried was Mary Ann Stover.

Karen James listened to the tape and said that it sounded like a girl who lived near Lisa on Pine Street. Her name was Mary Ann Stover.

The tape was then taken to Tim Braddock at the Walker County Department of Family and Children Services. He said that it was possible that the girl who'd called the Rome Police Department and spoken of Lisa Millican's death was Mary Ann Stover.

CHAPTER
10

Unraveling Threads

MARY ANN STOVER was picked up in Lafayette and brought to police headquarters late in the afternoon of October 2. She was seventeen years old, and when he first saw her, Kines could hardly believe his eyes. She was absolutely beautiful, as stunning a girl as he had ever seen. But the beauty remained in stark contrast to the life she had led. She had almost no education and appeared to have no desire to get one. Sullen and streetwise, she gave Kines short, crisp answers in the slurred, ungrammatical tones of Pine Street.

"You know Lisa Ann Millican?" Kines began.

Stover slumped down in her seat, her head at a cocky angle. "Yeah, I know her."

"You two live not too far apart, isn't that right?" Kines added.

"Not too far."

"So you know her pretty well?"

"I know her okay," Stover said in a tone that struck Kines as entirely uninterested, as if she were being asked questions about life on the moon.

Kines decided to bring her down to earth. "You know she's dead?"

Stover shrugged. "Yeah, I know that, but far as I know, she was just another girl that hung around the street."

Kines smiled thinly. "Well, that's not what we've heard, Mary Ann."

Stover tossed her head lightly. "Nothing I can do about what you've heard."

Kines looked at her determinedly. "Did you ever have a fight with Lisa Millican, Mary Ann?"

"Yeah," Stover admitted, "we had a fight."

"She kicked you, didn't she?"

"Yeah."

"And you were pregnant at that time, weren't you?" Kines asked.

"I was pregnant."

"And you lost the baby, right?"

"Yeah, but so what?" Stover said. "Girls always fighting on Pine Street. I don't hold no grudges against nobody."

Kines was not so sure of Stover's magnanimity. "Mary Ann, did you have anything to do with Lisa's death?"

"I didn't have nothing to do with it."

"Do you know anything about her death?"

"No."

After a long period of such questions and responses, Kines realized that it could go on in the same fruitless manner for hours. "Okay," he said at last, "let me ask you this. Would you be willing to take a lie detector test about Lisa?"

"Yeah, I would."

Kines nodded. "All right, Mary Ann," he said. "We'll be setting up a polygraph test for you in Rome."

At that, Stover merely shrugged, as if it was just another procedure she had to go through, nothing at all to worry about.

Once in Rome, Mary Ann Stover was taken to a phone booth on Turner-McCall Boulevard, one of the city's most heavily trafficked streets. She telephoned the Rome Police Department and read an exact transcript of the call they had received on September 28.

After that, Stover was returned to headquarters and

given what Kines later called a "very harsh" polygraph interrogation. "The guy was really good," he remembered later. "He really raked her over the coals. It went on and on. He gave her three separate polygraphs, and he was always very accusatory, a real 'bad guy' act."

After an hour and a half the polygrapher emerged from the room and walked over to the detective bullpen, where Kines sat waiting with other investigators. "That girl does not know one thing about the murder of Lisa Millican," he said.

Over the next two days a long line of witnesses and suspects were run through lie detector tests while investigators pursued any and every lead they had.

On October 2, Marlene Tubb told police officials that Lisa had called her on September 27, two days after her disappearance from the Riverbend Mall and one day before her murder. According to Tubb, the call had been made at approximately 10:00 A.M. on that Monday morning. During the conversation Lisa had told Tubb that she'd run away from the Harpst Home. After that, the two girls had made plans to go to the Playlate Club in Chattanooga, Tennessee, at around 7:30 P.M. on the night of October 2. Marlene was to pick Lisa up at the Krispy Kreme Donut Shop across from the Eastgate Shopping Center in Chattanooga. Lisa had not indicated that she was in any kind of trouble, Marlene said, but had told her that a lesbian at the home had been bothering her. Lisa had then gone on to describe the lesbian as being black-haired with her hair cut very short over her ears. She had been bothering Lisa so much that Lisa had decided to run away. Lisa had called long distance, collect, Marlene told investigators, and she had accepted the charges. "So there'll be a record at the phone company," she said.

Telephone records were checked immediately, and no such long-distance collect charges had been added to the monthly bill of Marlene Tubb.

*   *   *

One by one, the witnesses and suspects who had emerged from the Lafayette investigations were brought to Rome. Some were interrogated, while others were both interrogated and given polygraph tests. "The interrogations were very rough," Kines recalled. "Very rough. Some of these people were really put through the grinder. But when you've got suspects popping out of the woodwork like that, the list has to be narrowed down."

Under extensive interrogation, Fred Millican seemed unmoved by Lisa's death. He was casual until Kines pointed out that he, too, was a suspect. At that point he became very agitated, but he denied any involvement in his daughter's murder.

Frankie Millican also denied any knowledge of Lisa's death, but her attitude struck Kines as utterly untroubled, as if her daughter's murder were something she could simply take or leave, a matter of little consequence.

Slick Harris admitted that he was Frankie Millican's lover and that he hadn't really cared much for Lisa. Nonetheless, he said, he'd had absolutely nothing to do with her death. It was true that Frankie had always told him that Lisa didn't like him, he told Kines, but he'd never been sure of that. He'd been in prison for the last thirteen months, but since then he hadn't had any trouble.

Dale Bottomly said that he was a friend of Harris's, but that that was the only connection to Lisa he had. He'd had nothing to do with her death.

Each time the polygrapher's verdict was the same. None of them showed criminal knowledge of the death of Lisa Millican.

While the interrogations continued inside Rome police headquarters, other investigations went forward on the outside.

Detective Elaine Snow did extensive interviews with

the residents and staff of the Open Door Home. It had already been established that Lisa had made two calls to the Open Door on the morning of her death. Snow wanted to know why. In the resulting interview she learned that Lisa had not socialized well with the other children. She'd seemed to prefer the younger ones, however, spurning the kids who were closer to her own age. In general, she'd been a loner, but there had been one exception to this isolation. Lisa had become friendly with Trinity Merdez, a twelve-year-old girl who had been sexually abused by her stepfather. Merdez had lived an itinerant life, drifting with her family through various states from Michigan to Georgia. She had emotional problems, and at the time of her admittance she'd had no idea where her mother was.

As far as enemies, Lisa had had only one, a girl named Patty Chester, a fifteen-year-old white female from Bartow County. Chester had been at the Open Door for twenty-six of the thirty days that Lisa had been there, too. She'd had a black boyfriend named Don, staff members recalled, and this Don had spoken about some friends he had, one male, one female, at the Harpst Home.

Where was this Patty Chester now?

Snow was told that she'd been placed at the Southern Christian Home in Atlanta.

Snow asked about the other girls at the home. Were there any who were particularly difficult?

A second name emerged: Sandra Connack. She was very tough, very hard, a girl who had repeatedly boasted that nothing ever scared her. She hated the police and often bragged about fighting them. She often threatened to hurt people.

As far as her own behavior was concerned, Lisa was a bit stubborn, Open Door informants said, but she had committed only common minor infractions during her thirty days at the home. Her only problem was in personal hygiene, Snow was told, but that was no doubt one of the legacies of her home life in Lafayette.

Thus, the portrait of Lisa Millican that finally emerged was one of an abused child who had been in and out of foster care since December of 1980. Since that time, she'd been placed and removed from four separate foster homes. In January of 1982, she'd been returned to her mother in Lafayette. After a six-month stay, she had been removed once again.

Snow left the Open Door with the names of all sixteen children who'd been there with Lisa. Their ages ranged from fifteen years to eight months, but the one that needed to be checked first was Patty Chester.

Back at headquarters, Snow telephoned the Southern Christian Home, and the final Patty Chester lead vanished immediately. Chester, officials of the home told Snow, had been nowhere near the Riverbend Mall on September 25. She could not have had anything to do with Lisa's death or disappearance.

Like Snow, other detectives continued to work the case, following even the smallest clues. No matter how tangential the connection, every lead was pursued rigorously. When an eleven-year-old girl reported that she'd been raped by two men from California, David Burkhalter was sent to investigate. The girl claimed that one of the men had worked at the Coosa Valley Fair only a few days before. He had a great many tattoos, she said, and he drove a dark blue Nova.

Burkhalter went to Coosa Valley Fair officials and traced the route of the fair since leaving Rome. He found that it was operating currently in Tuscaloosa, Alabama. Three cars of detectives then headed toward Tuscaloosa. Once there, the men fanned out around the fairgrounds. A few minutes later, Burkhalter located the man with the tattoos, then questioned him thoroughly. The conclusion was that he could not have had anything to do either with Lisa's disappearance or the rape of the girl in Rome, a rape, as it turned out, that had not actually occurred at all.

* * *

Hour by hour, the threads, some of them tenuous at best, unraveled. In the end Burkhalter was reduced to interviewing a young boy simply because he'd been Lisa's boyfriend in the fifth grade.

Lisa had now been dead for several days. The trail was growing cold, and as the men continued to follow it, they were aware of the old truth of homicide investigation, that a murder case that doesn't break within twenty-four hours may never break at all.

Sitting in the squad room to the early hours of the morning, Kines continued to go over the unraveling threads of the case while the mound of cigarettes grew in the ashtray and the line of empty coffee cups lengthened across the edge of his desk. He could feel that everything was dissolving into a kaleidoscope of witnesses, accusations, and irrelevant details. He was losing it, and he was desperate to reach toward some new element that would focus his concentration. He kept thinking about the woman's phraseology, the way she'd described Lisa as being "on run" from the Harpst Home instead of having "run away," the more familiar usage. Since investigators had learned of the term used in the juvenile justice system, it had grown more and more faint as a clue in the case. And yet to Kines, it still seemed almost as important as a fingerprint. Still, he could only shake his head in frustration at the hundreds of girls who had gone through the state's sprawling criminal justice system. The caller could have been located anywhere inside that system—places as far-flung as the Open Door, the Youth Development Centers, the varied juvenile detention institutions that dotted the state, even the vast prison system itself. How could he possibly sort it out?

CHAPTER
11

"Are You Patricia?"

ON THE AFTERNOON of October 3, 1982, twenty-two-year-old Diane Bobo was headed down Shorter Avenue to her job at Hardee's, a fast-food joint located in the north section of Rome. She was in a hurry and did not notice the gas gauge until the truck began to sputter slightly as she approached the Thornwood School. Then she knew, but not fast enough to maneuver her way out of the heavy traffic and onto a side road. She glanced about, her eyes settling on the driveway at the far end of the school. If she could make it there, she would be all right.

The truck had stopped on a slight incline, and so she quickly put it in neutral and guided it carefully as it began to roll gently backward. The truck rolled well for a while, then slowed and finally stopped dead in the middle of the road. It was now blocking two full lanes of traffic and something had to be done. She got out quickly, walked to the front of the truck, and began to push it backward.

Suddenly she heard a man call to her. "Don't hurt yourself," he said.

She turned toward the voice and saw a man in a brown car with light-toned stripes running down the side. As he got out, she could see a small child in the backseat.

"I ran out of gas," Bobo said as the man approached her.

He was of medium height and looked to be in his late twenties. He looked well groomed, his short hair parted on the left.

The man joined her at the front of the truck and the two of them finally managed to maneuver it back into the driveway of the Thornwood School.

"Well, do you need me to take you somewhere?" the man asked when they'd finished.

Diane shook her head. "That's okay," she told him. "I'll just find a phone somewhere."

"You sure?" the man persisted. "I wouldn't mind."

Diane shrugged. "Well, if you wouldn't mind. I could use a ride to the nearest telephone."

"Okay," the man said. Then he turned and headed back across the street toward his car.

Diane quickly grabbed her purse, locked the truck, and joined the man in his car. As they drove away, she glanced back at the child. "Boy, this is terrible, isn't it?" she said. The child stared at her expressionlessly.

Diane glanced at the man. He was staring straight ahead, unsmiling.

After a moment the man's eyes drifted over toward her. "I believe there's a telephone right up here in this shopping center," he said.

Up ahead, Diane could see the parking lot of the Alto Shopping Center. "Yeah, I believe there's one in there, too," she said.

"Do you have change for the phone?" the man asked.

"Well, uh," Diane sputtered. It was the first time it had occurred to her. She began looking through her purse. There were a few pennies, but not enough to make a quarter. She had three one-dollar bills, but they would be no help. She started looking through the bottom of her purse, but there wasn't enough there either to make a quarter. She looked at the

91

man. "If you've got some change for a dollar, you know . . ."

The man started going through his pockets as he pulled into the Alto Shopping Center, but he found only two dimes and a nickel.

"I don't have a quarter," he told her. "But I have enough to make a telephone call."

Diane felt relieved. "Well, I sure do appreciate it," she said. Then she took the money and got out of the car. As she headed toward the phone, she saw the man drive away.

She walked immediately to the phone booth near the avenue. She called her husband and told him what had happened. "I'm late for work," she said insistently, "so you better hurry up."

There was a rock base not too far away. It was in the parking lot, and it would be easy for her husband to see her there. She immediately walked over to it and sat down.

The first minute passed slowly as she watched the traffic whiz up and down Shorter Avenue. But there was nothing to do but wait. It was Sunday, and all the stores in the little shopping center were closed. A second minute crawled by, then a third. She looked at her watch. It was exactly 5:00 P.M. She was going to be late for work.

The parking lot was almost entirely deserted, and so she noticed when a brown Dodge with light-colored stripes pulled into the lot. It had a CB antenna coming from the middle of the trunk.

Bobo's eyes followed the car as it swung over to the curb and stopped. She saw a woman get out and approach the newspaper vending machine not far away, then she returned her eyes to the traffic on Shorter Avenue, still looking for her husband.

Only a few seconds passed before she heard a noise, turned, and saw a woman standing very close to her. She wore blue jeans and a T-shirt, but her clothes looked too big for her. It also appeared as if she'd been wearing them for several days. As for the woman herself, she didn't seem in much better shape than her clothes. She looked as if she hadn't bathed in a long time, and there were dark circles under her eyes, as if she hadn't slept in quite a while either.

"Don't I know you?" the woman asked.

Diane shook her head. "No, I don't believe so."

"Are you Patricia?"

"No."

"Aren't you Patricia Alexander?"

"No, I'm not. My name's Diane."

The woman continued to look at her. "Well, I was just riding around," she said, "and I saw you, and I thought I knew you, and I thought maybe you might want to go riding around."

"No," Diane repeated, "I'm not that person." She studied the woman while she spoke, and noticed that although she'd gone up to the newspaper machine, she hadn't bought one. "I'm not the person you thought I was," she said.

The woman didn't seem bothered by that fact. "Well, I'm just out riding around," she said again. "Maybe you'd like to go riding around with me. I'm kind of lonely right now. I don't have nobody to talk to."

Diane shook her head. "I'd like to," she said politely, "but I can't. I have to go to work."

"Well, I could take you where you need to go," the woman offered quickly. She seemed anxious, as if she wanted Diane to go very badly.

"No," Diane said firmly, "I can't leave here. I've already called my husband. He'll be here in a minute. He's picking me up and taking me to work."

"Well, I'll take you," the woman persisted. "Really. It won't be no trouble."

"No," Diane said again. "I'd like to, but really, I can't. My husband's going to be here in just a minute and he wouldn't know where I was."

"Wouldn't he know you're at work or where'er you're supposed to be?" the woman asked insistently.

93

Again Diane refused. "No, I can't leave. I ran out of gas up the road, and I have to tell him where the truck is. You know, where to pick it up and everything."

The woman grew silent. She stared at Diane a few minutes.

"Really," Diane said to her after a moment, "I'd like to go with you, but I've got to sit here and wait for my husband."

The woman continued to watch her. "Okay," she said after a moment, but still she didn't move.

Not far away, in the brown Dodge with the CB antenna, Diane could see a small child hanging playfully over the front seat.

Suddenly the woman moved away from her, walked to her car, and started to drive away in the direction of east Rome. Diane watched the woman as the car drifted out toward Shorter Avenue. When she was near the end of the parking lot, Diane waved at her politely, and the woman politely waved back.

A few minutes later Diane's husband arrived on his motorcycle. She told him that a strange woman had tried to get her to go riding around, but that she'd refused.

When she arrived at Hardee's, she told her fellow workers the same story, how strange the whole incident had been, how the woman had kept after her with a weird persistence.

Later that same day, twenty-six-year-old John William Hancock, a cemetery worker for the city of Rome, and Janice Kay Chatman, twenty-two, the woman with whom he had been living, were walking down Shorter Avenue toward their home on Pike Street.

By the fall of 1982, Hancock and Chatman had been living together for nearly eighteen months. They'd met more or less by accident. Hancock's sister had moved in with Chatman's mother, and on one of his visits to his sister, Hancock had become acquainted with Janice. She was a quiet young woman who spoke very rarely about her life, her answers to his questions usually no more than a word or two, sometimes just a nod. Still, as the weeks went by, Hancock learned that she'd been married, but was now divorced, and that custody of her two children had been given to her former husband, a truck driver who still lived in Rome.

Janice had an easygoing manner that appealed to Hancock, himself a soft-spoken man who thought of nothing more than settling down with someone and raising a family. He thought Janice might be that special someone.

There were problems, however, and Hancock quickly realized what they were. Janice appeared to have had strikingly little education. In addition, it became clear that she'd been badly used throughout most of her life. She'd often been picked up by strangers, then simply let go on the street some hours later by men who'd not even had the decency to bring her home. On those occasions she'd trudged back to her mother's house, her feet sometimes sore from the long walk, but still utterly quiet and uncomplaining.

This was a form of meekness that powerfully elicited Hancock's sympathy, however, and after a time he decided that he should help Janice in any way he could. It was obvious to him that she would be better off with him to look after her than to continue living with her mother. Consequently, he asked Janice to move in with him, and she accepted immediately.

For the next few months John and Janice lived together in what newspapers would later describe as a "common law" marriage, although it was not exactly that. To Hancock, Janice remained curiously reticent, gentle as a kitten, almost childlike, and he looked after her as much like an older friend as a lover. Still, he did enjoy her company, the games she liked to play, the way nothing ever seemed to bother her. For recreation they sometimes drove around. But when there was no money for gas, they simply walked here and there around Rome, visiting relatives or friends.

On the night of October 3, they had been returning from a visit to Janice's mother's when Hancock glanced toward the ground where he saw a scattering of nuts and bolts. They looked like they could still be used, and so he bent down to pick them up. When he straightened up, he saw that a car had pulled up alongside Janice and that she was talking to the woman inside. As he glanced toward the front of the car, he noticed that it bore an out-of-state license plate, one that was too dusty, however, for him to determine which state. The colors looked like those of Kentucky, or was it Tennessee?

As he stepped closer to the car, he could hear the woman speaking while Janice gazed at her blankly.

"I'm from out of town," the woman said. "And I'm sort of lonely."

Janice looked helplessly at John, and he stepped up closer beside her, bent down slightly, and peered into the car. He could see a Cobra CB mounted on the floorboard, its coiled black cord dangling from a dark plastic microphone.

"I was just riding around," the woman said to him. "I was hoping you might want to ride around for a while, too."

Hancock hesitated. There was something about the woman. She looked rough, as if she hadn't slept in a long time. "We was just walking home," Hancock told her.

"I could take you home," the woman offered immediately.

John waved his hand. "Wouldn't be no need for that," he told her. "We don't need no ride. We just live three blocks down the road."

The woman persisted. "I wish you'd ride around with me," she said. "I'm new in town, like I said. I don't have nobody to talk to."

Hancock hesitated again, then glanced at Janice. She was grinning childishly. It made him feel sorry for her. Only a few days before he'd come home to find her playing pin-the-tail-on-the-donkey with no one but herself. He'd told her to do something useful, like picking up cans along the side of the road and selling them for thirteen cents a pound. The following afternoon he'd come home to discover several huge black plastic bags filled with discarded cans crowding the front porch and Janice lying exhausted on the sofa in the living room. He shrugged, thinking that maybe tonight she might like to ride around.

"It wouldn't be for long," the woman promised.

Hancock looked at her a moment longer. She seemed like she really needed somebody, and he'd only recently become a Christian. Maybe it was time to be a Good Samaritan all around, to help Janice as well as the stranger in his midst.

"I wish you would," the woman said softly.

Hancock nodded. "Okay, I guess," he said. Then he opened the door of the passenger side, guided Janice into the backseat, and crawled in himself, close, but not too close, to the woman behind the wheel.

On the other side of the city, Linda Adair was still unpacking her things. She'd just gotten back from the Bahamas. She and her husband had gone there on September 25 for a one-week stay. She'd hoped that the trip would get the firebombing off her mind, but she found that she still jumped a little each time the phone rang.

Still, all in all, things seemed to have calmed down quite a bit. Her work and her life appeared to be getting back to normal. Only one thing still reminded her of that night. Brent continued to sleep fitfully on the back steps, stubbornly refusing to go home.

Several hours later, on a rural highway in Gordon County, Georgia, a truck driver saw a tall, slender man step out onto the road directly in front of him. He was waving frantically as he staggered forward. The driver pulled over immediately and watched as the man rushed forward and hauled himself into the truck. "You got to help me!" he said breathlessly. "I been shot!"

The driver pressed the accelerator and roared off toward the nearest hospital. He arrived only a few minutes later at the Gordon County Medical Center, and the wounded man rushed into its emergency room.

"I been shot!" he repeated.

Several medical personnel came toward him.

"What's your name?" one of them asked him routinely.

"John Hancock!" he blurted, and then listened, amazed, as a burst of laughter swept the room.

At around midnight Ken Kines and David Burkhalter arrived back at headquarters. They'd been in Lafayette, Georgia, all day, interviewing everyone they could find who'd ever seen or heard of Lisa Millican. It had been a long, dreary day, with no breaks, no leads, nothing.

Still, Kines didn't want to go directly home. Instead, he decided to check the log of radio dispatches for the day. That way he could get an idea of what had been going on in the city while he'd been away. As he flipped casually through the log, he could hear the radio traffic filtering into the room. A man was being brought to the Floyd County Medical Center. He'd been shot in Gordon County and given emergency treatment there. But now he was coming to Rome.

Kines finished reviewing the log. He was still geared up, but he decided to go home, since it was shaping up to be a quiet night in the city. There'd only been that one shooting, and it was in Gordon County. Besides, that was the sort of thing that happened all the time.

CHAPTER
12

Bearing Witness

ON THE MORNING of October 4, Georgia Bureau of Investigation Agent Jim Carver received a call from Lester Stuck, an investigator for the Gordon County Sheriff's Department. Stuck told Carver that a man had been shot a short time earlier and that he had been transported first to a local medical facility and then on to the Floyd County Medical Center in Rome.

At 9:10 A.M. Carver and Stuck arrived at the emergency room of the Floyd County Medical Center. They talked to Jackie Newby, the supervisor of nurses at the center, and she showed them a copy of the medical report on John William Hancock. The report stated that Hancock had been brought in at about 3:00 A.M. and released about an hour and a half later at 4:24 A.M. He had been shot in the right shoulder through the scapula, and the bullet had been removed by the attending physician.

Carver asked for the bullet, and Newby gave it to him in a clear plastic specimen bottle with a blue screw-on cap. Carver put the bottle in his pocket, then he and Stuck made their way to 5A Pike Street, Rome, the address the report had listed as home of John Hancock.

Stuck and Carver arrived at Hancock's residence

only a few minutes later. Hancock received them politely when they told him they'd come to investigate the shooting. He said that he would be glad to talk with them, and the interview began.

Two hours later Stuck and Carver emerged from the house on Pike Street. Neither of them was in the least convinced by the bizarre story Hancock had related of being abducted by a woman who had then communicated via CB radio with a man, and who still later had walked him into the woods of Chattooga County, shot him in the back, and left him for dead while spiriting off Janice Chatman, the woman with whom he had been living at the time.

As they drove back toward Gordon County, the two officers discussed what they'd heard and observed during the interview with Hancock. First of all, his manner had struck them as very strange indeed. He had seemed very little affected by the abduction of the woman he'd been living with. He had not even seemed particularly interested in her present whereabouts.

Beyond these curiosities, however, there was a further one. When Hancock had come to relate the details of his own shooting, he had used the same flat, featureless voice as he had used during the interview to that point. He had seemed utterly without the normal emotions of rage, fear, or sorrow, and had simply talked about the whole incident in a casual, off-the-cuff tone that struck both men as nothing less than bizarre.

But beyond these obvious oddities of style there were other, perhaps more substantial problems with his story. It seemed to Carver and Stuck that Hancock and Chatman had gotten into the car too quickly, that they had exhibited too little hesitation or suspicion. Perhaps one of them had already known the car was going to stop. It was possible that Hancock had planned Chatman's murder, then shot himself.

Or perhaps Chatman had planned to have Hancock killed, then disappeared with what would appear to be her abductors. But if this were true, Hancock certainly appeared to have no suspicion of it.

Finally, there was this: Hancock had walked off into the woods in the middle of the night with a woman who held a gun to his back. A woman? Wouldn't he have been able to overpower her? If he could have, why didn't he?

In addition to these larger speculations, there were still other smaller ones. The spot had been secluded, the shooting had been carried out quickly, in what appeared to Carver and Stuck as an execution-style assault. They wondered if perhaps Hancock had been the victim of a drug burn of some kind, one whose true facts he was willfully concealing.

Still, Carver and Stuck agreed that Hancock's story could not be entirely dismissed. They decided they had only one card to play, and that was Hancock.

"Think he'll agree to a polygraph?" Carver asked.

"I don't know," Stuck said. "Why don't we go see."

As Stuck and Carver made their way back toward Rome, Diane Bobo began to talk to her landlady. She'd had an interesting experience just the day before, she said. A woman had tried to pick her up at the Alto Shopping Center.

The woman listened attentively. She was not simply Diane's landlord. She was also a police officer. "You should report that right away," she said. Then she told her how.

A few minutes later on that same afternoon, Monday, October 4, 1982, thirteen-year-old Debbie Smith got off her school bus at her stop on Shorter Avenue and headed toward her home on Magnolia Avenue, a walk of approximately one quarter of a mile. She was tired and anxious to get home. It had been a busy day. Mondays were always busy because each Monday there was a football game and she was one of the school team's eighth-grade cheerleaders. On that afternoon, as she made her way down Leon Street, she was still wearing her cheerleader's uniform.

She had made her way only a few yards down the block when she saw a car pull up to her, moving slowly, keeping pace with her as she continued to walk.

A woman was driving the car, and as Debbie continued to make her way home, the woman glanced toward her and asked a question.

"Are you Michelle?"

Debbie did not turn toward the woman, and so she repeated the question, this time a bit more insistently.

"Is your name Michelle?"

"No," Debbie said, looking over toward her for the first time. She was very near, and she could see the woman very clearly. She looked young, around nineteen or twenty, and had long hair and buckteeth. She wore a T-shirt and blue jeans, and her face was pale, with no makeup, which made her look as if she'd just gotten out of bed. A small child, around two years old, played happily in the front seat beside her.

"What's your name?" the woman asked.

"Debbie Smith."

"How old are you?"

"I'm thirteen," Debbie answered, and strangely, the woman giggled.

Then, after a few seconds, she resumed her questioning. "What school do you go to?"

"West Rome Junior High."

"Do you live down the block?"

"Yes."

"Well, I was just riding around and I was looking for somebody to ride around with me. Would you like to ride around?"

"No," Debbie said as she continued toward home, still walking at her same pace, the brown car inching along beside her while the woman persisted, talking steadily until she approached the Open Door Home.

Then suddenly she stopped, pressed the accelerator of the brown car down firmly, and sped away.

Debbie Smith arrived home at a few minutes after four in the afternoon. She immediately told her mother about the incident on Leon Street. Mrs. Smith told her she needed to talk to the police. Then she went to the phone and called one of the men she knew at police headquarters. His name was Kenneth Kines.

Diane Bobo came to Rome police headquarters late that same afternoon. Kines and other officers questioned her extensively, and during her interrogation she gave a full description of the car the woman had driven and the conversation she had had with her.

A few minutes later Debbie Smith arrived and was taken into the detective squad room. During a two-hour interview she amazed Kines and other detectives with the detail she was able to recall of her brief meeting with the woman in the brown car.

During the course of the interview Kines played the tape that the police department had received on September 28. As it was being played, Carver and Stuck arrived with John Hancock, who had agreed to be polygraphed. As he passed the room in which Kines and Debbie Smith sat listening to the tape, he stopped suddenly, as if caught sharp by an electrifying sound, turned toward the small black tape recorder that rested on the desk between them. His eyes widened incredulously as his finger stretched out toward the recorder.

"That's the damn woman that shot me!" he exclaimed.

Kines leveled his eyes on Hancock's astonished face. "What's your name?" he asked.

"John Hancock."

Kines suppressed a smile. "Well, sit down, John," he said, "I need to talk to you."

For the next several hours John Hancock related in immense detail the events of the preceding night, while Kines and other officers gathered around him, quietly taking him through his story again and again, each time hoping to dredge up some small additional detail.

At around six o'clock, he said, he'd been walking home with Janice Kay Chatman, the woman with whom he'd been living at the time. He'd seen some nuts and bolts scattered on the ground and had bent down to retrieve them. By the time he'd straightened up, Janice had been talking to a woman. The woman told him that she was a stranger in Rome and that she wanted to talk to someone. After a few minutes he and Janice had gotten in the car with her. Janice had gotten into the back while he had slid into the front passenger seat.

The car was a brown Dodge, Hancock said, with some kind of light-colored stripes running front to rear. The woman who drove it was wearing a gray jogging suit.

Hancock introduced himself and Janice while the woman continued to move forward. She passed the street where Hancock lived.

"I've got to go to my aunt's," she explained. "I got to get some money for gas."

"I'd pay for the gas," Hancock told her. "But right now, I don't have no money."

The woman didn't seem concerned. She picked up the mike on the Cobra CB at her right. "10-36," she said.

Hancock recognized the code. She was asking for the time.

The call was answered immediately. It was a man's voice. He gave the woman the time, and she asked him who he was.

The man responded with his CB handle. "Nightrider," he said. Then he asked the woman who she was.

She replied immediately, giving him her handle. "I'm Lady Sundown," she told him, then glanced back at Chatman. "You got any children?" she asked.

Janice nodded. "I got three."

Lady Sundown returned immediately to the CB.

She asked Nightrider for his 10-20. She wanted to know exactly where he was.

Nightrider answered that he was at the Dunkin Donuts, and as he did so, Hancock glanced at the CB. It was on Channel 40, a weak frequency that could not broadcast far. Nightrider was nowhere near the Dunkin Donuts. That would have put him a good five minutes' drive away, far beyond the range of Channel 40. Instead, he had to be very close by, perhaps no more than a car length away. Hancock wondered why Nightrider had lied.

Lady Sundown gave her location, then they talked awhile longer. They seemed to get along well, and in the end they decided to meet at the Old Coosa Post Office north of Rome.

Lady Sundown headed toward it immediately, moving north toward the Alabama state line.

At Highway 100 she swung left, as if she were going toward the small village of Cave Springs.

Nightrider told her that she'd see a narrow dirt road on her right. He said that she should pull off onto it and that he would meet her there.

She followed his directions, then stopped and waited. Within a few seconds another car pulled in behind her, its headlights shining brightly into her car.

The woman started to get out. "I'll go back and meet him," she said.

In the Dodge's rearview mirror, Hancock could see the two of them talking. The man remained in the car while the woman stood beside it, low over the driver's side. For a little while she hovered there. Then she returned to the Dodge.

"Nightrider wants to meet you," she said.

Hancock and Chatman got out of the Dodge and walked back toward the second car.

As they neared it, the man got out. He was very large, with a round fat face and small eyes. "I'm Nightrider," he told them quietly.

Hancock introduced himself and Chatman by their

CB handles. "I'm Fortune Teller," he said, "and this here is Lady Rose."

The man did not seem to care about the names. "We need to get something to drink," he said.

"I don't drink much," Hancock told him. "I think I'd rather just go home."

Neither the man nor the woman appeared to hear him. The woman immediately opened the door of the red car and gathered two small children into her arms. One was a boy, the other a girl. They looked to be around two years old. As the woman spirited the children away, he thought he heard her call the little boy Jeffrey and the little girl something that sounded like Dawn.

"I'm baby-sitting my brother's children," Nightrider explained as the woman headed toward her car with the children. "And Lady Sundown there looks a lot like my brother's wife." Then he opened his car door. "Get in," he said.

Hancock hesitated. He could feel a cold knot growing in his stomach. He glanced toward the Dodge. Chatman was already inside, sitting contentedly beside the passenger door. The children had already been hustled into its backseat. He turned toward the second car. Nightrider was maneuvering himself in behind the wheel. For a moment he tried to think of something to say or do, but there seemed nothing left for him to do but to climb into the car.

They started off immediately. Nightrider was in front, followed by Lady Sundown in the brown Dodge. Hancock could see its headlights close behind them. They filled the lead car's red interior with a yellowish light.

After a time the man picked up the CB. "Are the children asleep yet?" he asked.

"Yes," the woman replied immediately.

Nightrider looked pleased.

The little caravan headed north. Hancock noticed that the man rarely looked at him, rarely spoke except to the woman on the CB, never smiled.

He simply drove, leading them northward toward the Alabama line while he chatted periodically with the woman. "I think I met you at a party once," he told her.

The woman thought so, too. "Yeah, that's right," she said. "We danced some and had a few drinks."

Soon they passed a liquor store on the left, and the man snapped up the CB and told the woman that it was closed, that there was no need to stop. Then he turned back to Hancock. "I know a bootlegger," he said. "We can go find him."

He drove on a while, crossing into Alabama, then wheeled backward in the opposite direction, crossing once again into Georgia. They passed into Floyd County, then swung north on Highway 100, moving into Chattooga County, then through its slumbering county seat of Summerville.

Once through Summerville, they turned again, this time south on Highway 27. Now they were heading back toward Rome. But not for long. Another abrupt turn onto Highway 156 led them out into the wilds of rural Gordon County.

"Look for a red mailbox," the man told Hancock. "That's where the bootlegger lives."

They continued to search for the red mailbox. Once Hancock spotted one, but the man assured him that it wasn't the one they were looking for.

After a time the inevitable happened. "I got to piss," Hancock said.

Nightrider understood. "Me too," he said. Then he radioed the woman, explaining the situation to her politely. "We have to be excused," he told her. "We have to go to the little boys' room." Modesty had to be protected, and so he gave the woman specific instructions. "Pull in behind me when I stop," he told her, "and turn off your lights. We don't want nobody to see us."

The little convoy stopped only a few minutes later. Hancock got out and began to urinate, but Nightrider

didn't. Instead he walked back to the woman's car.
She got out, and the two of them then walked even
farther back, all the way to the rear of the Dodge.

Even so, Hancock could still hear them talking. But
their voices were low, and he couldn't make out what
they were saying. He turned away and went on about
his business. When he looked back again, he could see
that both of them were staring silently toward him. He
heard Nightrider say, "If we're going to do it, let's get
it over with," and suddenly the woman came toward
him. He noticed that she was wearing a gray jogging
suit, but that was not what captured his attention. It
was the gun in her hand, cocked and pointed directly
at his heart.

"Walk down the road," she told him, "and keep
your back toward me."

Hancock put up his hands, turned, and headed down
the narrow dirt road. They walked about three hundred feet down the middle of the road and finally
came upon a small stream. The woman told him to
stop and turn right, into the woods.

Hancock followed her directions, moving off at an
angle into the woods, but she suddenly told him to
stop and come back out again. She motioned him back
across the road and into a small clearing.

"Stop," the woman commanded.

Hancock froze.

He heard the man call to the woman from up the
road. "Hurry up and get it over with," he yelled in a
voice that struck Hancock as oddly frightened, almost
pleading. "We have to go."

"Okay, just a minute," the woman called back
sharply, as if impatient with his cowardice.

Hancock moved to turn toward her. "Can I ask you
a question?"

"Hell, no," the woman snapped. "Just keep your
back to me and don't say nothing."

Hancock turned and faced the empty woods. He

thought of the one question he had wanted to ask her, and never would: *Why are you doing this to me?*

"And don't worry about your girlfriend," he heard the woman say from behind him. "We'll take care of her."

Once again, the man called from up the road, demanding that the woman hurry up.

Hancock shifted slightly to the left, and just as he did so, he heard a shot, and felt the bullet tear into his right shoulder. He fell forward. The breath was knocked out of him, but he remained conscious. He could hear the woman hurrying out of the woods. The man was calling to her again, begging her to move faster. "I'm hurrying," she snapped back in a voice that Hancock thought unbelievably cold and hateful.

He remained on the ground. In the distance he could hear the engines start in the two cars. Their headlights swept the surrounding forest as they sped away.

For a long time Hancock continued to lie facedown in the woods. He could feel the blood running down his back, soaking his shirt, but he remained in place until he was certain they were gone. Then he slowly pulled himself to his feet and staggered toward the road. Several cars passed him as he trudged along the side of the highway, and so after a moment he decided to make someone stop no matter what. He stepped out in front of the next pair of headlights he saw. "They were either going to stop and pick me up," he told Kines determinedly, "or they were going to have to run right over me."

Kines nodded silently. He had listened closely as Hancock told his story, sometimes stopping him to ask questions or clarify details. He knew that he would have to take him through all the steps necessary to verify his story, but he also knew that he'd believed every word of it.

"Would you be able to identify these two people?" he asked.

Hancock nodded.

"We'd like to make a composite sketch," Kines said, "a drawing of what the man and woman looked like. Some other people have seen the woman, and they could help you with that."

"Okay," Hancock said casually. "Anytime you say."

The time, Kines thought, was now.

CHAPTER
13

Voices

THE NEXT DAY, October 5, Agent Carver handed the small specimen bottle with the bullet that had been taken from Hancock's shoulder to Kelly Fite, firearms expert for the Georgia Crime Lab. Fite examined it closely and made his determination. The bullet was a .38/.357-caliber Winchester wad cutter, and it probably had been fired either from a Smith & Wesson or a Ruger revolver. Carver relayed this information to Rome and Dekalb County police authorities.

On the same day, Hancock was taken to Atlanta to be hypnotized. It was hoped that under hypnosis, he would remember details that could become critical to the apprehension of the man and woman who had tried to kill him. The session produced only one additional detail. Hancock remembered that one of the cars had had a bumper sticker affixed to it. The sticker showed a cat hanging from a limb, and under the cat, the words "Hang in thar."

It wasn't the sort of detail that would break a case, but it was nonetheless obvious to Kines that Hancock remained the closest thing they were ever likely to get to a living witness. He intended to work him to the bone.

Consequently, when Hancock returned to police headquarters from Atlanta, Kines approached him immediately. "Come with me, John," he said. "I want us to go for a little ride around town."

Hancock accompanied Kines to a police car and the two of them got in.

"We're going to drive around for a while, John," Kines said. "I want you to look around and see if you spot any cars that look like the two they were driving the night you got shot."

"Okay," Hancock said.

Kines and Hancock headed out of the police parking lot. As they did, Kines pointed to the Polaroid camera that rested beside him on the seat. "If you see a car that looks like either one of the two you saw that night," he told Hancock, "just tell me, and I'll take a picture of it."

With those last instructions, Kines headed out into Rome. They had not gone two blocks before Hancock told Kines to stop the car.

"The man," he said hurriedly, "Nightrider. He was driving a car exactly like that one right there."

The car was parked behind the Floyd County Police Department, and Kines recognized it as belonging to an investigator in the department. "That's a cop's car," he said to Hancock. He pulled into the parking lot, stepped out of the car, and took several pictures of the car Hancock had indicated. He photographed the front, sides, and rear. He wanted no one to mistake the car for anything other than what it was: a red 1975 Ford Granada.

Kines then returned to his car and continued the process. He drove across Broad and started up a hill. Just as he turned to the left, he drifted past another parking lot and decided to turn into it. As they cruised slowly among the parked cars, Hancock stopped him again. "That one looks like it," he said, "the one the woman drove."

Kines again photographed the car from all angles. It was a brown Dodge Charger with cream-colored stripes running along the sides from front to rear.

Kines realized that it matched the description previously given by Debbie Smith. Because of that, it was very likely that whoever had shot Hancock and abducted Chatman were still cruising the streets of Rome. He returned to headquarters immediately and put on a BOLO ("Be On Lookout") notifying all units to be on the alert, but to exercise caution, that the woman behind the wheel was armed and dangerous.

Kines returned to the detective squad room and sat down. To his amazement the whole process had taken less than thirty minutes.

Other aspects of the case were going more slowly. The paperwork involved in scores of interviews and interrogations was becoming overwhelming. Still, it had to be done, and Kines was busily doing it later that afternoon when Floyd County Investigator Bill Whitner walked into the squad room. By then, the local media had been covering the case for days, and one aspect of it had gotten Whitner's attention.

"You know, Ken," he said as he came into the room, "we've had a girl calling us over at the sheriff's department, too."

Kines looked up immediately. "Calling the sheriff's department? What about?"

"A firebombing."

"What firebombing?"

"Somebody firebombed a YDC worker's house a couple weeks ago," Whitner told him. "Somebody shot into another one's house, too."

"When was this?"

"Early last month."

"And a girl called up about it?"

"Yeah, some girl said she'd done it. She threatened to kill them, too."

Kines let the paperwork slide. "And these people she threatened to kill, they were YDC workers?"

"That's right."

In his mind Kines heard the woman's voice on the tape again. *On run.* He leaned back in his chair and focused all his attention on Whitner. "And this was a shooting and a firebombing?" he asked cautiously, almost afraid to think he'd stumbled over the answer to where the woman had picked up her institutional jargon.

"Yeah."

"Of two YDC workers?"

Whitner nodded. "We think it's a domestic thing," he said. "The guy that got his house shot into and the woman who got her house firebombed, they both worked at the same place. We figure they're connected in some way, like a love affair or something like that."

"What are their names?"

"The guy is named Dooley," Whitner told him. "Ken Dooley. The woman's name is Linda Adair."

Kines nodded. "What about that call? Did you tape it?"

"Yeah."

"Get me a copy," Kines told him, "as fast as you can."

Whitner returned with the tape almost immediately. Its quality was disappointingly poor, but after Kines had listened to it repeatedly, he had no doubt that the woman who'd shot into Ken Dooley's house and tried to burn out Linda Adair was the same one who'd made the original calls about Lisa Millican.

Other investigators who'd heard the tape were not so sure, however. To convince them, Kines started playing one tape alternately with the other, a few words of each tape at a time.

Still, some of the investigators remained unpersuaded.

"Well, look at this," Kines said. "See how she used the same expression. Both tapes begin the same, with that 'uh, yes.' "

Resistance continued, and so all that night, until nearly dawn, Kines analyzed the tapes that the Floyd County Sheriff's Department had received, and compared them in the most minute detail with the ones recorded by the Rome Police Department. He recorded every similarity between them, every pause, grammatical peculiarity, or nuance of accent. He did not finish until three in the morning. Then he went home and for the next three hours tossed restlessly on his bed, the woman's voice whispering incessantly in his mind until he finally gave up on sleep, pulled himself to his feet, showered, dressed, and returned to headquarters. He was already there by seven in the morning, a mere four hours after he'd left.

As soon as a police-department secretary got to work, he asked her to type up his versions of the tape transcripts. Then, when other investigators arrived, he ushered them into the squad room and presented his evidence once again, this time backing up the recordings with the typed transcripts and his accompanying analysis.

Danny Smith and Darrell Collins agreed at once. "It was amazing," Smith said later, "how obvious it was that the two voices were the same once you'd seen the transcripts. No one could doubt one woman had made all the calls."

Later that day Kines listened to all the tapes once again. He still noticed the words "on run" in the call made about Lisa Millican, but now he felt reasonably sure that that part of the mystery had been solved: the caller had entered the criminal justice system at the level of the YDC, the Youth Development Center that she'd specifically mentioned in the calls following the shooting and firebombing. But in those calls she had mentioned something more as well—sexual abuse.

To Kines it seemed at least possible that the caller had, in fact, been sexually abused while under the jurisdiction of the Rome YDC and that for reasons that still could not be determined, she had sought vengeance against Ken Dooley and Linda Adair. Now, all roads led to them.

CHAPTER
14

Full Court Press

AT SIX O'CLOCK in the evening on October 7, the telephone rang at the house of Linda Adair.

"Hello."

"Is this Linda Adair?"

"Yes, it is."

"This is Kenneth Kines at the Rome Police Department."

"Yes."

"I'd like for you to come down to headquarters, please."

"Headquarters? You mean now?"

"Yes."

"But I was going to a ballgame."

"Be here at seven," Kines said.

"You mean in an hour? Do I have to?"

"Be here at seven," Kines told her firmly, "or I'll have you picked up."

"All right," Adair agreed reluctantly, then started to hang up.

"By the way," Kines asked quickly, "you know where Ken Dooley is?"

"He's probably at a ballgame tonight, too," Adair said.

"Which one?"

"Between Pepperell and Coosa," Adair answered.

"Where's it being played?"

"At Coosa," she told him. Then Kines hung up.

Ken Dooley was sitting in the Coosa High School football stands seven miles from Rome when someone from the field house motioned him to the phone.

"Ken Dooley?" the man asked as Dooley stepped up to the phone.

"Yes."

"This is Kenneth Kines. I want you to come down to the Rome Police Department."

"Now? I'm at a football game."

"Now," Kines said.

"But I'm a coach for Pepperell," Dooley protested. "I came with the team. I don't even have a car."

"Just stay where you are, then," Kines said adamantly. "I'll send one for you."

Minutes later, when Adair and Dooley arrived at police headquarters, they were immediately escorted into the detective squad room. They sat down side by side at a long table. Danny Smith, Bill Whitner, David Burkhalter, and Kines were already waiting for them.

Kines led the questioning. He was determined to get to the bottom of any sexual abuse that might have occurred at the Rome YDC. Only Dooley and Adair had been mentioned in the woman's calls, and he intended to find out what they knew, if anything, about such abuse. His interrogation would be a full court press.

"We think there's some kind of connection between what happened to you two, the shooting and the firebombing," he began, "between those two incidents and the murder of Lisa Millican over in Dekalb County, Alabama."

Neither Dooley nor Adair spoke as Kines continued.

"We have a positive link between the calls that were made to the police involving your situations," he told them, "and the calls that were made to the Rome police in regard to the Millican girl."

"The voice is the same," Smith added. "The same girl."

Dooley and Adair nodded, but said nothing.

Kines began to bear in upon them. "Did either of you know Lisa Ann Millican?" he asked.

"No."

"You never had any contact with her?"

Dooley and Adair shook their heads.

"Well, she was in the juvenile system," Kines added doubtfully. "Are you sure neither one of you ever ran across her?"

They were sure.

"But Millican had been at the Open Door," Kines went on. "That was just a little ways from the Rome YDC, wasn't it?"

Yes, it was only a little ways, Dooley and Adair agreed, but the two facilities were not related.

"And so both of you are absolutely certain that you never had anything to do with Millican?"

Dooley and Adair were sure. As the questioning continued, they remained firm. They had never met or heard of Lisa Ann Millican before her death.

Kines pursued the matter a few minutes longer, then abruptly switched directions. "Well, what about the things that happened to you," he said, "the shooting and the firebombing. Got any idea who would do anything like that to you?"

They did not.

Could they think of anyone who might want to do them harm?

No.

Everyone had enemies, of course. Didn't they?

Enemies, perhaps, but not people who would shoot at them or try to firebomb a house.

Perhaps not, but at the YDC they had to have contact with some pretty rough customers.

Yes, they did.

Might any of them have done the shooting and the firebombing?

Not anyone they could think of.

Kines and the other detectives continued on in this vein for over an hour, hitting at the same questions again and again. Then suddenly Adair was asked to leave. She walked out into the corridor, leaving Dooley alone with the investigators.

Kines began again. "Now look," he said darkly. "We have reason to believe that the killing of Lisa Millican had something to do with the YDC."

Dooley was astonished. "The YDC?"

"That's right," Kines told him. He went over the tapes again, the fact that it was the same voice on both tapes, and that in one of them the woman had specifically stated that she'd been sexually abused at the YDC.

But that had been in connection with the shooting into his house, Dooley said, and the firebombing of Linda Adair's house.

"But what about the girl who made the calls?" Kines asked. "What about her? She's been associated with the YDC."

That was possible, Dooley said. He told Kines that he'd never denied that there were some rough girls in the YDC. It wasn't a Sunday school, after all, it was a juvenile detention center. Of course it was possible that the girl who'd shot into his house and firebombed Linda Adair's house was connected to the YDC.

Kines insisted that it was a good deal more than possible. "Hell, she mentions the goddamn YDC," he said loudly. "She says she's doing this stuff to you and Linda because she was sexually abused at the YDC."

Dooley reiterated that he did not recognize the voice.

Kines pressed forward. "Well, how about the sex, then?" he asked pointedly. "Was there sexual abuse at the YDC?"

Many of the girls had been sexually abused, Dooley told him, but not while at the YDC. At least none that he knew of.

Kines looked at Dooley accusingly. "Well, what about you, Ken?" he said.

Dooley shook his head. "Never."

"Hell, I know how it is," Kines said. "Those girls out there. Tell the truth now, Ken, have you ever had anything to do with them?"

Absolutely not, Dooley said.

"Have you ever touched any of those girls?" Kines persisted.

"No."

"Touched their breasts, anything like that?"

Dooley was shaking with rage. "No!" he blurted. "Never!"

"We have reason to believe otherwise, Ken," Kines told him matter-of-factly.

"I've never touched one of those girls," Dooley insisted.

"That's a damn lie!" Kines said loudly. "You know who that girl is, Ken. You know the girl who shot into your house, and you know why she did it."

"I'm not lying," Dooley replied helplessly. "Why would I jeopardize my family if I knew who she was? She shot into my house. She could have killed my wife and children. You think that if I knew who she was, I wouldn't tell you?"

"I want to know who she is," Kines said sternly.

"I don't know who she is," Dooley answered. "I just don't know."

Kines's manner remained stern. "Now look," he said, "I don't care about your sex life, but I've got to know who that girl is."

"I don't know who she is," Dooley said.

"You realize that if you're lying to me, you can be charged with perjury, don't you?" Kines asked. "You could get a year, do you know that?"

"Yes, I do."

"And it could be worse than that," Kines added. "You could be charged as an accessory to murder."

Dooley shook his head. "I don't know who that girl

is," he said. "I don't recognize her voice. I don't know who she is."

"Okay, how about Linda Adair?" Kines asked.

"What about her?"

"What's your relationship with her?"

"We work at the same place."

"Well, let me ask you this," Kines said. "Are you having an affair with her?"

"No!" Dooley blurted.

"Just a professional relationship, is that it?" Kines asked.

"Yes."

"Never had anything to do with her besides at work?"

"No. Nothing."

"Well, we got a phone call from somebody who said that you and Linda were more than friendly, Ken. That you two were, in fact, having an affair."

Dooley shook his head. "We're not having an affair. Linda is the assistant director of the YDC where I work. That's the only relationship I have with her."

"Strictly professional," Kines said doubtfully.

"That's right."

"And you and the girls out there at the YDC," Kines said, "nothing between you and them?"

"No. Nothing."

"And how about in the past? How about with a girl who may not be at the YDC anymore?"

"I've never had anything like that to do with any of the girls at the YDC," Dooley said adamantly.

Kines continued, going back over the same ground, hammering at Dooley relentlessly.

Almost four hours after he arrived at police headquarters, Dooley staggered back into a patrol car to be taken home. He felt as if he'd been *in* a football game that night instead of simply coaching one.

The following evening, it was Adair's turn to be questioned more vigorously. Like Dooley the night before, she was asked about their relationship. Then the interrogation began to center on Dooley himself. How long had he been teaching in the short-term treatment program? Did he flirt with the girls at YDC? Had he ever gone out with any of them? Did he touch them? Had any of the girls ever complained about him? Did he show particular attention to the females? Did he favor them over the boys? Did any of the girls have crushes on him?

Repeatedly Adair told detectives that she knew of no inappropriate behavior on Dooley's part. He was liked by the girls, and some of them probably had crushes on him. But that was only natural for a male in that situation, being with girls who were confined, who had been taken away from the other male figures in their lives. There was nothing really wrong with it. And more, there was nothing that Ken Dooley could do about it. If you expected to teach teenage girls without them getting crushes on you, you were living in a dreamworld.

Like Dooley before her, Adair was told that an informer had said that she and Dooley were having an affair.

"You've got to be kidding," Adair replied.

The questioning continued, the detectives once again, going over the same ground.

Then, toward the end of the evening, Kines produced the composites that had been made from the descriptions of Hancock, Smith, and Bobo.

"Do you recognize either one of these people?" he asked.

Adair studied the drawings closely, then shook her head. "No," she said, "I don't recognize them."

"Are you sure?"

"Yes."

"Look at the girl again."

Adair did as she was told.

"You've never seen her?"

Adair shook her head determinedly. "No."

Kines tried not to show his frustration. Instead, he simply drew in a quick breath and began again.

For the next few nights Adair and Dooley were brought back to police headquarters again and again. One at a time, bits of information were fed to them. They learned that CB radios had been involved in the abduction of John Hancock, that there were two cars involved as well, one of them a brown Dodge Charger with white stripes, the other more than likely a red Ford Granada. They learned the handles of the man and woman, Nightrider and Lady Sundown.

At the same time, background checks were done on both of them, friends and associates questioned, anything that might break through what appeared to be an impregnable wall of virtue and innocence.

In the end, after all the questions had been asked and the background checks completed, Kines was left with one inescapable conclusion: Ken Dooley and Linda Adair had not had an affair, and neither one of them had had anything to do with the death of Lisa Millican.

As he drove toward home after his final interrogation of Adair, he once again considered all the evidence. Some tiny piece still eluded him. Tomorrow, he would begin again.

CHAPTER
15

Twenty-five to One

FRIDAY, OCTOBER 8, was a long day for Kenneth Kines. He had felt sure he was nearing a solution when he made the connection between the voices on the tapes, but the long interrogations of Dooley and Adair had brought him to another dead end. Weary with the long sleepless hours, he busied himself by rereading the various investigative reports that made up the thickening case file on the murder of Lisa Millican.

By around five in the evening, he had had enough. He'd reviewed everything again, scrutinizing each detail. The YDC connection still seemed the most important, and in his mind he added it to other details that had been gathered during the last few days, especially Hancock's certainty that the woman's car had borne Tennessee or Kentucky license plates. This, added to the fact that Millican had been transported from Georgia to Alabama, gave him another idea. He stood up immediately and walked over to the office of Juvenile Officer Elaine Snow. It was early evening, and Snow was preparing to go home for the night.

"Elaine," he said, "before you go home, I want you to search your files and get me the name of all the female offenders who have been placed in the YDC from out of state."

An hour later Snow handed him a list of approximately twenty-five names. He glanced briefly at the list, then told Snow to have Dooley and Adair brought to police headquarters once again.

They arrived two hours later.

Kines took Adair into Ragland's office and interviewed her separately. He showed her the list of girls that Snow had compiled.

"These girls all have two things in common," he told her. "They're all in the juvenile system, and they're all from out of state. I want us to go through them one by one to see if you think any of these girls could be the one that firebombed your house."

Slowly and meticulously over the next several hours, Kines and Adair went through the files, discussing each girl in as much detail as possible. At the end of the process the list of twenty-five names had dwindled considerably. Some of the girls didn't have the temperament necessary for the crimes. Others could be placed far away from Rome at the critical moments of abduction. Some were incarcerated. Some were black. Still others, though white, did not fit the physical descriptions given by Hancock, Smith, and Bobo. Their hair was the wrong color or the wrong texture. They were too fat, too thin, too tall, too short. One suffered from a severe speech impediment and would not have been able to have made the calls to the various law enforcement agencies the woman had telephoned.

By the end of the night of interviews with both Adair and Dooley, the long list originally given to Kines had been reduced to five names: Sara Klemper, Dora Madson, Judith Ann Neelley, Sue McKillan and Nell Pitts whose sister, Jane, was currently on Georgia's death row for the murder and sexual molestation of a young woman only a few miles from Rome.

The following day, Linda Adair tried, as she'd been trying since the firebombing, to have what would pass for a normal day. Still, the events of the last few

weeks lay heavily upon her, and not even the brief
vacation she'd taken in the Bahamas had given her
very much relief. Her friends had begun to worry, and
on that day two of them managed to get her out for a
brief walk.

Reluctantly Adair agreed to accompany them to the
mile-long circular drive that went around one of the
local schools. It was something she really needed, a
brisk, vigorous walk. As she headed around the back
of the school, her friends at her side, she felt almost as
if the long night were over. Then, just as she rounded
one of the drive's sweeping curves, she saw it, a car
parked just behind the school. It was a red Ford
Granada that looked exactly like the one the police
had described as belonging to the kidnappers of Lisa
Millican. She froze as if she'd suddenly come upon a
snake coiled in the grass.

"I've got to get out of here," she told her friends.

"What? What do you mean?"

With no further explanation, Adair turned and ran
full speed back to her friend's car.

"Just get me out of here," she said when her friends
joined her. She glanced back toward the school parking lot. She could see the red car still motionless in the
distance. Then just as another car pulled into the
deserted lot, it fired its engine and raced away.

Over the next several days Kines and other investigators began to track down the five women they thought
most likely to have murdered Lisa Millican. It was
tedious work, but through it all Kines could feel his
energy steadily building. "I felt that somewhere on the
list we had her," he recalled, "but there was so little
time."

Very little time. Janice Chatman was still alive as far
as any of the officers knew. Lisa Millican had been
killed three days after her abduction. Almost a week
had now passed since Chatman's disappearance. Time
was clearly running out, and as Kines and the other

officers moved through the tedious steps of locating each of the five women on the list, they could almost feel Chatman's breath growing fainter with each passing hour.

Feverishly, they worked on, eliminating one name at a time, closing in, each remaining name growing more sinister as the others dropped from the list.

Sue McKillan, sixteen, was questioned. In addition to fitting other aspects of the profile, she had a record of telephoning the police. But she had not been in Rome at the time of the disappearance. Nor did she fit the woman's physical description closely enough.

Like McKillan, Dora Madson could prove that she had not been in Rome at the time of the disappearance. Also, like McKillan, she did not have the necessary physical characteristics.

Nell Pitts was also eliminated when investigators admitted they'd put her on the list more out of their knowledge of her sister's criminal activities than out of anything Nell had done herself.

Sara Klemper had been arrested in Bartow County, Georgia, just to the south of Rome, for carrying a concealed weapon. She was eighteen years old, and a psychiatric report classified her as a paranoid schizophrenic with "possible suicidal and homicidal tendencies." She had, in fact, attempted suicide while at the YDC. In the past she'd also been arrested for public drunkenness, and she was known to walk the roads and to disappear with truck drivers for days on end. Such associations made it likely that she was acquainted with the operation of CB radios. It was also discovered that she had relatives in Lisa Ann Millican's hometown of Lafayette and was known to visit them there.

Within hours, Sara Klemper arrived with her mother at Rome police headquarters. Kines and the other investigators shook their heads in despair as she lumbered through the door. She weighed nearly two hundred pounds, and her hair was blond, physical characteristics that hardly matched those given by Hancock, Smith, and Bobo. Clearly, Sara Klemper had not been the woman in the brown Dodge.

Kines looked down at the list, his eyes now focusing on the only name that still remained on it: Judith Ann Neelley.

At Kines's request, Snow pulled her file on Neelley. It was a case she remembered well, and she had no trouble relating it to Kines.

Neelley had been involved in an armed robbery at the Riverbend Mall on October 31, 1980. She'd taken a purse containing both cash and checks and had fled the scene in a car driven by a man who turned out to be her husband, a chubby, soft-spoken fellow named Alvin. Ten days later, on November 10, the Rome Police Department had been contacted by employees of the Big Star, a large grocery store at Central Plaza. A white female had just left the store after trying to cash a stolen check in the name of Jackie Wells. Employees had followed the woman out of the store, and while she had gone inside a Laundromat, they had taken down a full description of the car, along with its license-plate number.

A lookout had been placed on the car, and in less than five minutes it had been spotted on Second Avenue. Police officers had found a fully loaded .25-caliber pistol resting quietly inside. The woman who'd been driving the car had been taken immediately to police headquarters. Once inside, she had been interviewed by Detective Tommy Pruitt. He'd confronted her with the checks, along with a composite drawing that Wells had helped police construct at the time of the robbery. She had confessed immediately, and said that her husband had known about the robbery as well. Her name, she'd said, was Judy Neelley. Her husband was Alvin Neelley, and they had been living in Room 3 of the Seven Hills Motel.

Pruitt and other officers had gone to the motel and

had advised Alvin Howard Neelley, Jr., that he was under arrest. They had also checked his car and found Wells's purse and identification cards. Later, a trace run on Alvin had disclosed that he was wanted in various Georgia counties for theft by conversion, for fraud, and felony theft; and in addition, there were also other outstanding warrants for his arrest in Albany, Georgia, and Whitfield County.

Snow produced a transcript of the separate and joint interrogations of Alvin and Judith Neelley concerning the armed robbery, and Kines went over each of them carefully.

The interrogation of Alvin Neelley had occurred on November 14. It had been conducted by Officer Tommy Pruitt, and during it, Neelley had claimed that he hadn't known that his wife was going to commit an armed robbery.

"Well, me an' my wife was over at the Riverbend Mall," he'd told Pruitt, "and I had played the pinballs earlier at Aladdin's over there and I was going to play some more. Me and my wife got to talking about being broke and she thought maybe she could get a purse off some woman or something. I told her it wouldn't work. We'd be caught and be in a mess of trouble. Said she was going to do it anyway and we got in an argument and I thought she had just gotten out of the car to go and walk awhile and cool off. She come running back and jumped in the car and said let's go and told me she had just took a purse from a woman. I panicked and went."

They'd left for Tennessee, then headed to Columbus, Georgia, to look for work. Alvin reported that he had not helped his wife cash any of the checks. He had even tried to stop her. "I knew she was doing them," he'd told Pruitt, "and I told her she better stop. We were going to get in trouble or something if she didn't stop."

Detective Pruitt had then told Alvin that Wells had said the getaway car was waiting, running, when the girl had hopped into it.

Alvin emphatically denied that he had been waiting for his wife. "I was sitting the car because I didn't know what to do," he told Pruitt. "The car was acting up a little bit. The car wouldn't run, it had been running hot, and I had to let it cool down. . . . I didn't think she was serious."

In her interview with Elaine Snow, Judith Ann Neelley had related a somewhat different version of the events leading to her arrest. Although at first she had denied trying to pass a check at the Big Star, during the interview she admitted it. She had been living at the Seven Hills Motel with her husband, she said, but had been in Rome for only a few days. At the Riverbend Mall she and her husband had begun to talk about how they needed money, and she had suggested a robbery. Alvin had doubted that she would do it, but at the time of the robbery he had been aware of what she was doing. Further contradicting her husband's story, she admitted that they had planned it together. After the robbery they'd driven to the Shangri-la Motel on Cave Springs Road. Not long after that, she started trying to pass the checks. She'd done this on her own, without Alvin's knowledge.

After giving her statement, Judith Neelley had been charged with fourteen counts of forgery and one count of forgery, criminal attempt.

Two days later she had given birth to twins, a boy and a girl, at the Floyd County Medical Center. She'd named the girl April and the boy Jeremy. Five days later, on November 17, 1980, she had been placed in the custody of the Rome Youth Development Center. Subsequently she had been transferred to the larger facility in Macon, where she had remained until her release six months later.

Kines thought all of this over. There were connections—the Riverbend Mall, the fact that they'd driven up Cave Springs Road, the same place where Hancock said they'd stopped to meet the night that he'd been shot.

He decided that this was the one name still worth pursuing, and that it had to be pursued immediately: Judith Ann Neelley.

Over a hundred miles away, in the Jackson Heights section of Murfreesboro, Tennessee, a young woman whose street name was Casey sat idly on the steps in front of a Sears Roebuck. She was braless, dressed in shorts and a sleeveless shirt. After a time she stood up and headed slowly down the sidewalk. As she passed a brown car, she heard a female voice call to her from inside the car.

"Are you Teresa?"

She turned and looked at the woman behind the wheel. "No," she said, "my name's Casey."

"What are you doing?" the woman asked.

"I'm just looking for somebody to ride around with," Casey answered.

"Me too," the woman said. "You want to ride around with me?"

Casey nodded quickly, then got in.

The brown car pulled away, and after a moment the woman asked for a 10-36.

A man's voice answered immediately, telling the woman that the time was a little after seven.

The man and woman began to talk. By that time Casey had mentioned that she was into drugs, and over the CB the man said that he could get some if they'd agree to meet him at a motel.

The woman turned to Casey. "You want to meet him?" she asked.

"Yeah, okay," Casey said. "I used to hang around truck stops. I'm used to guys like him, meeting people, stuff like that."

A few minutes later the brown Dodge pulled into the parking lot of a small motel on the Nashville Highway. The red Ford Granada was not far behind.

*   *   *

On Tuesday, October 12, David Burkhalter and Danny Smith arrived at the Rome YDC to interview Linda Adair once again. Adair met the two men in the lobby, then led them back to her office. She sat down behind her desk and watched Burkhalter place a tape recorder on it.

"I want you to listen to this," he said, "and tell me if you recognize the voice."

Adair listened quietly, but did not recognize it.

"Does it sound like the woman who called you up the night of the firebombing?" Burkhalter asked.

Adair shook her head. "No. Who is it?"

Burkhalter began to put the tape recorder away. "It's that woman who owned that motel in Cave Springs," he said. "Remember? The fire your husband was investigating?"

Adair nodded. That now seemed like a million years ago.

For a moment they began to talk about another case, the shooting of John Hancock.

"It was definitely a man and a woman who did that," Burkhalter told her. "Hancock said they met out near Highway 100. A bridge out there."

Adair felt a twinge of fear. "That's near my house," she said.

Burkhalter nodded. "Well, yeah, they've hung around in there, I guess. We've had reports of two cars cruising around the Coosa school. That night they met by the bridge. Hancock got in the car with the man. Chatman got in the other car with the woman and the two kids."

"Kids?" Adair asked unbelievingly. "They had children?"

"Two of them," Burkhalter told her. "A boy and a girl. Little ones, around two years old."

Adair thought a moment, her mind whirling. Then she opened her desk drawer and withdrew a photograph of two small children.

"Are these the children?" she asked as she handed the picture to Burkhalter.

Burkhalter looked at the photograph, then glanced back up at Adair. "Whose kids are these?"

"They're twins," Adair told him. "A boy and a girl. I took the mother to the Floyd County Medical Center when she was in labor. Those kids are Judy Neelley's."

Burkhalter drove Adair back to police headquarters as fast as he could, and for the next few minutes she answered a battery of questions about Judith Neelley. Neelley had been at the Rome YDC, Adair said, but she was originally from Tennessee, a small town called Murfreesboro, not too far from Nashville. In addition to the robbery at the Riverbend Mall, she said that Neelley had gotten into some sort of trouble in Albany, although she could not remember what the trouble was. As for the robbery at the mall, she added, Judy had been the aggressor, the one who had the gun.

Kines instantly rethought Hancock's account of his abduction. In this case, too, it had been the woman who had the gun. He immediately called the Albany Police Department and asked them if they had pictures of Alvin Howard Neelley, Jr., and his wife, Judith Ann Neelley. A few moments later he was informed that the Albany police did have pictures of the two of them.

"I need them right away," Kines said urgently. "They're prime suspects in a murder case."

Albany understood. "We'll relay it by way of the state patrol."

For the next hour Georgia State Patrol cars, their sirens blaring, raced through the rural countryside of southern and central Georgia, toward Rome, relaying the photographs through various jurisdictions for the two-hundred-mile-plus journey.

While he waited for the pictures to arrive, Kines scrounged around headquarters in search of other pictures he could use in a photographic lineup. He had assembled all he needed by the time the pictures of Alvin and Judith Neelley arrived on his desk.

It was 6:00 P.M., Tuesday, October 12, 1982.

Within a few minutes of their arrival, Kines had arranged the Neelley pictures in a photo lineup. While he and Burkhalter watched, John Hancock went through the photographs that Kines had assembled. After looking at the picture of Alvin Neelley, he said that if the beard and mustache were removed, along with twenty or thirty pounds, it could be the same man he'd ridden with on the night of October 3. As to Judith Neelley's photograph, he said that she definitely looked "similar" to the woman who'd shot him, but that he would need to see her in person.

The following day identical photo spreads were shown to Diane Bobo. When she came to the picture of Judith Neelley, she hesitated, then said that the girl in the picture looked like the woman who'd tried to pick her up, except that she didn't look quite run-down enough. Still, she said, the picture and the woman had the same facial features. Nonetheless, she could not make a positive identification because the picture was in black-and-white and she couldn't tell the actual color of the woman's hair.

Debbie Smith arrived a few minutes later and reviewed the same selection of photographs. One by one, she looked at the pictures while detectives, now somewhat disappointed by Hancock and Bobo, waited attentively.

Smith glanced quickly at picture number one, then did the same to numbers two and three. Then, suddenly, at picture number four, she stopped dead. "That's her," she said. "Absolutely."

The silent, grim-faced detectives who'd surrounded her suddenly broke into smiles. "I felt my heart stop," Kines said later. Picture number four was Judith Ann Neelley.

*   *   *

On Oregburg Road Linda Adair felt no relief. She glanced out her kitchen window, toward the small walkway that led inside the house. Brent was still sleeping there.

Once the identification had been made, GBI Agent Jim Carver walked briskly to his car at the rear of Rome police headquarters. He got in and drove quickly to Gordon County, where John Hancock had been shot, and obtained aggravated-assault warrants on Alvin and Judith Neelley. With the warrants in hand, he headed toward Cleveland, Tennessee, where Alvin Neelley's parents lived, in the hope of apprehending him.

Kines sent Alcohol, Tobacco and Firearms Agents Taylor and Dorling to Cleveland for the same purpose. Once in Cleveland, they searched the Neelley family property, but could not locate Judith or Alvin.

During his stay in Cleveland, however, Dorling established a good rapport with other investigators there, and they promised to put out a BOLO for all of Tennessee and to contact him should the Neelleys be located.

Several days before, on October 9, 1982, Detective David Gresham had arrived at one of the rooms of a seedy motel on the Nashville Highway not far from Murfreesboro, Tennessee. He knocked loudly, and a few seconds later the door opened and a large woman stood calmly before him. She didn't speak, and so he asked her a question that at the time, he didn't realize was a variant of the one she herself had asked so many other girls. "Are you Judith Neelley?"

"Yes."

"I have a warrant for your arrest," Gresham told her.

"Why?"

"For passing bad checks."

The woman did not respond.

"You have a right to remain silent," Gresham began.

A few minutes later a red Ford Granada pulled up to a shopping center in Murfreesboro. Casey got out quickly and waved to the man behind the wheel, the one whose wife had suddenly been arrested. He smiled and waved back. Then he pulled away.

Three days later the same man arrived to visit his wife at the Rutherford County Jail. By then, the police had come to suspect that he'd also been involved in the larcenies with which his wife had already been charged. One of them approached him as he got out of his car in the visitors' parking lot. *You have a right to remain silent.*

On the morning of Thursday, October 14, 1982, Kines and several other investigators were sitting in the detective squad room, all of them huddled in a strategy meeting. While the meeting was still in progress, ATF Agent Taylor walked into the room.

"Well, we got 'em," he said proudly. "The Neelleys are in custody in Murfreesboro, Tennessee."

For an instant the room exploded with the kind of electrifying joy that only long weariness followed by sudden triumph can inspire. Then, almost immediately, the jubilation dissipated as one by one, the men and women in the room turned their minds away from the Neelleys, whose capture now seemed curiously irrelevant, to Janice Chatman, her fate no longer in doubt. "Since she hadn't been with the Neelleys in Murfreesboro, it was obvious that something very bad had happened to her," Kines later recalled. "The only question for us now was what and where."

CHAPTER
16

"I'll Take Him"

KINES ARRIVED AT the Rutherford County Jail in Murfreesboro, Tennessee, at around six o'clock in the evening. As he was getting out of the car, an Alcohol, Tobacco and Firearms agent approached him.

"You'd better get in there, Kenneth," the agent said urgently.

"What do you mean?"

"Son, they're about to fuck up your case."

Kines sprinted up the steps of the courthouse and found fifteen to twenty men from various law enforcement agencies gathered in a small room on the first floor. There were FBI, GBI, ABI, and ATF agents, officers from Floyd, Gordon, and Dekalb counties, most of them involved in an effort to determine who would or would not interview the Neelleys.

Kines stepped forward determinedly and all eyes turned toward him. "Now, listen," he said firmly. "Nobody knows more about this case than I do, and if anybody tries to interview one of them before I do, he'll have to whip my ass to do it!"

No one challenged him, and after a moment Kines added, "I'll take him," meaning Alvin Howard Neelley, Jr. "Somebody else can take the woman."

A few minutes later, Neelley was brought down into

one of the first-floor offices of the Rutherford County Courthouse. He sat down behind a desk and waited for Kines and GBI Agent Jim Carver to begin their interrogation.

To Kines, Neelley was a tremendous disappointment, and when he saw him for the first time, he could hardly believe his eyes. Ponderous, overweight, with a decidedly halting gait, Neelley trudged to a waiting chair and lowered himself into it. He had light brown thinning hair, and his blue eyes seemed perpetually tearful. His face was chubby, even cherubic. Shaved, and in a size-44 diaper, he would have looked like an enormous baby. He reminded Kines of the cartoon character Little Huey.

"You're Alvin Neelley?" Kines asked incredulously.

"Yes, sir," Neelley answered in a soft, Southern accent.

"Judith Neelley's husband?"

"Yes, sir," Neelley said.

For a moment Kines stared at him silently. He could hardly comprehend the full extent of Neelley's quiet, ingratiating manner. He'd expected something entirely different from the curiously diffident fat man who sat before him and looked not only temperamentally but physically incapable of committing the crimes for which he had been arrested. "He was just a complete wimp," Kines recalled later, "a pathetic character if there ever was one. Not too bright. More or less a fat slob. He just didn't fit the picture at all, and right then I thought there must be something real strange in all of this."

Kines read Neelley his rights, then listened as Neelley gave the routine answer that he understood them.

"Okay, let's begin then," Kines said. "You know you've been charged with murder."

"Yes, sir," Neelley said, "but I didn't do no murder. I ain't never killed nobody."

"You want to tell me about it?"

Neelley reacted without emotion, almost confidently, as if he had nothing to hide. "I'll tell you everything you want to know," he said, "but I was wondering if I could see Sam House."

"Who's Sam House?" Kines asked.

"He's a GBI agent," Neelley said. "I've done some work for him."

"We could see about that," Kines told him.

"One more thing," Neelley added. "It wouldn't take no time, and I don't think it'd be no problem, but I'd like to see my lawyer, too."

Kines terminated the interrogation immediately. "Okay," he said, "we'll send for your lawyer."

For the next few minutes Kines and Carver waited for Neelley's lawyer to arrive. Carver remained with Neelley, but Kines left the room, lit a cigarette, and strolled down the corridor to where Judith Ann Neelley was being interviewed by other investigators. He could hear her answering questions, stating quite clearly from time to time that she did not wish to see a lawyer. He lingered outside for a moment, then walked into the room. It was the first time he'd ever seen Judith Neelley. She looked haggard, her hair hanging to her shoulders in dirty tangles, dark circles underneath her eyes. But at the time it was her voice he noticed most. It was as cold a voice as he had ever heard. "I knew right then that I'd really fucked up," he recalled later. "I should have taken her."

A few miles away, other officers fanned out to search the Neelley residence and their two cars.

Detective Burkhalter, ATF Agent Ernest Dorling, and David Gresham, a Murfreesboro police investigator, proceeded to the house of Barbara Adams on Manness Road in Murfreesboro. Adams was Judith Neelley's mother, and investigators had already learned that Judy and Alvin had been living at the house since returning to Murfreesboro.

They arrived around 6:30 in the evening. Mrs. Adams met them at the door. She did not appear unduly disturbed when the officers told her that they had come to search her house. She gave her consent, then stepped aside and allowed the officers to enter.

Burkhalter was one of the first men to enter the house, and as he stepped inside, his eyes drifted over to a small shelf of what appeared to be a scattering of bric-a-brac. Nestled quietly among them, entirely visible from almost any place in the room, was a pair of steel handcuffs.

During the next few hours, the house and both cars, the Granada at the Adams house and the Dodge, which had been sold to a used-car dealership in Murfreesboro, were thoroughly searched.

Among a great many other items, the search netted:

1) one Halloween mask
2) a pair of handcuffs
3) six spent cartridges
4) two police-call radio directories
5) five spent, six unspent .38 cartridges
6) one box .38-caliber Smith & Wesson shells
7) one box .38-caliber shells with six shells missing
8) two CB radios and manuals
9) $1,128 in bills and $2.39 in change
10) three knives
11) one box .38-caliber ammunition with ten shells
12) one 7mm clip loaded with three shells
13) two .22-caliber RG pistols
14) two Smith & Wesson Airweights
15) one 7mm Remington nylon
16) one 30-30 rifle
17) a letter from Jim Bakker and other literature associated with the Praise the Lord Club
18) a stack of new-car titles
19) various materials related to a place in Berkeley, California, that supplied blank identification cards that could be used to establish false identities
20) a vast number of letters, virtually the entire body of correspondence between Judith and

Alvin Neelley during their respective periods of incarceration.

Alvin's lawyer, William Burton, arrived not long after he was called, and he and his client discussed Alvin's situation. Burton told him that he was going to be charged with murder. Under those circumstances, Alvin thought, it would be a good idea to talk. Burton thought so, too, and moments later Neelley signed a waiver certificate and agreed to make a statement.

That done, Kines and Carver began their interrogation. At the end of it Alvin Neelley had told his story very thoroughly, and as Kines read it over to himself, he tried to imagine just how much of it he was willing to believe.

It had all begun in Rome on the night of October 3, Alvin said. It was around 10:00 P.M., and he'd been riding around in his car, a red 1975 Ford Granada. His two kids, Jeremy and April, were with him, and just as he'd come up to the Wendy's on Martha Berry Boulevard, he'd gotten a call from his wife on the CB. She was in her own car, a brown Dodge, and she told him she'd just picked up a man and woman. She even told him their names, John and (Janice) Kay. She wanted him to meet them. That sounded okay to him, and so he fell in behind his wife's car somewhere on Shorter Avenue. They headed west out of Rome, toward Alabama. On the way they passed a "big factory," then turned left onto a dirt road that led to a river. They stopped near the bridge that spanned it. The people in the two cars introduced themselves, and John got in the car with him while Kay got in the car with Judy. Judy took the children, too, and then they all took off again, this time traveling toward Summerville, all of them looking for a place to buy something to drink. There was a bootlegger in the area, Alvin said, and he thought he'd be able to find his place. Since it was a Sunday, he was probably their only hope, and so they all kept looking for him, for the big red mailbox that he remembered from an earlier time.

They kept driving, and after a while they moved through Summerville, then out of it down Highway 27. His car was in the front, leading the way toward Rome.

They rode on for a while, then made a turn onto Subligna Road. They kept going, crossing the line into Gordon County.

They'd been riding a long time by then, and John needed to urinate. They finally found a place where they could let him out and so both cars pulled off the road together.

He and John got out and urinated. When John finished, he started to take a walk down the dirt road.

"Why did he do that?" Kines asked.

"I don't know," Neelley said. "But Judy followed him."

"Down the road?"

"That's right," Neelley said. "And I was pretty worried about it, too, because he was strange, that John guy, and I was afraid he might try to rip Judy off."

"So you were worried about Judy?"

"I just had a strange feeling something was going to happen," Neelley said, "so I went to Judy's car and took the children out again. I seen Kay sitting in the passenger's seat. She was handcuffed to the seat."

"Was she afraid?" Kines asked.

"No," Alvin told him. "She was just sitting there in the dark. She was real quiet. She didn't seem worried about nothing."

"Okay, what happened?"

"I put the kids in my car," Alvin said, "then I got in, too. I couldn't see Judy, so I yelled for her to come on."

"What happened then?"

"She yelled back that she was coming."

At that point, Neelley said, he pulled away and went back to the Oak Hurst Motel in Rome, where he and his wife had been staying. He'd just put the children inside the room when he saw Judy pull up to the room. Kay was with her, but John was not.

"Did you ask about John?" Kines asked.

Neelley nodded. "Yeah. I met her outside the room, and I asked her where he was. She said she shot him."

"Did she say anything else."

"No," Neelley answered. "But she smiled."

All of them stayed at the motel that night, Neelley went on. "Kay was real strange," he added, "and Judy started mocking her a little, making fun about how she couldn't talk plain."

"How'd Kay react to that?"

"She didn't seem to care one way or the other," Neelley said. "She just sat on the bed like it was just another night to her, like it didn't make no difference where she was."

Kines nodded. "All right, go ahead."

The next morning, Alvin continued, they agreed to go to Cleveland, Tennessee, but didn't leave right away. Judy and Kay rode around Rome in her car, while he took the children with him.

They all got back together around lunch, ate at the Dairy King on Highway 27, then traveled north.

Neelley's face tensed suddenly. "Then she just turned east, onto this paved road near the old Armuchee High School. I didn't know where she was going, so I just followed her, and she went across these two intersections, then swung left onto another road I didn't know." He shifted uneasily. "It made me real nervous, her doing that, so I grabbed up the CB and told Judy to pull over. I mean, what with all that happened the night before, John and all, I didn't know what to expect."

"This was all her doing?" Kines asked.

"She was out of control," Neelley said. "I was afraid she might shoot me this time. I didn't know what she was going to do."

Kines looked at him dubiously.

"She's a dangerous person," Neelley said emphatically. "She's already told me about things she done before. She firebombed this house in Rome."

"Whose house?"

"A woman named Linda Adair."

"Why'd she do that?"

"She had her reasons," Neelley said assuredly. " 'Cause while she was at the YDC in Rome, Linda Adair forced her to have sex with one of the teachers. Judy tried to get even with him, too." He nodded vigorously. "She shot into his house." He glanced toward Carver. "Judy's got plenty of guns. She's got two rifles, a .22 pistol, an RG, and a couple of .38s."

"Where's she keep them?" Kines asked.

"In my car," Neelley answered. "It's a red Granada. She keeps a few at my mother's house, too." He added that he'd be willing to sign a constitutional waiver so they could search both places.

"Okay," Kines said, "what happened after you pulled your wife over?"

"Well, I didn't want to go off onto some strange road with her," Alvin said, "so I just guided my car over to the right side of the road and stopped near a big house with a fancy fence in front of it."

He'd waited there for a long time, he continued, then he saw Judy coming toward him again. When she stopped, he asked her what she was going to do.

"What'd she say?" Kines asked.

"That she was going to get rid of the girl."

"Kay Chatman?"

"That's right."

"Where was Kay Chatman?"

"Just sitting in the car," Neelley said. "She wasn't doing nothing, just sitting there."

"What did you do?"

"Nothing," Neelley admitted. "I was too scared of Judy. I just drove back to Rome, and about fifteen or twenty minutes later, when I was passing Jim Walter Homes on Highway 27, Judy come up behind me. She was alone."

"Did you ask about Kay Chatman?"

Neelley nodded. "Later I did. Judy told me that she'd shot her."

"Did she leave the body down that road you stopped at?"

"Yeah, she went on down there, and that's where she shot her."

"Could you draw me a little map of where you think that shooting was?"

"Yeah, I guess."

Kines supplied the paper, then watched silently as Neelley drew a crude map, his short, beefy fingers clutching at the pencil as he struggled to draw straight lines.

"How about signing it, too," Kines said when Neelley had finished the map.

Alvin shrugged indifferently. "No problem," he said. Then he signed it.

Kines smiled as he drew the map from Neelley's fingers. Alvin Howard Neelley, Jr., had just drawn a map to the body of a murdered woman in his own hand, then put the cherry on top by signing it with his own name.

Outside Neelley's interrogation room, Kines looked closely at the map. He thought that one of the lines, the one that indicated a road whose name Neelley had not been able to remember, was probably Haywood Valley Road. He walked to a phone and called Mike Ragland back in Floyd County.

Within minutes a contingent of Floyd County and Rome City police began to converge on Haywood Valley Road. As they drove, they talked back and forth on their radios, and these transmissions were picked up by Chattooga County officials, who then began to converge on the scene as well.

Within a short time, despite working through a solid darkness, the badly decomposed body of Janice Kay Chatman was discovered beside a small creek bed approximately two and one half miles inside Chattooga County.

Since Chatman was dead, no background check would ever be run on her. Carver and Stuck would never know why their initial idea that she might have been involved in a contract on John Hancock was entirely absurd. They would never go to her school and read her file. Because of that, they would never see that she'd been enrolled in EMR classes for almost her entire life, never realize that Janice Kay Chatman had been mentally retarded.

Back in Murfreesboro, Kines stood in the cold early-morning air of the parking area behind the Rutherford County Courthouse and watched as Alvin Neelley was handcuffed and placed in the back of the patrol car that would take him to Rome. Bill Whitner and Ernest Dorling then climbed into the front seat.

"See you boys back in Rome," Kines told them. He stepped away and watched the car make its way out of the lot. "It'll take them about three hours," he said to Burkhalter, who stood beside him. "I guess we better start back, too."

"I just want to make a call first," Burkhalter said as he turned and walked into the courthouse. Once there, he telephoned Linda Adair. "Well, Linda," he said, "we've got them. You can rest easy tonight."

"Thank you," Linda said. Then she hung up. It had been thoughtful of Burkhalter to call, but she realized that she still did not feel entirely safe. She looked out the back window, her eyes drifting down toward the back steps. For the first time since that horrible night when she'd looked out to see the air aflame, her back steps were vacant. After his long vigil, Brent had finally gone home.

Kenneth Kines and David Burkhalter arrived back in Rome at approximately five o'clock the same morning. At police headquarters Kines gave strict instructions regarding Alvin Neelley. "I'm going home to grab a few hours' sleep," he said, "and I don't want anybody talking to Neelley until I get back." To the men gathered at headquarters, both Kines and Burkhalter looked too tired to drive their own cars, and so patrolmen were dispatched to take them home.

A few minutes later, as Kines dropped into his bed, he realized that neither he nor Burkhalter had changed clothes, bathed, or slept for the last thirty-three hours.

But even now, Kines found it hard to rest. Within a few hours he was back at headquarters. By then everyone knew from the final statements taken from Alvin and Judith Neelley in Murfreesboro that John Hancock had been shot in Chattooga County, Georgia, that Lisa Ann Millican had been murdered in Dekalb County, Alabama, and that Janice Kay Chatman had been shot in Gordon County, Georgia. Thus, none of the crimes Kines had investigated so tirelessly had occurred within his jurisdiction. He had no choice but to turn Alvin Neelley over to other officials.

Before doing that, Kines walked over to the short line of holding cells across the hall from the detective squad room. Alvin Neelley stepped up to the bars as he approached.

"You better start getting ready," Kines told him. "They're going to take you back over to Summerville this morning."

Alvin nodded.

"Well, I'll check on you later," he added.

But he never did. He simply walked away.

"Before this case," he would recall many years later, "I had been very ambitious. My dream was to become chief of detectives. But after it was over, I lost that dream. I knew that this was the one case I'd been waiting for all my life, and that from now on, no matter how high I might rise in the department, everything would be routine, all the burglaries and forgeries, even the murders, would be routine, and I would just be putting in my time."

PART

THREE

THE DIVERGENCE OF THE TWAIN

CHAPTER
17

Judy

IN MURFREESBORO, NOT long after advising Alvin to cooperate with the police, his attorney, William Burton, walked down the corridor toward a second interrogation room, where he assumed that Judith Neelley was currently being interviewed. Smudgy clouds of cigarette smoke made the hallway seem to undulate eerily. Crowded with police officers, it looked more like a command center than a simple county courthouse. In all directions, various officers slouched in open doors, hunkered down in the adjoining rooms, or simply squatted alongside the walls, in uniform and out, all of them tired, but still tense, energized, not yet able to rest in the aftermath of capture.

Burton's presence drew their attention instantly, and like a group of slightly roused guard dogs, several of them converged immediately upon him, blocking his path. One of them was Danny Smith, short, wiry, determined, and not in the least in the mood to let someone lightly interfere with Judith Neelley's interrogation.

"Where you going?" he asked Burton.

"To see Judy Neelley," Burton replied. "I'm her lawyer."

Smith stood his ground directly in front of Burton,

the other lawmen now huddled around the two of them, listening carefully.

"She hasn't asked for a lawyer," Smith said. "Until she does, we're going to keep talking to her."

Burton did not intend to give in easily. At forty-one years of age, an associate in the five-member firm of Daniel, Burton and Thomas, he had been practicing law since 1968, handling a general list of legal services that included divorces, wills and estates, collections, criminal practice, accident litigation, and malpractice. For many years he had represented the family of Judith Neelley, and on this particular occasion he saw no reason why he could not continue to do so, despite the small army of police officers who blocked his path.

"Is Judy being interviewed right now?" Burton asked. Smith nodded.

"Where is she being interviewed?"

"Down the hall," Smith replied without budging, "but like I said before, she hasn't asked for a lawyer."

"Well, Judy's uncle, Ron Adams, called me a few days ago and asked me to represent her," Burton said. "As a matter of fact, I've already interviewed her in connection with her arrest a few days ago."

"What was she charged with?" Smith asked.

"Forged money orders."

"Well, she's not being interviewed about forged money orders at this time," Smith said. "She's being interviewed about her possible involvement in a murder."

Burton told Smith he'd come to the courthouse because Alvin Neelley had telephoned him just after supper and asked him to come down. Alvin had told him that out-of-state officers had arrived to question him and he wanted to talk to Burton before talking to them. "And now I want to talk to Judy," Burton added.

"So Alvin asked for you, is that right?" Smith asked.

"Yes."

"Well, that's the point," Smith said. "Judy hasn't

asked for anybody. And we don't have to let you see her until she asks for an attorney."

Burton did not relent. "You know, you could be endangering any case you're building right now," he warned. "Any evidence you get after this may be tainted."

One of the officers who stood beside Smith, FBI Agent Everett Steward, thought Burton might be right. He told Burton to wait while he called the local United States attorney, then elbowed his way to the nearest phone. The U.S. attorney promptly confirmed exactly what Smith had told Burton.

"The U.S. attorney says you don't have a right to see Judith Neelley unless she asks for you," Stewart told Burton after returning to the corridor.

Smith smiled quietly at the lawyer. "If she asks for you, we'll let you know," he said.

At that point, there was nothing left for Burton to do but keep an eye on how the U.S. attorney's decision fared in later court proceedings.

In the meantime, Judith Neelley continued to sit calmly in one of the courthouse's interrogation rooms. Two men stood nearby, FBI Agent Bill O. Burns and Gordon County Sheriff's Investigator Lester Stuck. They had begun their interrogation at 6:45 P.M. It would not be over until past midnight.

Despite her bedraggled appearance, the shapeless sweater and tangled hair, Neelley appeared fully conscious, completely lucid in every respect. She did not seem concerned about her present circumstances or intimidated by the men around her. In a clear, utterly calm voice, she proceeded to lie her head off, denying that she had ever been in trouble with the law and giving off the general sense of a simple, forthright girl, several months pregnant and clearly living in a state of reduced circumstances, but otherwise quiet, sincere, her manner entirely uncontrived.

But as the questioning continued, Neelley admitted that she'd been arrested for armed robbery in December of 1980. Not long after that, she said, her twins had been born. She'd only been sixteen at the time, and so, having been found guilty of armed robbery, she'd been placed at the Rome YDC. She'd stayed there for about a month before being sent to Macon, where she'd remained for the rest of her term, six months. Upon release, she said, she'd gone to the FBI office in Atlanta and complained about the YDC to a female agent there. She was curiously reticent to discuss the reason for her visit, but hinted darkly that it involved sexual matters, things she'd rather not go into. She added that the FBI had done nothing about it.

"What about your husband?" Burns asked, suddenly shifting the questioning to another topic.

Neelley looked at him quizzically, her voice a kind of verbal shrug. "What about him?"

"How long you two been together?"

"Since 1978."

"Are you afraid of him?"

"No," Neelley said flatly. "He's the only person in the world I ever trusted."

"What about that black eye?" Burns asked. "He do that?"

"No," Judy told him, "I got that in a fight."

"Where was this fight?"

"Jackson Heights Shopping Center in Murfreesboro."

"Who'd you get in a fight with?"

"A girl named Kathy," Neelley replied. "I'd been driving around. That's when I spotted her. I knew her from back when we was in school together, so I got out of the car and we started talking. That's when we got in a fight."

Neelley was just finishing her brief description of the fight when Danny Smith entered the room. For a moment, he let his eyes linger on her while Stuck and Burns continued their interrogation. She was a large woman, close to six feet tall, with broad shoulders and thick bones. Her eyes were small and set close together. They appeared utterly blank as she either stared straight ahead, or down at her hands, or let them drift idly, following the men as they shifted around her. Her nose was narrow and pointed, with a bump about a third of the way down the bridge that gave it a jagged look. Deep shadows hung in crescents beneath her eyes, and her skin was very pale, as if she'd rarely ventured into the sunlight. Her voice was as flat as her eyes were blank. It was almost entirely without intonation, so emotionless that it seemed unable even to imitate emotion.

But as Smith watched and listened, he continued to think of a second voice, the one captured on the thin brown tape in the recorder beneath his arm. He considered how best to approach her in order to break through the blank stare and featureless voice. After a moment, he stepped over to the table. "I got something I want you to look at, Judy," he said. Then he showed her a picture of Lisa Ann Millican.

Neelley looked at the picture dully, as if it were the photograph of a basket of fruit.

"Do you know this girl?" Smith asked, then waited for the lie he fully expected to hear. Instead, her answer, and the lack of hesitation before giving it, stunned him.

"Yeah, I know her," she said, almost offhandedly, her thick, somewhat rural Southern accent stretching out the vowels. "I met her at an arcade in Rome. She was playing Pac-Man there. I noticed her because she looked like Joanie Cunningham."

"Joanie Cunningham?"

"That little girl on television."

"When did you see her in the mall?"

"About two months ago. I talked to her for five or ten minutes, I guess."

"And you didn't see her after that?"

"No, I didn't."

Smith showed Neelley a second picture of Lisa Ann.

"She was murdered," he said coolly. "Her body was found at the bottom of Little River Canyon."

Neelley did not react, and so Smith decided to play his next card. "How about Ken Dooley?" he asked. "Do you know him?"

"Yes."

Smith placed the tape recorder on the table, then began to play the tape that had been made by the Floyd County Sheriff's Department the night of the firebombing.

Only the first few words rose from the tape before Neelley waved her hand, indicating she did not want to hear the rest.

Smith snapped off the machine. "Did you shoot into Ken Dooley's house?" he asked.

"Yes," Neelley said.

"How many times?"

"Four."

"What'd you use?"

"It was a .22-caliber pistol," Neelley said. "I think it was an RG."

"How about the firebombing, did you do that?"

"Yes."

Smith was astonished. She was admitting everything. "What did you have against Adair and Dooley?" he asked, before moving on to the final tape, the one that would require a far more profound admission.

"Well, Dooley, he raped me," Neelley said. "And Linda Adair, she come down to Macon and told one of the workers at the YDC down there to set me up for him. He come down twice after that, and he raped me. And Linda, when I was at the Rome YDC, she stopped me from writing my husband when he was in prison."

Smith nodded quietly and inserted a tape in the recorder. If he were ever going to play it, it seemed to him that now was the time. "I want you to listen to this now," he said as he began to play the tape that had been made by the Rome Police Department, the one that gave the location of Lisa Millican's body.

As before, after a few seconds, Neelley indicated she did not want to hear the rest of the tape. She waited until the recorder had been turned off, then asked a startling question. "Did you tape the one I made to Fort Payne, too?"

Smith felt his breath stop. He did not have a tape of the Fort Payne calls, and now he would never need one. "Why don't you just tell us about those calls, Judy," he said.

Neelley complied without reluctance, and in a voice that continued to strike Smith as the coldest he had ever heard, she gave a horrifying account of the last days of Lisa Millican and the death of Janice Chatman.

At twenty minutes after midnight, Judith Ann Neelley signed an extradition waiver to be transported to Alabama. She was handcuffed in the front, then placed alone in the backseat of Eddie Wright's car. Wright slid in behind the wheel, with Dekalb County Sheriff's Deputy Cecil Reed in the passenger seat.

Not far out of Murfreesboro, Reed began to feel about the front seat. "Eddie," he said after a moment. "Have you seen my gun?"

Wright shook his head. "Did you leave it at the jail?"

Reed didn't think so. He checked the seat, the front floorboard, the glove compartment.

Suddenly Wright remembered something. On the way down, Reed, a large man folded uncomfortably in the cramped backseat of the car, had complained about the feel of his gunbelt. He had then taken it off and dropped it into the backseat floorboard only a few inches from where Judith Neelley now sat, staring silently toward the front of the car.

Wright's fingers squeezed the steering wheel. His eyes shot to the rearview mirror. He could see Neelley's head, backlit by streetlights, her hair falling in a tangled mass toward her shoulders. Instantly, he leaned to the side, trying to get Reed's attention. When he did, he whispered, "Didn't you take that thing off in the backseat on the way up here this morning?"

Reed nodded, and the two men stared at each other tensely.

Wright then guided the car over to the side of the road, and both men got out, went to their respective rear doors, and quickly opened them.

Wright saw it first, a .357 Magnum nestled in the darkness only a few inches from Neelley's feet. He snapped it up quickly and both men returned to their seats. "It was just laying there like a snake on a log," Wright remembered. "And handcuffed like she was, with her hands in front of her, she could have bent right over, picked it up, and shot us both in the back, just like she'd already done to two other people."

But Neelley had not moved for the Magnum. Instead she sat quietly as it was snatched from the floorboard, her manner so oblivious that Wright could not be sure whether she even knew it was there at all. After that, she spoke to Wright and Reed only once during the remainder of the early-morning journey to Fort Payne. She told them she had a headache, and they stopped again, this time at an all-night convenience store to buy a packet of aspirin.

CHAPTER
18

"Why?"

ON THE DAY following her return to Alabama, Judith Neelley was questioned again about the events surrounding the deaths of Lisa Ann Millican and Janice Kay Chatman.

After reading Neelley her Miranda rights, Smith and Alabama Bureau of Investigation Agent Pat Wetzel slowly and meticulously took her back over the events she had previously described. This time, however, a third person was hearing them for the first time. His name was Richard Igou and he was district attorney for the Ninth Judicial Circuit of Alabama. A tall, bespectacled man in his midthirties, he leaned silently against the wall of the interrogation room as the questioning began. As he watched, his eyes were almost as unemotional as Neelley's, but he was studying her carefully, noting her face, her eyes, her hands, listening to every intonation of her voice. He had been a prosecutor for several years, but if he decided to bring a capital-murder charge against Judith Neelley, it would be the first he had ever brought, and he did not want to do that lightly.

Igou was neither a vengeful nor a vainglorious man. Unlike many district attorneys, he was satisfied with his office and had no dreams of a larger political career. As a person, he was decidedly uncharismatic, a man of flat, solid-colored suits and striped ties who had never—either in anger or passion or for the sake of grandstanding—raised his voice in a court of law. Soft-spoken and almost determinedly mild-mannered, he seemed to embody in his person the purposeful and reverential decorum of the law. No lawyer ever looked or acted more in accordance with a book of sacred rules. Now, in complete silence, asking her not a single question, he was taking his first look at Judith Neelley, working to discover the nature of someone he would either prosecute vigorously or extend an unexpected mercy. What he saw amazed him. "You can read the details of the trial until you're blue in the face," he would say many years later. "You can go over the transcripts forever, but you can never get the feeling she gave off when she was under interrogation or on the witness stand. It took me a long time to figure out what she meant to me."

"Now, Judy," Smith began as Igou stood off to the side a few feet away, his arms folded over his chest, "you've told us a lot of things, but now what we want to know is why, Judy? That's what we want to know right now."

Neelley looked at Smith with an expression that struck Igou as almost utterly uncomprehending, as if the question were meaningless or immaterial, or even curiously eccentric, an inquiry made from some distant other world. She did not answer.

To get a response Smith offered her the only enticement he thought might prove helpful, the ultimate carrot, her love for her husband. "Now you know that Alvin's not coming to Alabama, don't you?" he told her. "So the only way you could see him would be if you were taken back over to Georgia, too."

Neelley seemed to understand, so Smith continued.

"Now you've admitted picking up Lisa in the mall, right?" he asked.

"Uh-huh."

"And you offered her a ride?"

"Yes."

"And you were driving?"

"The Dodge."

"Your husband was somewhere in the parking lot out there in the Ford?" Smith asked.

Neelley did not respond.

"Did you talk to Lisa?" Smith asked. "What did she say?"

"That she was from the Harpst Home," Neelley told him. "She didn't like it there. She said that whenever they punished her, they gave her more severe punishment than the rest of the girls, and she didn't like it. She didn't want to go back."

"And you started driving toward Cedartown?"

"Yes."

"Did you stop anyplace?"

"I stopped and got us a Coke. I had no intentions of hurting her."

Igou's eyes bore into her. If she had not intended to hurt Lisa, why had she picked her up at all, and why, a few days later had she attempted to pick up several other young girls before settling, as it seemed to him, for Janice Chatman. Why? Why? Why? He continued to listen, hoping for an answer.

"Where was your husband at this time?" Smith asked.

"I don't know."

"You know how long you drove around toward Cedartown?"

"About three hours."

Neelley added that she had checked into the motel sometime after midnight, but she did not know the name of the motel or the number of the room.

"And it was just you and Lisa?" Smith asked.

"And the two kids."

"Okay, this was on Saturday night; on Sunday morning do you know what you did?"

Yes, Neelley said. She remembered that they had gone to Alabama, but she did not know which town, or even if it was a large or small one. The investigators offered to supply her with a map, but she declined. A map wouldn't help, she said, or even calling the names of the towns in that part of Alabama. Nothing would help because she hadn't been paying attention to where she was. "I was just driving around," she said.

She drove for hours, she continued, then stopped at a motel. She thought the motel was small, and although she could not be sure, she suspected it was in Alabama. It had an L-shape, but she could not remember her room number. She and Lisa and the twins had stayed there Sunday night and all day Monday. They'd only gone out to eat at a little restaurant nearby.

Then, on Tuesday morning, September 28, something suddenly changed.

"On Tuesday morning you got up," Smith said. "You and Lisa and the children got up, and you all got in the car and started driving."

"Yes," Neelley answered.

"That night," Wetzel asked, "was Lisa afraid of you?"

"No."

But in an earlier description of the last days of Lisa Millican, Neelley had mentioned handcuffs.

"Well, you told us about some handcuffs," Smith reminded her. "At what point did you put handcuffs on her?"

"I'm not really sure," Judy told him, "but I didn't want her to run off on me, because I knew the people at the Harpst Home were out looking for her."

"Okay," Smith said. "The next day when you got ready to leave, did you keep the handcuffs on her?"

Yes, Neelley said, she'd had them on for a long time. She'd bought the handcuffs at a pawnshop. There were two sets, but she'd used only one of them to handcuff Lisa both inside the car and earlier to the bed.

In his mind Igou could see the handcuffs locked

"Boney and Claude": Judith and
Alvin Neelley in happier times.

Alvin Neelley: "He was always
smiling."

The first physical link: Judith Neelley's jeans caught in the trees only a few yards from Lisa Millican's body.

Lisa Ann Millican: The first victim.

Little River Canyon: The eerie site of Millican's death. (PHOTO CREDIT: *Mickey Strickland*)

The precipice at which Lisa Ann Millican stood, facing out over the canyon, a few moments before her murder. Safety rail was constructed not long after the murder. (PHOTO CREDIT: *Mickey Strickland*)

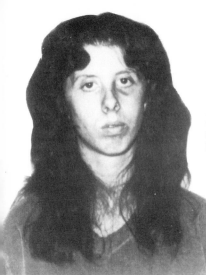

Judith Neelley as she appeared at her arrest in Murfreesboro, Tennessee.

Judy transformed at her trial in Fort Payne, Alabama. (PHOTO CREDIT: *Dennis Benefield, Fort Payne Times Journal*)

The faces of Judith Neelley. (PHOTO CREDIT: *Dave Dieter, Huntsville Times*)

John Hancock: The only living witness. (PHOTO CREDIT: *Donna Hancock*)

Detective Sergeant Kenneth Kines: The Roman Centurion in uniform.

The prosecution team. Foreground: Mike O'Dell followed by District Attorney Richard Igou and Investigator Danny Smith. (PHOTO CREDIT: *Dennis Benefield, Fort Payne Times Journal*)

The defense: Robert French escorts his client to court. (PHOTO CREDIT: *Dennis Benefield, Fort Payne Times Journal*)

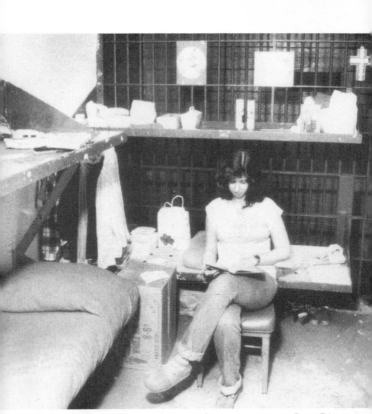

Judith Neelley waiting out her appeals. (PHOTO CREDIT: *Dave Dieter, Huntsville Times*)

around Millican's small wrists. Now he knew that Lisa had slept on the floor, handcuffed to the bed, while Neelley's two small children must have played around her or slept on another bed a few feet away. He wondered if the sounds of the steel handcuffs as they jangled against the bed had ever wakened them.

"I told her that I handcuffed her so she wouldn't run off and get me in trouble," Neelley said.

But at some point that reasoning must have become transparent to Lisa, and Pat Wetzel wanted to know precisely when that was.

"At what point did she become afraid of you?" he asked.

Lisa was afraid when they met, Neelley answered. "She was scared when I first saw her," she told Wetzel. "She thought the people from the home had left her there, and she was scared, didn't know what to do because of the way some guys had been staring at her. I guess she got more scared of me when she saw I had a gun."

"When did she see it?"

"When I took her to the motel."

"What kind of gun was it?"

Neelley replied with a crisply detailed description. "A .38 with a four-inch barrel."

"Did you do anything at all to her that whole time?" Wetzel asked.

Igou braced himself for her answer. Had she tortured her, sexually violated her, committed any of those acts that the human mind considers almost as bad as murder.

"Talked to her," Neelley answered flatly.

"What'd you talk to her about?"

"She talked about her family, about her being in the Harpst Home."

"Did she try to run?" Smith asked.

"No."

"Did you threaten to do anything to her if she did run?"

"I just told her not to try to run," Neelley replied. "I always kept the gun on the front seat when I was driving. When I was at the motel, I laid it up on the dresser."

The questioning then switched directions again, inching steadily toward the fatal moment on the canyon rim. Because of Neelley's previous statement, the investigators already knew what had happened there. But as he leaned unobtrusively against the far wall, barely a blur in Judith Neelley's field of vision, Igou was hearing it for the first time. He had seen the pictures Smith had taken of a little girl broken over a fallen tree, then later, the other photographs of her face, scraped and bruised in the fall, the white skin dotted with tiny red ant bites, her bare chest beneath the open blouse, the single red gash just below her left breast. But Lisa Millican as she had lived the last minutes of her life still lay beyond his imagining. He had seen her dead, now he was about to see her in the last few minutes of her life, feel the cool fall breeze that had doubtlessly played in her hair as she stared out over the gray distances, hear her voice, weak, plaintive, whimpering softly as she begged for her life.

"When did you know as to what you were going to have to do?" Smith asked.

"I'd been thinking about it since that morning when I got up," Neelley said. Lisa could not be turned loose, she added. If she were, she'd have ended up at the YDC. "And I liked the girl," she said. "I didn't want to hurt her."

Igou shifted on his feet. Did not want to hurt her, he thought, with Drano and Liquid Plumr?

"So you'd rather she be dead than have to go to the YDC, is that it?" Smith asked.

"Yeah."

And so the brown Dodge had moved steadily up the mountain, toward the canyon, then swung right onto a winding road, heading west until it passed under a net of power lines, then stopped a few yards beyond an isolated picnic area, a place for families to rest, eat, observe the high granite walls.

"So you pulled on down by the picnic tables," Smith said. "And you and her got out of the car and there was some trees off to the right. Where were your children?"

"Asleep in the car."

"Where was Lisa?"

"She was in the front seat, handcuffed to the door," Neelley said. "She stayed there while I got up and looked around."

Igou had visited Rocky Glade, and it was easy for him to visualize the car there, its dusty grille edged into a grove of stunted pine. That Neelley's children were sleeping in the backseat was harder to imagine. In her telling, they seemed always asleep. Had they never awakened to see the strange, frightened girl in their presence? Had they never wondered who she was, or why she trembled as she lay curled on the hard motel-room floor or sat handcuffed to the car door? Perhaps they had slept through it all, he thought, but one child had been awake throughout, and he found himself focusing on her, a thirteen-year-old girl handcuffed in the car, silently watching as Neelley paced the area, large and looming in the distance, perhaps stopping here and there to lean cautiously over the canyon wall, glance down, then back up at Lisa, making dreadful calculations.

Igou knew what she was looking for, a place out of the way, with a sharp edge, a precipitous drop. But he wondered if Lisa had known that, too, as she sat in the car, listening to the little hissing breezes that seemed never entirely to abandon the canyon edge. Perhaps, instead, Lisa had tried to tell herself that Neelley was looking for something else, a place where she could safely let her go, or let the children play, or, much more simply, perhaps only a mountain flower to bring back to them, something soft and pretty to greet them when they woke.

But if Lisa had harbored such comforting hopes, they were quickly to be dashed.

"What happened after you went back to the car?" Smith asked.

"I told her to get out," Neelley said. "And I took her over to the tree and I told her to lay down right there and I told her I was going to give her a shot to put her to sleep so I could leave and she wouldn't know where I was going."

Lisa did as she was told, Neelley continued, and while she lay on the ground, handcuffed to a tree, Neelley bent over her and gave her a shot in the left side of her neck, pressing down on the small black plunger, releasing a caustic drain cleaner, Liquid Drano, into Lisa Millican's throat.

Igou closed his eyes slowly as he listened. He could almost hear her tiny moan.

The Liquid Drano hadn't worked, Neelley went on, "So I got the Liquid Plumr."

There followed another shot on the other side of the neck, but it didn't work either.

Lisa continued to lie facedown on the ground, Neelley said. She was moaning softly and complaining that the shots were hurting her. Neelley administered another shot, this one in Lisa's left arm, then, after a short interval, another into her right arm.

Neither of them worked, and so the next one went in to Lisa's right buttock, and still another into her left buttock.

And still, it didn't work.

"She said it was hurting," Neelley said matter-of-factly. But Lisa was still alive, she added, the shots were not killing her.

Igou glanced toward the window. It was mid-October, but the cold outside the room seemed like nothing compared to the cold within it.

"Why did you think about Liquid Plumr and Drano?" Smith asked.

" 'Cause it had lye in it."

"So at this point, you'd given her six different shots," Wetzel said. "Was she handcuffed at this point?"

"The first one she was handcuffed 'cause I didn't know what it was going to do," Neelley explained. "I kept them on 'cause she might get violent."

"Do you know how long you waited to see if it was going to do anything?"

"About a half an hour," Judy answered.

Igou felt his breath stop. Half an hour. Terror lengthens seconds into days. He could not imagine the eternity of half an hour.

"Did the shots have any effect?" Smith asked.

"She said they burned," Neelley answered dully. "She said she was cold. She wanted me to give her a shirt and let her lay down."

"Did you?"

"Yes."

Lisa was burning, and she was cold, but she wouldn't die. Because of that, it was time to take the next step, so Neelley told Lisa to get up and walk out to the edge of the canyon.

Once again Lisa did as she was told, but by now she'd caught on to what was happening to her, and she began to plead for her life.

"She begged me to take her back to the Harpst Home," Neelley said. "She said she wouldn't say nothing."

"What'd you tell her?"

"I told her I couldn't."

"Did she say anything else?"

"No."

"Did you say anything else to her?"

"I told her to turn her back to me."

"Did she do that?"

"Yes."

"Then what happened?" Smith asked.

Neelley's answer was clipped and quick. "Then I shot her."

As the interrogation continued, she described the

gun she'd used, and how Lisa's body had tumbled backward, instead of plunging over the canyon wall as planned. Because of that, she'd had to get down on her knees to push the body over, and in the process she'd gotten blood on her jeans. She'd changed into another pair and thrown the old pair, along with the towel and the syringes, over the edge of the canyon.

Then the brown Dodge had moved off the mountain, with Judy at the wheel, the children still sleeping soundly in the backseat.

"When you called Fort Payne the first time," Smith asked, "do you remember where you were at?"

Neelley gave her location on the first call, then the second. She was at Jack's, a local hamburger joint, then at the Piggly Wiggly parking lot. She fell silent after that.

Smith waited a moment for the third location, then reminded her that she had made three calls to the Dekalb County Sheriff's Department that day.

For an instant Neelley seemed genuinely surprised at herself for the first time, amazed by something she had done.

"Three in one day?" she asked. How odd.

Igou let his eyes settle upon her. It would be many months before he finally told someone what he saw.

CHAPTER
19

"I Thought He Would Throw Up"

ON THE EVENING of October 18, Danny Smith and Darrell Collins arrived at the Chattooga County Courthouse in order to get hair and saliva samples from Alvin Neelley. Neelley was under interrogation when they arrived, and the two men joined in the interview being conducted by GBI Agent Sam House, ABI Agent Pat Wetzel, and Chattooga County Investigators Ron Turner and Tony Gilleland.

Smith again advised Neelley of his rights, and he again waived them.

Smith's questioning began at approximately 7:50 P.M. "We want to know what happened," he said firmly, "the whole story about Lisa Millican."

Neelley was exhausted from hours of previous interrogation. He'd lost weight on the lean prison meals, and his eyes were red-rimmed and glistening. He shifted nervously in his seat, and Smith pulled his own chair up close to him, staring at him fiercely. Gilleland immediately followed suit, bringing his chair up beside Neelley in classic interrogation style, boxing him in, creating a powerful physical rendering of Neelley's present circumstances.

"How did you end up with Lisa Millican on Saturday afternoon, Alvin?" Smith asked. "And don't give us any more bullshit. We've heard enough of that."

Neelley shook his head. "That was Judy that done that," he said adamantly. "I didn't have nothing to do with it."

Smith glared at him unbelievingly. "You're telling me she did all that by herself?"

Neelley nodded quickly, nervously, his eyes darting from side to side.

"How'd she do it, then?" Smith demanded.

"She just picked her up, that's what she done."

"When was that?" Gilleland demanded.

"When we come back from Macon," Neelley said, "we was in different cars. We was sort of separated, you know. We wasn't together, but I seen that somebody was in her car."

"Did you know who it was?" Smith asked.

Neelley shook his head again, his hands shifting restlessly in his lap. "We was talking on the CB, and she just said it was some friend of hers. It didn't make no difference to me, 'cause I had something else to do."

"What was that, Alvin?" Smith asked. "You didn't have a job. You were just roaming around. What did you have to do that was so important?"

"I was supposed to meet this other girl," Alvin told him.

"Girl?" Smith asked doubtfully. "What other girl?"

"I don't remember her name."

"You're bullshitting me, Alvin," Smith said darkly. "And I told you before, I'm tired of that."

"This girl didn't never show," Neelley answered, almost sweetly.

"Bullshit," Smith snapped.

"I ain't lying," Neelley whined. "I mean it. She didn't ever show up." He shrugged. "So after a while I met up with Judy again and she was with this other girl."

"Where'd you meet up with her?" Smith asked sharply.

"Franklin, Georgia," Alvin told him. "And Judy and this girl, they was talking, and Judy asked her, she said, 'Are you a virgin?' And the girl, she said she wasn't no virgin. She said she was on the pill."

"Pill?" Smith snapped. "She was thirteen years old. She was living at a Methodist home. Where the hell would she get a pill?"

Neelley shrugged. "That's what she said."

Smith let his eyes narrow. "Did you have sex with Lisa Millican?"

Neelley shook his head. "I didn't have no sex with her," he said, almost pleadingly.

"They found semen in her vagina, Alvin," Smith said. "Where do you think that came from?"

"I don't have no idea."

"Well, it didn't just get there by itself," Gilleland said.

"No, it sure didn't," Smith said angrily. "And we can test it, Alvin. That's the reason Collins and I came over here, to get samples of blood and hair and saliva. We know you were with that girl, and we know you had sex with her."

"I didn't have sex with her," Neelley said. He drew in a deep, trembling breath, then added nothing else.

Smith bore into him. "Where'd the semen come from, then?"

"Well, it was mine," Neelley admitted haltingly. "But I didn't have no sex with her."

Smith's head shot forward. "What the hell are you talking about?"

"She jerked me off," Neelley said.

"Who did?"

"Judy. She done it in a Dixie cup, then she poured it into Lisa."

Smith leaned back slightly. Even for a battle-hardened investigator, this was a new one. "Why'd she do that?"

"So she could . . . could . . ."

"Could what?" Smith snapped.

"So she could have sex with Lisa like that."

"You mean go down on her?" Smith asked.

"Yeah."

Smith drew his chair in closer to Neelley, still sitting directly in front of him, their faces nearly touching. "Don't tell me one more lie, Alvin," he warned. "Not one more."

Gilleland closed in on him, too. "You expect us to believe a disgusting story like that."

"What kind of fool would believe that, Alvin?" Smith demanded. "What kind of idiots do you think we are?"

"I just . . . just . . ."

"What kind of man takes a little girl and does something like that?" Smith said angrily. "Pours semen into her, then watches his wife go down on her?"

Neelley began to sputter, starting sentences, then stopping them abruptly, his words left dangling in midair.

"We're tired of hearing this bullshit," Smith said hotly. "I'll tell you that, Alvin. We're sick of it."

Neelley tried to draw away slightly, leaning back, as if to draw a breath of unencumbered air.

Smith leaned in toward him, immediately closing the space that had opened between them. "You had sex with Lisa Millican and we damn well know it!" he said. "And I'll tell you something else, we can prove it!"

Neelley began to shift in his seat, his legs trembling.

"And we're going to prove it," Smith added resolutely.

"At first I didn't," Alvin said weakly, breaking visibly for the first time.

Smith's eyes snapped over to him.

"She wanted to," Neelley said, his lips now trembling, too, "but I said no."

"You said you wouldn't have sex with her?" Gilleland asked.

"I told her I'd already been with this one girl that

day, you know," Neelley said. "And the way I am, I ain't good for but once."

"So what happened?" Smith demanded.

"Nothing," Neelley answered. "We didn't have sex right then. Judy and her, they went to the Kwikie Mart for some food, and me, I just laid down and went to sleep. I didn't even take off my clothes. I just slept right there in my jeans."

"So nothing happened that night in Franklin?" Gilleland asked.

"No, wasn't nothing happened then," Neelley said.

"What happened the next morning?"

"Well, Judy, she went off to get the kids," Neelley said. "To my mama's house in Cleveland, Tennessee."

"Where'd you go?"

"Just riding around," Neelley said. "I met her back up on Highway 64, but we didn't stay together long. I went on off to Chattanooga, and Judy, she went up to Murfreesboro to pick up her sister."

"What's her sister's name?" Gilleland asked.

"Dottie," Alvin said. "She likes girls. She's one of them, you know, lesbians, just like Judy is."

"Judy's a lesbian?" Smith asked.

"She likes them both," Alvin said. "Men and women."

"When did you see her again?"

"Sunday night at around ten or eleven," Alvin answered. "They was at the Dairy Bar in Scottsboro, Alabama. It was Judy, and Lisa and the twins. We all sat on the car outside the Dairy Bar for a while, then we went to this motel on Highway 35. Judy checked us all in. It was Room 12, I remember that, and I turned on the TV, and the news was on, and while I was watching it, Judy and Lisa, they went into the bathroom for a while, and when they come back out, they was both naked." He took a deep, shaky breath. "They wanted us all to have sex, and Lisa, she crawled up next to me, and she started rubbing on me and kissing me, and she put her hand in my pants, you know, feeling of me; she grabbed my penis and she was rubbing it." He stopped, and his eyes watered and grew red at the rims. "And we . . . we . . ."

"What?"

Suddenly Neelley's body began to shake uncontrollably. His eyes seemed to pop out of his head, and he began to cough and choke, his body heaving forward as he struggled to get air.

The men in the room drew toward him as he continued to gasp. His body jerked forward, and he started to heave so violently that Smith and the others stepped back. "I thought he would throw up all over the place," Smith remembered years later. "I had never seen anybody react to testimony that way, that violently, with such a physical revulsion."

Finally, the racking movements grew more subtle, and Neelley regained his breath. "Anyway," he began again, quietly, still laboring to get his breath, "we all had sex. I did it first, and then Lisa got down on the floor, and I could see that Judy was doing it to her, you know, between her legs, licking her down there."

"This was after you'd had sex with her?" Gilleland asked.

Alvin nodded. "But I didn't do nothing else. I just went to sleep after that."

"Did anything else happen that night?" Smith asked.

"No," Neelley said. "The next morning Judy and Lisa went out, and when they come back, they was in the bathroom again, and I could hear them talking. When they come out, they was naked and they asked me if I wanted to do it again, and I said no."

"Why didn't you want to do it again?" Smith asked.

" 'Cause I figured they'd been out that morning screwing around," Neelley answered, "and I didn't want to catch nothing."

"What happened then?" Gilleland asked.

"They said they was going to the K-Mart to buy some new clothes," Alvin said, "but when they come back, they didn't have none. They got naked again, and we all watched television, and I went to sleep, and the next morning when I woke up, Judy, she was already loading up the car."

"Is that when you left Scottsboro?" Smith asked.

"That's right," Alvin told him. "Me and the kids, we went to Gadsden. And Judy, her and the girl, they said they was going to Fort Payne to meet up with this guy named Charles that had dated Lisa's mother before."

"When did you see them again?"

"I didn't never see Lisa again," Alvin said. "But me and the kids was eating breakfast at the Omelet Shop, and Judy come up, and Lisa ain't with her, and I noticed right then that she'd changed her clothes."

"What happened when you left the Omelet Shop?" Gilleland asked.

"We went on up to Cleveland to see my parents," Alvin said. "But they wasn't home, and so we come on back to Rome, and Judy checked us in at the Oak Hurst Motel, and we stayed there about three days, and on the last day, Judy, she picked up this boy and girl."

"Okay," Smith said. "What happened after she told you she'd picked up these two people?"

"Well, we all met at this big plant," Alvin said. "And it was near a bridge and some water and the guy, he said that he'd done some fishing in that creek. Then the guy, he got in my car, and the girl, she went with Judy, and we went off."

"What were you planning to do?" Gilleland asked.

"Nothing," Alvin said. "But I was getting afraid of Judy, 'cause I thought she was going to set me up, you know, 'cause she'd already told me that she was going to get me burned."

"Why?"

"Because she'd been after some people in Macon," Alvin explained, "and she said I hadn't pinned them, and she was mad about that."

"What happened after you left the bridge?"

"We was looking for a liquor store," Alvin said, "but the one we come to, it was closed, and so we started looking for the bootlegger, and the guy, he started saying he had to go to the bathroom, and then Judy come on the CB and she told me she wanted to stop, that she had to do something."

"Did you stop?"

"Not right then," Alvin said. "I told Judy that John had to go to the bathroom, and then the guy, he said to pull over at this little road he seen, and so I pulled over and he got out and started using the bathroom, and while he done that Judy swung around in front, and John, he headed off down the road, and I got Judy to give me the kids, and I drove off."

"Where was your wife?" Smith asked.

"She followed John down the road."

"When did you see her again?"

"It didn't take no time, and she come back up behind me," Alvin said. "I stopped at the Golden Gallons, where Highway 225 comes into Highway 27, and I bought thirty dollars' worth of gas."

"What happened then?"

"We drove on down Highway 53 back to Rome," Neelley said. "And we was back at the Oak Hurst, and Judy and Kay, they come in right behind me, but the guy, he wasn't with them."

"Did you ask Judy where he was?" Smith asked.

Alvin nodded. "She said she shot him."

"And then you all went into the motel room?" Smith asked.

"Yeah," Alvin said, "and Judy and Kay, they got playing with each other and they did that for a while, and then Judy went to this Waffle House on Shorter Avenue, 'cause she said she knew some people there that was from the YDC."

"She left Kay Chatman with you?"

"Yeah, and she come over to me, and she said something like 'Hey, you want to get it on?' Something like that, and she took off her clothes, and she wadn't wearing no bra or no panties, and she got into the bed and we had sex right there."

"What happened after that?" Gilleland asked.

"Well, I got dressed, and then Judy come back," Alvin told him. "And Kay was still naked, and they both went into the bathroom, and they had sex, too, and when it was over, Judy come back out, and she had a towel around her, but Kay, she still didn't have no clothes on."

"Did they crawl in bed with you?"

"No, they was in bed with each other," Alvin answered. "And the kids was in bed with me."

"Did anything else happen that night?"

Alvin shrugged. "We just all went to sleep, and the next morning, when I woke up, Judy was already loading up the car, and Kay was just standing at the door, doing nothing."

"And you left the motel that morning?" Smith asked.

"Yeah," Alvin said. "Judy told me she wanted to ride around with the girl a while, and she did that, and then she come back around lunch time, and then we all went riding around."

"In the same car?"

Alvin shook his head. "No, in two cars. Judy headed off down Highway 27, and I sort of hung around Rome."

"When did you see Judy again?"

"I drove up to Summerville," Alvin said, "and I hollered for her on the CB, and we all met up at the Dairy King and ate in our cars. I told Judy not to do nothing to the girl, to just drop her off in Rome. But she said no, and we was driving around again, and I stopped and told Judy again, but she said no, and so I drove on off, and not long after that I heard on the police scanner that a guy had been shot."

"What did you do then?"

"I drove back toward the Dairy King, but before I got there, I come up on Judy and the girl wasn't with her no more, and so I asked her where the girl was, and Judy just said that she got rid of her down the road."

"And you were nowhere around when Lisa and Janice were murdered?" Smith asked.

Neelley shook his head.

"Why did she pick up the girls?" Smith asked.

"Well, she just said she'd do it for me," Neelley answered. "She told me that when she come back from Macon, 'cause when she was in Macon, she'd gotten into screwing blacks, and I didn't go with that, and so she said, well, she'd pick me up some girls, and then she'd just let them out so they could get to a phone."

"She didn't say she was going to kill them?" Gilleland asked.

"No," Neelley said. "But she's done it before."

"How do you know that?"

"She showed me some clippings."

"Where were they from?"

"Albany, around in there, and Columbus," Neelley said. "And one time she told me she was going to rip off a Magic Market in Chattanooga. She bought a Halloween mask, and she was going to use it to rob some place. That's when she showed me them clippings from Fort Payne, the ones about Lisa. And she showed me them, and she said, 'I've got you now. You're going to help me rob some places.'"

"And that's why she killed Lisa Millican?" Smith asked. "To get you to do that?"

Alvin nodded his head vigorously. "To set me up so she could have control over me, that's right." He glanced from one officer to another. "That's the whole thing with Judy," he said. "She likes to have control over people."

Following the interview, Alvin was transported to the Chattooga County Hospital, where Smith and Collins obtained hair and saliva samples before returning him to the Chattooga County Jail.

Once in his cell, Neelley began a letter to Agent House, for whom he had served as a small-time snitch. It would finally take up twenty-six handwritten pages and detail an enormous number of accusations against both Judith Neelley and the Rome and Macon YDCs.

"Here's what I know and have been told by Judy Neelley, my wife, and to [sic] girls who were locked up with Judy," the letter began.

On November 10, 1980, Alvin wrote, he and Judy had been arrested in Rome for armed robbery. Judy had been sent to the Rome YDC while he had been taken first to the Rome City Jail then the Floyd County Jail.

While separated, they had written letters to each other until the correspondence had been stopped by YDC staff. Their mail had been interrupted, Alvin contended, because Judy had been "trying to tell me something was wrong at the time, without just saying it in plain words."

Judy had later been released briefly and had visited him in prison, Alvin went on, and during that visit she had told him that Linda Adair had talked to her encouragingly about "messing" with men who made late-night visits to the Rome YDC. Other YDC officials promised her special favors for her cooperation, while Juvenile Officer Elaine Snow assured her that she could not become pregnant because she had been sterilized after the birth of her twins. In addition to these outrages, Alvin went on, Judy had been sexually abused by a Rome YDC teacher named Ken Dooley at both the Rome and Macon YDCs.

Under YDC pressure, Judy had finally become a member of a prostitution ring that YDC staff had organized and that worked out of several motels in the area. After a time the pressure was no longer necessary. Judy had become a willing participant. Parenthetically, Alvin added that Judy had also been raped by her attorney and a courthouse guard in January of

1981 while at the Floyd County Courthouse, a story Judy herself later denied.

Still later, Alvin said, Judy had become an enthusiastic member of a sophisticated prostitution ring run by YDC staff in Rome and Macon. As a member of this criminal underground, she'd come to prefer a life of prostitution, pornography, blackmail, and violence to the better life she'd lived with him.

Neelley added that for the last four months he'd been conducting his own investigation of the YDC prostitution ring. Later he would give dramatic details of stationing himself outside the Rome YDC and watching through the night as Rome police officials arrived for their nocturnal liaisons with selected YDC girls.

In this letter alone, the first Alvin wrote after he'd been charged with murder and incarcerated at the Rutherford County Jail in Murfreesboro, Tennessee, there were enough falsehoods, conjectures, and deceptions to keep investigators working for weeks in an attempt either to disprove or corroborate them.

But the letter was just the beginning of a story that was slowly being elaborated. During the next few weeks, while Georgia officials pondered their case against him, Alvin would talk again and again, but he would never admit to having been involved in the actual murders of either Millican or Chatman. That had been Judy's doing, he maintained, and it had flowed from an incomprehensible rage he'd always noticed in her. "She was always mad," he said years later from prison, "but I couldn't ever figure out why."

CHAPTER
20

Advisaries

SMITH AND COLLINS reported the results of their interrogation of Alvin Neelley to Igou the next day.

"He admitted everything," Smith told him. "That he raped Lisa in Scottsboro, that he knew about her murder, everything."

"Except that he was at the canyon when Lisa was killed," Igou said. "He didn't admit that."

"He denies it," Collins said. "My guess is, he always will."

Igou nodded. "But is he telling the truth?"

Smith shook his head. "The fact is, we don't have any physical evidence linking him to that canyon at all."

"And Judy backs him up one hundred percent," Collins added. "According to her, Alvin was nowhere near the canyon."

Igou sat back, letting his eyes roll toward the ceiling. "Why was she picking up girls? What was in it for her?"

"Sex," Smith answered. "At least that's the way Alvin tells it."

Igou had his doubts. "It's possible," he said, "but I'm not sure we're looking for a sexual motive in her case. Maybe it was part of it, but I think the sex was for Alvin. With Judy, it was something else."

"But what?" Smith asked.

It was a question whose answer Igou would ponder for a long time.

Only a few hundred yards away, Robert French, Jr., Judith Neelley's defense attorney, had questions of his own. Only a few days before, Judge Randall Cole had asked him to serve as Neelley's court-appointed defense. Reluctantly, after voicing his protests, he'd acceded to Cole's request. Not long after that, he'd actually met Judith Neelley in her cell in the basement of the Dekalb County Sheriff's Office. They'd spoken for some time, and she'd given him a letter to be delivered to her husband, one that exonerated him from having any part in her crimes.

At the end of this initial interview, French could hardly remember having had a more negative reaction to a client. That evening, when his wife asked him what Judith Neelley was like, he described her as "the real thing, a cold-blooded killer." A night's sleep had not softened his opinion, and the next morning, when members of his staff asked him what he thought of his new client, he told them that as far as he was concerned, Halloween had come early. Still later that same day, he told his co-counsel, Steve Bussman, that he did not like Neelley, but that he would do the best he could for her, then let them cart her off to Georgia where they'd "fry her eyeballs out."

At fifty years of age, a slender, classically handsome man, French had risen to become one of the South's most successful attorneys. He was also one of its most politically active. A Republican in a state that voted largely Democratic at the local level, he had twice run and twice been defeated in bids for a seat in the United States Congress.

But his legal practice had flourished, and the rewards of his success surrounded him. At the beginning of the trial, as he would later say, he had been a millionaire several times over, the owner of a private plane, with which he'd actually buzzed the town, and a white Rolls-Royce, surely noticeable symbols of his position in a town as small as Fort Payne, Alabama. In addition, he owned a three-hundred-thousand-dollar house on the mountain, various residential properties, a fifty-two car rail siding, thirty-two acres of prime industrial real estate, and a half-million dollars worth of industrial machinery.

For the last few years French had lived lavishly and well, and as he freely stated, he had developed an ideology to go with his status. His politics were those of a staunch conservative Republican, and he was a strong advocate of the death penalty.

But all of this was about to change as French launched into his defense of Judith Neelley, surely one of the most passionate ever offered in an American court.

Like the local earthquake it would finally produce, it began, as it were, with a series of motions. The first was that Neelley be considered under the Youth Offenders Act. Under this statute, an offender under the age of twenty-one could make application for youthful-offender status and waive the right to a jury trial.

On December 1, Judge Cole allowed the motion and ordered that a probationary report be done to determine whether she should be granted youthful-offender status.

Within a few days the report was finished. It noted that Neelley had committed, been charged with, and convicted for numerous criminal offenses. She had lived as an adult, committed the crimes of an adult, and in the judgment of the report, she should not be regarded as a youthful offender.

On the basis of the report, Judge Cole denied Neelley status as a youthful offender on December 17, a step which, in effect, ordered that she be tried as an adult.

At that point Igou read the state of Alabama's three-count indictment of murder, abduction with intent to harm, and abduction with intent to terrorize and sexually violate.

To this indictment, Neelley pleaded not guilty and not guilty by reason of insanity, a double plea that would allow the jury the option of freeing her entirely with a not-guilty verdict or remanding her to the custody of a mental institution in the event of a finding of insanity.

The defense then asked for a ten-day continuance in order to make an additional plea. Cole granted the motion and set a trial date of March 7, 1983.

The defense also requested that a psychiatric examination be done, and Judge Cole granted the motion.

Pursuant to this motion, Neelley arrived at Bryce Psychiatric Hospital in Tuscaloosa, Alabama, on January 18, 1983. For the next two days she was subjected to examinations of her mental status on the day of her admission, an evaluation of her mental condition by the three-member Lunacy Commission, psychological assessments, a social history, a physical examination, and a general extended observation.

The findings in Tuscaloosa were not encouraging to the defense. Neelley was found to be, in the technical language of the commission's subsequent report, "oriented in good contact and cooperative."

In addition, her general demeanor struck her observers as appropriate to her "thought content." She told members of the staff that she had trouble sleeping, but that she had no desire to commit or tendency toward suicide. There did not appear to be any disturbance in the content of her thought processes. She was not delusional, and her memory was good for both recent and distant events. Upon examination, she was able to give a chronology of events in her life from the time she left home to get married to her arrest and incarceration.

Psychological tests administered on January 20

showed Neelley to be in the superior range of intelligence, "with no indications of organic involvement."

There was, however, some suggestion of a personality disorder that the report classified as "either of the passive-aggressive or dependent type." She was also said to suffer from "situational depression."

Still, according to the report that the Lunacy Commission submitted to Judge Cole on February 9, Neelley did not suffer from any mental deficiency or disorder that would serve to "diminish her criminal responsibility."

Judith Neelley could stand trial.

It was now four and one half months since the death of Lisa Millican.

While French filed motions and Judith Neelley sat for psychiatric evaluations, Igou continued to make those decisions that were necessary in the case. His first determination was that a charge of murder could not be made against Alvin Neelley. The problem was in the physical evidence; there was not one thing to connect him to Lisa's murder. Time and time again Judith Neelley had exonerated her husband. Repeatedly, in statement after statement, she had declared that Alvin had had nothing to do with the killing, that, in fact, he had been miles away, barreling down Highway 59 toward Gadsden, Alabama, at the very moment when Lisa Millican had been marched to the edge of the canyon and shot in the back. On the first night of her incarceration in Fort Payne, she had written a letter that the FBI had later seized and in which she stated once again, this time in writing, that Alvin had not been involved in Millican's death. Such statements, along with the utter lack of any physical evidence against Alvin Neelley, made it impossible to press an indictment for murder. He could be charged with rape by Scottsboro officials and with various other crimes connected with the kidnapping of John Hancock and the shooting of Janice Chatman in Georgia, but as regarded his activities in Dekalb County, Alabama, no case could be made.

"It's just Judith Neelley now," Igou told Smith and Collins. "She's the one we've got a case against. We'll have to leave Alvin to other jurisdictions and hope they've got enough to nail him."

During the next few weeks, the prosecution began to build its case in earnest, assembling, cataloging, going over the forensic and other physical evidence, interviewing witnesses, then deciding on the order of their presentation.

As part of the process, Smith began to read the vast correspondence that Judith and Alvin had written to one another during the time of their respective incarcerations. There were hundreds of letters, all written in neat, curiously similar scripts. "I spent hours and hours reading those letters," Smith recalled. "And at the end of it, I really felt like I knew Judy Neelley, what she was like and what her relationship with Alvin was like, and I can tell you this, it didn't make me one bit less determined to prosecute her."

CHAPTER
21

Life and Letters

AS HER LETTERS along with subsequent testimony and investigation would reveal, Judith Neelley's life had been relatively ordinary until her father's death threw the family's economic and social conditions into radical decline. He'd left them with only a small Social Security pension and eight acres of land on the outskirts of Murfreesboro. For a time the family depended on other relatives for support. Then Judy's mother, Barbara Adams, decided to use the otherwise useless eight acres as a large wooded parking space for a double-wide house trailer.

Mrs. Adams also took a job at Heatcraft, a local factory, trying as best she could to support the family alone. As her husband's memory inevitably faded, however, she began to see other men. Not long after that, she was involved in a car accident and Judy was dealt the humiliating blow of learning that her mother was "running around" with a teenage boy. Formally charged with contributing to the delinquency of a minor, Mrs. Adams's life took a steadily downward turn. She stopped working at Heatcraft and simply hung around the trailer while Judy did the chores.

By then, it had become clear that Mr. Adams's

death had done more than undermine the family's finances. It had entirely changed their way of life, and increasingly, as Judy moved into her teenage years, she saw it as a terrible dive toward trashiness. The discipline and order her father had imposed was replaced by a "white trash" life-style she despised. Her brother and sister grew lazy, staying out of school and guzzling beer in front of the television set or taking long, pointless rides around Murfreesboro. To Judy, it seemed that the whole family had become trapped in a low-class existence, sloppy, brutish, lumpishly stupid, a world of losers.

To the rest of the family, however, such a world seemed perfectly acceptable. Mrs. Adams yammered mindlessly on the CB she'd installed in the trailer, and pretty soon an assortment of men began turning up at the double-wide, beers in hand, their bellies pouring over their trousers, all of them looking for the Indian Princess, Mrs. Adams's CB handle.

Judy avoided them by taking long walks in the woods around the trailer. She liked the cool shade, the sway of the trees, the quiet and the solitude. It gave her the chance to think about what she wanted for herself.

Already she knew she was unwilling to accept the world her family accepted. For a time her ambition focused on being a nurse, and she pursued that goal relentlessly, passing through the predictable stages of education in Murfreesboro: Walter Hill School, Kettrell School, Oakland High School. She was a good student, and even made the honor roll. She was active in the 4-H Club and in the Future Homemakers of America. In the eighth grade she became a cheerleader, something that made her so proud she posed triumphantly in her new uniform, legs apart, arms uplifted, a chrome baton held firmly in her hand. It is not the picture of a wallflower, a shy retiring nature waiting to be overwhelmed. In it, Judith Neelley looks entirely in command.

It was a command that did not stop in the photograph. By the time she was fifteen, a continual stream of men was flowing through the double-wide. Since nothing more than a sheet separated Judy's room from her mother's, she could often hear their drunken sexual play. It disgusted her, and to avoid it, she sometimes left the trailer, climbed one of the trees in the surrounding woods, and stayed there through the night, cradled in the limbs, watching the darkness like an owl. Still, as she later claimed, not one of those men ever dared touch her. There was something about Judith Neelley that kept them cautiously at bay.

Through it all, Judy kept to her one ambition. The way out was education, and at school she remained the dutiful straight arrow, always working at her studies. She had come to think that she was pretty smart, and she liked others to know it, too. In subtle little ways she liked to outsmart people, demonstrate the superiority she was slowly recognizing. Physically, she was big, able to take care of herself. She was beginning to understand that her mind was just as large.

Still, she was only fifteen, and there were times when her whole body ached needfully. Fiercely virginal, repulsed by the men and boys around her, she'd had only two dates, and there were times when she felt her pinched estate—the trailer, her family, even her virginity—almost like a physical prison. Somehow, she had to break out of everything small and limited. The double-wide was cramped and dilapidated, her sister and brother were going nowhere. There seemed no escape, and so from time to time she found herself yearning romantically for what all the preachers called "a true deliverance," the mythical man, her knight in shining armor.

Judith Adams met Alvin Neelley for the first time on an afternoon in early summer 1979. He'd been riding around with his friend, Dan Hartley. For several days Hartley had been planning to look up a woman he'd met by CB. Her handle was Indian Princess, and she'd told him she lived in a trailer on Marboro Road. Her place would be easy to recognize, she'd added, because it was the only one around with a CB antenna.

But it wasn't the antenna Alvin Neelley noticed as he headed down the gravel road, looking intently at the trailers from behind the wheel of his yellow Gremlin. It was a girl who stood in front of a car, talking quietly to another man and woman. She was beautiful, the sort of girl he'd only seen in magazines, and it was only after he'd pulled into her driveway that he noticed the tall CB antenna on her trailer. It was the Indian Princess's trailer, he found out later, and the tall, dark-haired beauty was her fifteen-year-old daughter.

For a moment he sat behind the wheel, amazed at how she boldly strode up to the Gremlin and introduced herself. It was as if she'd been drawn to him suddenly by a vast, implacable force.

Everything that happened in the double-wide during the next few hours was out of character for both of them. While Dan and the Indian Princess talked, Alvin and Judy simply stared at each other from across the kitchen table.

Suddenly, without a word, Judy left the room, then returned a few minutes later in a completely different dress and with her hair in a completely different style. Then, without a word, they both got up and walked into the living room to be alone, to talk. They talked until four o'clock the next morning, at times in loud jolly voices, at times in steamy whispers. They had never experienced anything like each other. Alvin thought her beautiful, perfect, and marveled at how she seemed to know what he was thinking before he thought it. It was as if they could speak to each other without talking, feel the heat coming from each other's bodies. "If anyone had stepped in between us," he would say years later, "they'd have been burned up in the sparks."

Over the next few weeks they did everything together. They watched "Happy Days," "Solid Gold," and "American Bandstand." They talked about the latest songs, and the wild, feverish lyrics seemed to fit them perfectly. They saw movies together, but even the most romantic ones were unable to match what they felt for each other. It was as if both of them had spent their lives praying for what had just been handed to them.

The talk went on ceaselessly. Judy told Alvin about her father, about how much she'd loved him. She detailed the ways her life had been altered by his death.

As for Alvin, he had a good deal more to tell, since, at twenty-nine, he'd lived a longer life. He told her about how he'd had all the childhood diseases in one year—mumps, measles, chicken pox—one directly after the other. Judy had laughed at that, and over the years, it seemed that it was this laughter that defined them. Alvin had always been a prankster, pulling tricks, throwing frogs at girls, sneaking up on petting couples to scare them half to death. Now he'd found someone who could appreciate his oddball sense of humor, recognize as he always had that stupid people deserved the tricks played on them.

As Alvin had grown older, however, the tricks had turned a bit less harmless. He was proud of them anyway, however, and he wasn't shy about telling Judy about them. He'd stolen a few cars, been locked up a few times.

Of course, it hadn't all been fun and games. Alvin had suffered the slings and arrows of misfortune more deeply than most. Thus, as Judy listened night after night, he related the tragic episodes of his life. The most tragic, he said, had been his rejection from the navy. He'd gone to the recruiter in Danville, lied about his age, and joined up. But later, he'd been sent to Roanoke for the medical examination. The examination had taken almost all day, and at the end of it the navy doctors had stamped "PERMANENTLY DISABLED" in big black letters across his application. Somewhere in all those tests, he told Judy sorrowfully, they had found a murmur in his heart.

Judy was sympathetic. She continued to listen as he moved on through his life. He told about that day in the summer of 1968 when he and three others had decided to tow a hot rod over to a dirt racetrack in Blue Ridge, Georgia. On the way the tow had come loose and the two cars had drifted off the road. It was already dark, but he'd had enough light to stand between the two cars and secure the towing chain again. While he was doing it, one of the cars had shot forward suddenly, caught his legs between the two bumpers, crushing his left leg just above the knee, his right one at the knee itself. As a result, Alvin said, he'd spent the whole summer of his seventeenth year in Erlanger Hospital in Chattanooga.

Not long after that, Alvin went on, he'd stolen another car and been caught again. This time they'd tried him as an adult and given him two years. But there was a joke at the end of this story, too, Alvin added, because when the judge had explained that with good behavior he'd be out in only a few months, Alvin had looked the judge right in the eye, flashed him a great big happy-go-lucky smile, and said, "Well, in that case, Judge, see you in two years."

At last, as Judy and Alvin grew closer, Alvin admitted that he was already married. His wife's name was Jo Ann, he told her, and she wasn't much to look at or talk to. She was a liar and a cheat, and she'd still been married to another man when he married her. They'd had a lot of trouble, he said, and the marriage would soon be over.

As the summer ended, Judy and Alvin continued to see each other. They rode around for hours, talking constantly. There was never enough time to get it all out. For Judy it was wonderful to get away from the double-wide, from Dottie and her brothers and Dan Hartley, who'd never gone home after that first night with the Indian Princess. But it was not just getting away that made life more exciting, it was getting away with Alvin. They kept each other laughing all the time. She'd always complained that her nose looked like a ski slope, and once, when she'd done some stupid thing, he'd laughed and said she was just like a Polack. Then he started calling her Slopeski. She couldn't help it, whenever he called her that, it just broke her up.

Still, they agreed that the best thing between them was the way they could talk to each other through looks and facial expressions alone. It was magical the way they could communicate wordlessly, speak to each other silently, as if in a language no one else could hear. It was freaky, and it was wonderful. They were sure that none had ever loved like this.

Finally, Judy told him she was a virgin, that she'd been saving herself for the right man. Alvin was that man because he was different from all the others. He was generous and funny, but there was another side, too, a daring, criminal edge that intrigued her. It was an irresistible combination, the allure of gentleness and violence, sweetness and danger, security and peril, all mixed together in a base of sidesplitting humor. He was just the sort of man she wanted to give herself to.

After the first time they made love every chance they got. It didn't matter whether it was in his apartment or his car. Sometimes they would remember it as gentle and loving. At other times they would remind each other of how they could really tear the backseat of a Gremlin up.

Toward fall they began to plan for their elopement.

Alvin would stay in Murfreesboro, make a little more money for their nest egg, then join Judy in Cleveland, Tennessee, where he'd taken her to live with his parents.

Only a few weeks after she'd returned to school as a tenth-grader at Oakland High, Judy wrote her mother a harsh note, then eloped with Alvin. For a time they lived with his family, then moved first to Rome, then to the Smith's Motel in Kennesaw, Georgia, a small town about twenty miles north of Atlanta, where Alvin worked at a Magic Market just across the street on U.S. 41.

The motel room was small and cramped, so Judy often wandered over to the Magic Market to be with him. Alvin would always be sitting behind the cash register, fingering the keys or glancing down at the money drawer.

Sometimes Judy would stock the shelves or replenish the cooler with beer and soda. She'd even sweep the place once in a while or pick up the few discarded wrappers that blew listlessly across the parking area. Inside, she'd find Alvin still behind the cash register eating a sandwich or sipping at a can of Coke. She could tell when he wanted her, and at times they would lock the front door, go back behind the cooler, and lie down together on the cement floor.

When it was over, they'd return to the front and stare out the large glass windows, their eyes enviously following the traffic that whisked so freely up and down the road.

One night not long after he'd gotten the job at the Magic Market, a group of deposits turned up missing, and Judy and Alvin left Kennesaw, heading north into Alabama, then south again to Albany, Georgia.

Both of them went to work at the Zippy Market in nearby Dawson. Alvin worked the cash register as he always did, while Judy stocked the shelves, swept, kept an eye on the parking lot.

There were times when none of it seemed like the life they had imagined together, and they would watch the road longingly, then let their eyes drift down to the cash drawer of the register, its thick store of bills waiting for deposit.

Soon she was robbed. The owner suspected that she'd robbed herself, and so they were on the move again. This time they'd left without taking any money, and so they slept in their car at night and aimlessly wandered the local malls during the day. For food, they bought bread and peanut butter and stored them in the glove compartment. It was the kind of raw poverty that made life on the road miserable rather than romantic. It surprised them how much being poor made them think about money all the time. Days sometimes went by without a single laugh.

As the weeks passed, the robberies continued, along with their incessant movement. But on July 14, 1980, they stopped in Ringold, Georgia, long enough to get married. Then they struck out for Columbus, Georgia, where they had their honeymoon at the Econo Lodge in nearby Phenix City, Alabama. It was Room 13, with mirrors on the wall and ceiling. There was only one bed, a waterbed that rolled like a wave machine when they made love on it.

They left for Phenix City, Alabama, a day or two later, then moved on ceaselessly, finally reaching Cleveland, Tennessee, where they stayed overnight with his parents. The next morning they loaded themselves into a light blue Pinto and struck out for Texas. Alvin was feeling cramped and wanted to see the wide-open spaces. Judy was up for seeing anything as long as it wasn't another convenience store or cheap motel.

They didn't stop again until they reached the little town of Rustin, Louisiana. There was a Best Western Motel there, and it looked like a nice place. It had a pool, and while Alvin watched, Judy kept zooming down the waterslide, sometimes belly-down, which might have been a problem, since she was six months pregnant.

They headed on through Texas, then stopped at a

small town between Marshall and Dallas, where they stayed for four days, then turned back east, into Georgia, remained there a while, then headed south, finally stopping at Panama City, Florida, where Judy played in the ocean for the first time.

Alvin cared less about the sea. He'd started eating obsessively, hamburgers and french fries, Cokes and sandwiches, the junk food of the road. Because of that, he'd ballooned up to nearly two hundred pounds, and bouncing around in the surf was pretty much out of the question. And so, for the most part, he simply lay on the bed or sat slumped in a chair, reading the Bible or *Fortune* or any of a host of detective magazines. Nothing felt so good to him as an air-conditioned room.

Judy remained more playful, always in the waves or out on the beach, sunning herself. Once, she stretched out on a striped air mattress and posed for pictures. For some of them she reclined seductively, her skin very smooth and white against the blue bathing suit. For others, she posed in ways that were more blatantly suggestive, her hands behind her head, her legs spread wide apart for the camera's prurient eye, the kind of sexy poses Alvin liked.

By the time they got back to Georgia, they were running out of money, and so they stayed at the Oak Hurst, a fleabag motel on Martha Berry Boulevard in Rome.

For amusement, they sometimes went into Chattanooga. Both of them liked wrestling, and often they would go to the matches at the Gold Port Theater. Alvin had once served as a referee and knew very well how the whole scam worked. Once, while they were ringside at the Gold Port, he called to one of the wrestlers, an old acquaintance, Crazy Luke Graham, and told him to "throw the bum out." Graham accommodated in a flash, practically dropping his opponent to the floor at their feet.

They both loved wrestling. They even loved to cheer

or boo the same wrestlers. They always booed the "good guy," the namby-pamby one the crowd adored. And they always cheered for the one who'd been designated to play the "dirty wrestler" for the match, the one who scratched and bit and strangled, the one who never played by other people's rules.

Back in Rome, reality swept down on them again, and they began to think about money. Only a few days later, Judy robbed a woman at gunpoint in the parking area of the Riverbend Mall.

Both Alvin and Judy were subsequently charged with the robbery. Alvin was sentenced to five years in prison and was transported first to the Georgia Diagnostic and Classification Center in Jackson, Georgia, then to the Walker Correctional Institute in Lafayette. Judy, because she was under eighteen, was turned over to the Rome Youth Development Center. Two days after arriving there, she gave birth to twins. Still later, she was sent to the YDC in Macon, where she served the bulk of her sentence.

During this time of separation, Alvin and Judy wrote many letters to each other. It was this correspondence that Danny Smith laboriously read in the late fall of 1982.

As he subsequently discovered, the letters contained secret codes and secret names, Sundown, Lady Goodyear, Slopeski. In addition, Judy sometimes drew a sundown at the end of the letters, a way of drawing her CB handle of Lady Sundown, or Lady of Sundown, since Alvin had chosen Sundown as his handle because he usually worked the second shift at convenience stores, the one that more or less began at sundown.

In the letters, Alvin addressed Judy lovingly as "Sexy" or "My Beautiful Wife," while she addressed him as "My Big Bedroom-Blue-Eyed Husband."

They wrote continually, sometimes stating the obvious, while at other times writing things between the lines. They were obviously aware their letters were being read by watchful officials.

"I miss you so much," Judy wrote to him. "I miss your gentle touch and your sweet kisses. I miss the smile on your handsome face and the sexy look in those beautiful blue bedroom eyes. I miss your tender lovemaking more than any of that. You always knew how to make me feel like a woman."

Alvin responded passionately, often through sexual references to Judy's body.

"I blushed when I read what you said at the end of your letter," Judy answered him on one occasion. "You said that you missed my big, very big, almost bigger than life, you know, Gash. I got embarrassed just reading it. Just remember that is something that you can say is your fault! (smile)."

It was the letters that seemed to keep the relationship at a fever pitch, so much so that when Judy received a Valentine's Day card of red hearts and pink birds, she pasted Alvin's picture inside one of its large hearts and taped it to the wall.

And yet, as Smith discovered, the letters were not always so warm. At times the separation seemed to be tearing at them, driving them apart. Alvin often grew jealous and accusatory, lashing out in anger at her infidelities. On such occasions, his letters became threatening.

"I have enough on you to put you in prison for a long time," he warned at one point. But his greatest threat remained the withdrawal of his love. "I'll put my love where it will be returned," he told her. "You can't have me and play around too."

But Alvin was not the only jealous one. Judy was also convinced that Alvin was cheating on her, and she viciously made threats against these imagined lovers. "I'll take care of her when I get out!" she told him. "None of them are woman enough to try to take you from me when I get out." These women, Judy wrote, made up a "little bunch of nothings" who weren't "going to take anything from me! Don't worry, I can take care of myself. You showed me how, so don't worry."

It was a lesson she'd already taught the other girls in Macon, she told Alvin proudly. "But they don't give me any bull. . . . None of these other girls will run their mouth at me. I wonder why. Do you know? (smile)"

As for the girls outside, the ones who were trying to take him away from her, Judy assured her husband that they would get what they deserved. "Well, I noticed that you seem to admire this Janie," she wrote. "Saying that she is a 'beautiful sixteen year old,' and that she has more smarts that most 30 year old women . . . Well, let me tell you something, she might be trying to get you by what ever means she can. But she will Damn Well Have to Kill Me to do it. And I will sure as hell not give the little bitch the upper hand. I'll kill her before she ever gets you from me. Damn it, I Love You. And I will prove it to you! Just wait!"

But Janie was just the beginning. "And this little Betty has had it," Judy added later on. "I'm gonna raise some hell if I ever meet up with her. What is her last name?"

Again and again, Judy expressed her feelings of anger and betrayal. Alvin was even putting the little drawings they had always shared in letters to other girls, she wrote, little drawings that were supposed to be theirs alone, especially the one she really liked, the picture of a "Smile" with a tongue in it.

But Judy not only voiced her own accusations, she continually responded to the ones Alvin incessantly voiced against her. People were putting crazy ideas in his head, she told him, they had even gotten him to believe she would have relations with blacks, a possibility she emphatically denied. "For one thing," she wrote, "I'm not going to call any niggers, and there were only two white security guards." Alvin's idea that she would have sex with blacks was absurd for obvious reasons. "I hate niggers and you know it," she wrote angrily. "I always told Cindy what I thought about her messing with niggers. I never have been and I never will be like her."

But Alvin remained unappeased. "You said, it's been so long since we've been together," he wrote, "you've almost forgotten how. How what? You've not stopped anything. I get it! It's been so long with me, you've forgotten how with me. It may be alots longer with me than you think, like *never!* again."

But if Judy was having trouble with Alvin, she was also having trouble with her peers at the YDC, as well as its local staff. As for the other girls, they were wimps and meddlers, utterly incapable of playing Boney to Alvin's Clyde. "Well these little [YDC] girls wouldn't know how to help me if I wanted help," she wrote. "But I don't think my life is any of their business, so I don't talk to them about me. I think group is *stupid*. I don't think we should have it at all. All it does for me is give me a headache."

The staff was as bad as the girls, especially Mrs. Green, who was always trying to get Judy to write her family in Murfreesboro. "I don't want to write to anyone in that so-called family of mine," Judy hissed, and no one was going to make her do it. It was only Alvin she loved, but YDC staff had refused even to let her call him on their wedding anniversary. "These people sure are cold hearted," she wrote. "One day they will regret what they have done to us. It says in the bible that they will."

Phone calls were one thing, but later Judy wrote Alvin that YDC staff members were also interrupting their correspondence. "What kind of ass holes they can be," she wrote angrily. "I'm sending it back and this time it damn-well better get to you! I'm sick and tired of a bunch of weak-minded turkeys playing with our mail!" Everyone was trying to destroy them, Judy added, especially the "stinking, lying crooked law." She seemed mystified that anyone would want to break up such a perfect couple. "I don't know why everyone wants our marriage to end. But I do know that I'm not gonna let it end. I love you and you are mine, and I am yours forever! They haven't turned me against you. They have tried every way they can, but I could never turn against you, love. Never!"

In letter after letter, Judy fought to keep this love alive, particularly its erotic power. "Thinking back over all of those memories made me think back before we ever did 'anything,' (know what I mean?)" she wrote. "When we were sitting outside listening to Roger Whittaker and we were leaning up against the car. It was a warm night, but it sure did get *hotter*." There had been many such nights, she reminded him, and she wanted him to remember them. "And who says you can't make love on a Gremlin," she wrote. "We sure did . . . And it was great."

"I miss your sweet kisses and your gentle touch," she gushed. "I miss those sexy blue bedroom eyes. I miss that beautiful smile and the way your hypnotizing eyes shine when you laugh."

All she wanted was to be near him. "I miss holding you close to me and feeling the warmth of your body next to mine at night. I miss your wonderful lovemaking and the way you make me feel important and like a woman. I miss you!! I'm losing my mind being away from you. I'm looking forward to the wonderful day we are together again. It seems like it will never get here, but I know it will."

They had to remember what it was like between them, what they had shared, their codes and their ecstasy. "Are you puckered up?" she asked him. "Remember?"

As the days of separation lengthened, Judy continued to struggle to maintain her relationship with Alvin. "It seems like an eternity since I held you in my arms. When I see you again, I'm going to hold you so close you won't be able to breathe. I Love You,

Horney! I always have and I ALWAYS WILL! Understand me, Turkey?"

At times she could not seem to understand why he was jealous of her. "Why are you so jealous of me?" she asked him. "I'm not worth being jealous over. I'm just about as ugly as they come and I ain't worth a shit. But I have good reason to be jealous. You are the handsomest man I have ever met. You have dated a college full of women all at one time. You could have any woman you want and when you make love to me, I am so happy and feel so wonderful I can hardly stand it."

Judy was released in November of 1981. She took a bus all the way to Cleveland, Tennessee, to live with Alvin's parents and the twins. A little over a week after she returned she was arrested again, this time for the robbery of an Exxon station, but by March of 1982 she was back in Cleveland, living with Alvin's parents.

It was not the happiest of times. Judy did not like Alvin's father, and she minced no words in saying so. "I can't stand that S.O.B.," she raged to Alvin. "Your dad still raises hell every now and then. . . . But he won't say anything to me. If he ever does, he knows he will regret it."

But Mr. Neelley was not the only one Judy said should keep away from her. She was dangerous, and she meant for people to know it. As a sign of her devotion to Alvin and her inaccessibility to others, she donned a green T-shirt that said "Yes, I do, but not with you," on the front. If anyone tried to come on to her, she told Alvin, she'd "cuss him out in a heartbeat."

As the time neared for Alvin's release, Judy's letters grew cheerful and teasing. She promised to turn their bedroom into "a place for beautiful love making between a husband and a wife." She was sure that his mother would mind the kids, she added, but warned him that he'd need to be in good shape. "Take care of yourself," she teased him gently, "or I will turn you over my knee! -smile-"

Toward the end of his sentence, Alvin suddenly stopped writing. During the weeks of his silence, Judy's letters grew increasingly frantic. "To be honest, I feel very unloved," she wrote. "Could you at least write me one letter and let me know why your not writing? Please! I love you, Babe, and it is killing me not getting anything from you."

But Alvin did not write her, and as the days passed, Judy's tone became pleading. "I've gotten to the point where my nerves are on end," she wrote. "I'm going nuts. I toss and turn all night long."

To this, Alvin responded with another accusation. "I have only gotten 4 letters from you and two cards since you have been there," he wrote. "So I figure you have been awful busy with something (or someone) else. Right? I guess you are writing to all of your 'friends.' huh? Well, if you are, could you please tell them to send you stamps if they want to hear from you."

Judy was desperate, and she told him so. "I can't handle this," she wrote. "I'm going crazy."

When Alvin refused to answer her, desperation turned to anger. "I am gonna answer the letter the same way you wrote it, Smart!" she wrote. "If I wanted to leave, I wouldn't have to wait until I was 18. I could go anywhere I wanted to right now. But I am where I want to be."

As far as his jealousy was concerned, she was sick of it, sick of all his "bull." "I have always been true to you. And for what? For you to accuse me of everything under the sun! I might have talked and written to boys, but I have never put my hands on them, and they have never put their hands on me! And you know you can't say that, because you always had a reason, didn't you? And you always had a reason to write letters to your 'friends' like you did too. Right? Bull! You are so paranoid you will believe *anything* you hear about me. While you're talking to a counselor, why don't you tell him how paranoid and insanely jealous you are."

Only a few days later, her tone softened markedly. "Guess what I dreamed about the first night I was here?" she asked him. "Do you remember the bedroom we used to sleep in whenever we would come here. Well, I dreamed about us making love in there. *It Was Wonderful!!* I know that terrific dream will come true. I can hardly wait. I miss you so much. I miss *everything* about you. From that sexy smile to all of the wonderful love making. Damn I miss you! Listen here, Big 'D', when we get together again, I'm gonna lay a screwing on you like you've never had!! Understand, Horney??!!"

Alvin responded in kind, sending her a little poem he'd written just for them:

Prison walls may be between us
Prison walls may keep us apart,
But each letter I receive, darling,
Brings you closer to my heart.

Love, there's no need to worry,
There's no reason to fear,
When I offered you my heart,
I placed it in your care.

It won't be long now, sweetheart,
Our time is near.
I'll show you I love you,
And prove I'm sincere.

Alvin was released at the end of April 1982. Judy met him at the bus station. They went to a Richard Pryor movie and laughed and laughed. For a few hours it was like the old days when they'd first met, the same talk and laughter. They made love in their old bedroom, and it was very good, like old times.

But it didn't last. Over the next few weeks the sex

turned sour. Alvin told her that he didn't want her anymore.

The talking died away, too, and sometimes he would start to say something to her and then stop in midsentence.

And then there was the money. They didn't have any, and so they decided to get some. They broke into post office boxes and snatched the checks inside. They bought money orders, and Judy raised their amounts by writing in a script that looked like a computer's.

After cashing a few stolen checks, they went almost immediately to her mother's house in Murfreesboro. Then they got in a yellow Volkswagen van and went down to Panama City, Florida, for a couple of weeks to see her sister, Dottie. While there, Alvin bought Judy a final gift, a black T-shirt with white letters across the front: "Eat Your Heart Out, I'm Married."

Not long after Smith had finished reading the correspondence and then the various background checks that had been done on the Neelleys, the prosecution team sat down to hammer out their case. They had all the facts by then, and they were entirely confident they could prove beyond the shadow of a doubt that Judith Neelley had murdered Lisa Ann Millican at the rim of Little River Canyon. It was all they had to do, simply prove that she had done it. Still, her motive eluded them.

Igou posed the question. "Why did she do it?"

" 'Cause she's one mean bitch," Collins said.

Danny Smith agreed. "Yeah, very hard, no doubt about that."

Igou looked at him. "Was it the sex?"

"Maybe," Smith said. "That's Alvin's story."

"Anything else?"

"She liked scaring people, dominating them," Collins said. "We know that from the way she treated Hancock. Baiting him the way she did, cussing him, and teasing him about what they were going to do to his girlfriend."

Igou nodded, some part of him still unsatisfied. "Anything else?" he asked.

No one answered.

"What do you think French is going to say about why she did it?" Smith asked.

Igou shrugged. He could not imagine French's defense. He would soon experience it firsthand.

CHAPTER
22

The Little Chicago
of the South

THE TRIAL OF Judith Ann Neelley began at 9:30 A.M. on March 7, 1983, in the second-floor courtroom of the Dekalb County Courthouse. On that morning, Judge Randall Cole called twenty names from the list of prospective jurors, and the process of striking a jury began.

As his or her name was called, each juror walked to the elevated jury box that rested just to the left of the witness stand. From their slightly lifted position, the jurors could see Igou and Assistant District Attorney Michael O'Dell as they sat silently at the rectangular wooden table on the other side of the room. Robert French sat at the defense table, just to the right of Igou, nearer to the jury so that at any moment his client could be observed without obstruction.

Nearly all of the large room's remaining space was given over to rows of seats that had been set aside for the public, almost two hundred of them, now empty. It was a modern courtroom, brightly lit and without the adornment common to rural Southern courthouses. There were no paintings of the honored dead, no Confederate battle flags hung dramatically behind the judge's bench, no sweeping murals depicting famous episodes in state or local history. Instead, the room

looked like an architectural rendering of the old Quaker
notion of plain-speaking. The walls were painted in a
flat, unaccented pastel color, and they rose over a
stretch of low-pile gray carpet that might have been
used for a suburban patio. The high, galleried hall
where Hollywood had filmed the great courtroom battle of *To Kill a Mockingbird* was a memory, the galler-
ies themselves made obsolete by desegregation. Inside
Judge Cole's courtroom, spectators might have imagined themselves anywhere from Maine to California,
local color having yielded to judicial uniformity.

The same might have been said of the prospective
jurors. They had the plain look of rural or small-town
people everywhere. They dressed in flannel and acryl-
ics from Wal-Mart or one of the discount clothiers
located in the various towns they came from—small
crossroad villages like Rainsville, Fyffe, Collinsville,
Valley Head. The men cut their hair short and their
sideburns high. The women spun their long hair in
high beehive swirls or let it hang in short curls, sometimes dyed, sometimes "frosted," but always with the
modesty and conservatism typical of people who do
neither expect nor wish to be noticed. As individuals,
they might have been found in Wisconsin or Vermont
or the desert fringes of southeastern California, their
hearts and minds less defined by their region than by
their way of life. It was a modest and more or less
predictable life of work and play. For work, there
were the farms and textile mills along with various
small mercantile and service enterprises. For enter-
tainment there was vigorous intramural sports, video
movies, local television and its satellite-disk exten-
sions, church socials, and the eternal drama of family
relations.

This was the life shared by most of the jurors, and
as Igou watched them take their seats in the jury box,
he felt confident that he knew both it and them very
well indeed. Because of that, he also felt confident
that the case would be tried on its merits, the evidence

weighed reasonably and well. He would neither ask nor expect any more than that, but he felt sure it was all he needed, since from eyewitness to forensic testimony, everything served to substantiate the state's contentions.

The only mystery was Robert French, and Igou watched intently as French rose to begin his questioning of the jury venire.

At first, French merely asked the predictable questions any competent lawyer would ask of jurors in the case. Did any of them have daughters the same age as Lisa Millican? Had any read too much about the case to render a fair verdict? Were any disinclined to accept a defense based on mental defect?

Then he suddenly shifted to another theme, a move that gave Igou his first hint that French was planning an unusual defense.

"How many members of the jury generally feel that women are overemotional?" French asked.

There was no response.

"That they tend to overstate their problems when they talk about them?"

Again, there was no response.

"How many of you feel that men are better able to deal with their problems than women are?"

No response.

"How many of you women tend to feel that men usually don't understand the female point of view?"

No response.

French was doubtful. "Now, come on," he said, "let's get honest."

Two women raised their hands.

"How many of you feel that men are generally insensitive to pain that women experience during their lifetime?"

To this there was no response.

"How many of you men feel that women tend to complain too much?"

Once again, there was no response.

"How many jurors, by a show of the hand, feel that the husband should be the head of the house?"

Four jurors raised their hands, two men and two women.

"How many of you feel that as the head of the house the man should make the final decision in all matters affecting the life of your family?"

Igou sat back. Now he knew. French was going to defend Judith Neelley as a victim, one whose suffering was greater than those she victimized.

Throughout the rest of the afternoon and the following morning, the process of striking a jury continued until the original sixty-five members of the jury venire had been whittled down to twelve jurors and two alternates.

When it was completed, the composition of the jury and alternates was seven women and five men. For the next sixteen days, they would listen from the jury box to a proceeding whose bizarre aspects and curious turns would rock their community to its foundations.

Fort Payne, Alabama, the county seat of Dekalb County, had begun as a small fortified settlement in the middle of the Cherokee Nation. It had grown slowly until the removal of the Indians in the 1840's allowed whites to pour into the fertile mountain plateau that overlooked the town.

This growth could hardly have anticipated the boomtown that developed in the late 1880's, however, when rumors of rich mineral deposits similar to those already found in Birmingham, approximately ninety miles to the southwest, turned the entire area into a speculator's dream and generated its brief history as the "Little Chicago of the South."

Fueled by an advertising campaign of the newly created Fort Payne Coal and Iron Company and largely directed to the northern financial centers of Boston and New York, the boom miraculously turned a sleepy valley town into a bustling city. Virtually overnight, fifteen industrial companies, four banks, three investment centers, and a huge one-hundred-and-twenty-five-room hotel, said to be the largest wooden structure in the world, sprouted among the pine rushes and along the unpaved roads of the town.

Within a year or two, however, it was all over. The banks and investment houses withered, the northerners departed, and the hotel became an apartment building and rooming house that limped along until it burned to the ground in 1911 in a fire so immense that its ashes spread up and down the valley for seven miles.

It was the one and only boom, and after the bust Fort Payne returned to a slow, steady growth, one tied to agriculture and textiles, particularly sock mills, rather than to fantasies of mineral wealth and sudden riches, and its populace replaced the earlier, inflated reference to Chicago with the more modest sobriquet "Sock City."

By 1983, it was a town of approximately thirteen thousand people with a single business thoroughfare, Gault Avenue, a smattering of shopping centers at its extreme northern and southern perimeters, and a downtown area that was slowly falling into commercial abandonment and disrepair, a narrow haunt of shabby furniture stores, discount clothing shops, and already-empty buildings whose "For Rent" signs were already yellowing with age.

It was an ordinary town, known only for its concentration of sock mills and other textile factories. It had the usual number of churches, civic entertainments, parks, and schools. Its people lived lives that were closely tied to the community. It was a town where most people within a certain economic and social class knew all the other people in that class. The people called their officials by their first names, and the prevailing atmosphere was friendly and polite.

From time to time, of course, people got angry at each other. From time to time, passion or avarice took over and someone killed someone else. Still, within the last fifty years, no one had done anything so terrible, "so wanton, so outrageously inhuman"—to use the words of Judith Neelley's indictment—as to be charged with capital murder. The one time someone had, it had been a black man, the old-timers still recalled, not a white man, much less, of course, a woman. Thus, not since what the local population called "hanging times" had there been a case even remotely similar to the one that was about to break over them.

Because of that remoteness, the community was, in a sense, ill prepared for the case. The atrocity that had been committed at Rocky Glade was the kind they vaguely associated with that hazy netherworld known as "the City." They knew that such acts were committed, of course, but that knowledge remained at a distance from their lives, both physically and emotionally, images that fluttered briefly on their television screens then disappeared forever.

But Judith Neelley did not disappear. She remained a fixed presence in the town from the time of her arrival in October until the beginning of her trial the following March. Her story was not a headline glimpsed in the paper and immediately forgotten, but a drama that slowly transpired over many months within the community itself.

By March it was clear that living with Judith Neelley among them had not been an easy task for the people of Fort Payne. Even from the beginning, she'd been an outsider, a bit of trash brought in from the gutter and dropped on the living-room floor, where it had remained week after week, while the community waited for it finally to be picked up and tossed out the door again.

But inevitably, the tossing had gone slowly. And so, from October to March, Neelley's presence had hovered over them, gray and spectral, a small insistent ache forever in their minds, a dark humming in their conversations at the cafés and beauty parlors, always there, a name like a bad taste in their mouths, something that for months they'd been wanting to spit out: Judith Ann Neelley.

Over the months since her arrest, every detail of Neelley's aimless, sordid existence—the endless drifting from one cheap motel to the next, the steady diet of hamburgers at greasy fast-food restaurants and peanut butter sandwiches made from supplies kept in the glove compartment of her car, the children born in jail—all of this had become familiar to the people of Fort Payne, so familiar that by the time of the trial they had come to call her "Judy," no longer "she" or "her" or "Neelley," but "Judy" as if she'd been one of them all along.

The opening arguments in the trial of Judith Ann Neelley began on Wednesday, March 9, 1983, in a packed courtroom. Members of the press had already been given preferential seats in the first three rows, and the court had even issued a typed statement outlining their responsibilities and prerogatives while covering the case.

For the general public, the rules remained unchanged, and old courthouse habitués would have noticed only one difference between this and all the other trials that had been conducted in the room. A metal detector had been set up at the entrance, and trial spectators were required to pass through it before going to their seats. There were no exceptions to this rule, and even the sixty members of the eleventh-grade class whose history teacher had brought them down from Geraldine High School had to pass through it, glancing self-consciously at each other before taking their seats to hear the opening arguments in their region's most famous case.

Those remarks began at 9:30 A.M. when Igou walked to the lectern that had been placed before the jury. He preferred to speak behind the lectern, facing the jury directly, formally, with the dignity he associated with the presentation of a case. He arranged his notes carefully, then began describing the first phone call to the Rome Police Department and moving on to the discovery of the body.

It was Lisa Ann Millican, Igou told the jury, a thirteen-year-old girl, "who had not had most of the advantages, resources, good things in life that most of us have had from time to time." It was Millican Igou did not want the jury to forget, and if he had a strategy beyond the orderly presentation of the evidence, it was to keep her alive in the minds of the jury. Though dead in body, he told himself, she was alive in the law, crying for justice, and he wanted the jury to hear that cry. To make them hear it, he took them through her life, told them how she'd lived in an impoverished home, one that was physically filthy and emotionally disordered, how she'd been sexually abused by her father, and had finally been removed from the home itself. She was a child who had been placed in one foster home after another, shuttled from one institution to another, a child who, while on an outing from one of these very institutions, had fallen into the hands of Judith Ann Neelley.

Igou then shifted to Neelley. From the very beginning, he said, she had approached Lisa Millican with the intent to kidnap and terrorize her and to abet in her sexual violation and abuse. In the "four-day ordeal" that followed her abduction, Millican had suffered terribly, been raped, beaten, then taken to Little River Canyon, where she was systematically tortured and murdered.

Judith Neelley had not suffered from any mental defect when she had done these things, Igou concluded, and because of that, she was now subject to the penalties that the law had long ago prescribed for such a crime.

Defense Attorney Robert French then rose to address the jury, and while Igou sat at the prosecution table, waiting in anticipation, French declared the whole heart and substance of his defense for the first time.

"I will tell you in this statement," he said as he paced back and forth before the jury, "that every move, every act, every thought carrying out the perpetration of this heinous event was planned, calculated, instituted by Alvin Neelley."

Judith Neelley, he contended, had been responsible for nothing.

French asked Neelley to stand, and she did, to her full height of five feet ten inches, in a sleek, stylish dress and a pair of high-heeled shoes. The haggard, washed-out appearance of the woman arrested in Murfreesboro had disappeared entirely.

"I want you to meet Judith Neelley," French said. Then he introduced the jury to her life. She had been deprived of her father at the age of nine, he said, and during her early adolescence she had lived with a mother who continually entertained a host of gentleman callers in the family's double-wide house trailer. At times, French went on, these men had made advances toward Judy, but she had always rejected them. In the process she had become afraid of men, "particularly those with whiskey on their breath."

French described the arrival of Alvin Neelley into Judy's life. He had charmed a young girl, he said, taken her away from her family, and finally married her.

But it was a nightmare marriage, French added, one that began with "slaps and kicks and hair pullings, and from there escalated to punches all over her body and around the face," so that by the time Neelley was sixteen, she was a thoroughly battered woman. In the end, French told the jury, Judith Neelley had come to look "like some creature from a horror movie. Her eyes were purple slits, and her nose was flattened and beaten against her face and bloody, and her arms were twisted, and her fingers were broken."

The violence had continued to escalate all through

Neelley's married life, French went on. From using his hands only, Alvin had progressed to metal objects, to a saw, a gun butt. In the process he had "reduced a child to a vegetable, and once he had complete control over her, once he had broken her will, as you do in an animal, then she became the type of wife he wanted, and every night she bathed him, and every morning she tied his shoes, and every day she fed him, and she waited on him hand and foot all day long, and all day long, every day, he told her in no uncertain terms what would happen to her if she crossed him."

In the process of this brutal dehumanization, French declared, Judy Neelley had been "brainwashed if anyone was ever brainwashed." In the end, she had been reduced to nothing more than "Alvin Neelley's slave."

At the prosecution table, Igou continued to listen as French moved through increasingly graphic descriptions of the utter bestiality of Alvin Neelley. Over and over French hammered at the brutality inflicted with horrendous regularity upon the mind and body of his lost, subservient wife, and of her resulting reduction to "a robot at the hands of Alvin Neelley." From time to time his eyes drifted over to the tall woman who sat silently only a few feet away. He remembered the voice he'd heard in the grand-jury room, the look in her eyes as she'd talked that day.

Not far from where Neelley now sat, French continued his opening statement, moving on to the torture-murder of Lisa Millican.

"Judy begged him to let her go," French said, but Alvin had refused, and so "Judy, with tears in her eyes, told Lisa that she was going to give her some sleeping shots and leave her."

Once again, Igou's eyes swept over to Neelley. This time he looked at her eyes as he listened to French's argument.

"Judy Neelley was reduced to an instrument," French declared.

What bullshit, Igou thought.

*   *   *

After the opening arguments had been completed, the prosecution began its case by calling Melba Davis, the caseworker in the Walker County Department of Family and Children Services who had been in charge of the Millican family and who knew its emotional and economic distress intimately. Since it now appeared that French was going to put Alvin Neelley on trial in order to divert attention from Judith, it became even more important for Lisa Millican to be kept in the forefront of the jury's mind. They had to know the many ordeals through which she'd passed before enduring the final one.

Davis testified to her involvement with the Millican family since October 1980 when she'd received a referral concerning Tina Millican, Lisa's younger sister. Tina was being abused by her father and Davis had opened a protective services case on the family as a whole. Since then, she'd made regular visits to the family "home," a filthy trailer in a run-down district of Lafayette.

But trouble had continued in the Millican family, Davis went on, and in August of 1982, the Department of Family and Children Services again found it necessary to remove Lisa. After a series of foster homes, she was transported first to the Open Door in Rome and then, a month later, to the Ethel Harpst Home in Cedartown.

As to Lisa's life, Davis testified that it had been a very bleak one. Born in June of 1969, Lisa had been sexually abused by her father from the age of eleven. At the time of her disappearance, Mrs. Davis added—a strange, curiously tender detail, which Igou hoped would stick in the jury's mind—she'd had dark brown hair cut in a shag.

Igou next called Gail Henderson, the substitute houseparent who'd brought Lisa to the Riverbend Mall, then Lonnie Adcock, who'd taken Neelley's first telephone call to the Rome Police Department.

Igou then shifted his witness lineup to reflect the story as it had developed in Dekalb County, the calls that were received at the sheriff's department, the first unsuccessful attempt to find Lisa's body, then the later successful one. Slowly, witness by witness, the jury followed the officials as they arrived at Rocky Glade, the one who'd shone the flashlight down upon Lisa's body as night fell over the canyon, the firemen who'd first confirmed that she was dead, the police officer who'd watched over her during her last night on the canyon floor.

As morning passed into afternoon and then into the evening, the jurors followed the progress of Lisa Millican from her life on Pine Street to her agony at Rocky Glade. If his strategy had worked, Igou thought at the end of the day, then Lisa Millican had been firmly established in the jury's mind. The task now would be to keep her there until they could render judgment on her killer.

CHAPTER
23

The Ones Who Got Away

DURING THE NEXT few days Igou concentrated on presenting the physical evidence in the case, all the intricate linking of hair and blood samples, the classification of ammunition, the comparing of various carpet fibers taken from Neelley's car with others found at the crime scene. This was long, tedious testimony that French hardly needed to dispute, but when the prosecution began to call Neelley's would-be or actual victims, his defense went into high gear, as Igou knew it would. For it was the psychological rather than the physical evidence that was now in dispute—not what Neelley had done, but the circumstances under which she had done it.

The first prosecution witness who had knowledge of those circumstances was Suzanne Clonts.

Under Igou's questioning, Clonts went over the details of that Saturday in September when she had been approached by a woman near Aladdin's Castle in Riverbend Mall. She gave a physical description of the woman, along with the substance of their brief conversation. Then she positively identified Judith Neelley as the woman she had encountered on that fateful day.

It was now French's turn to begin to put in place the

building blocks of his defense. He began it with his sixth question.

"Now, when you were approached by the lady with long hair, you say that—would you tell the jury how she was dressed?"

"Yes, sir," Clonts replied. "She had on a loose T-shirt, and you could tell that she was not wearing a bra, and I don't remember what kind of pants she had on, but she had a generally unkempt appearance."

"Did she have on any makeup at all?"

"She didn't look like she did."

"Did you notice anything strange about her mouth?"

"Yes. It was shaped odd, and her teeth appeared to be bucked."

"Did you notice anything else about her teeth?"

"They were kind of shaped funny."

"Was a tooth broken?"

"I didn't notice."

"You didn't notice? And she had just struck up a conversation with you?"

"Right."

After a few additional questions about Neelley's appearance, French began to approach a more critical question. "That big heavy-set man, did you see her with him before the conversation ended?" French asked.

"No," Clonts answered. "I had noticed her earlier with him, and then she went back to him after I was talking to her."

"And you noticed her earlier with him where in the mall, Suzanne?"

"In the game room."

"All right, had he been playing the machines with her?"

"He was playing a game and she was watching."

"Did you ever see him talking to her?"

"No."

"He was a big man, wasn't he?" French asked.

"Right."

"He would weigh well over two hundred pounds, wouldn't he?"

"I'm a bad judge of weight."

"Well, was he as big as a high-school football player?"

"Yes."

"Bigger?"

"I guess."

"Did you ever see him turn around and look at you in any way before she approached you?"

"No."

"Did he ever approach you at all?"

"No . . . Before she ever talked to me he was playing Frogger. . . . He was in the back corner."

"He was in the back corner," French repeated. "Was that a darker part of the room?"

"It was the darkest."

"And he was back there mostly by himself with just this woman?" French said. "And would it be fair to say that if I walked by the arcade and looked in, he would be the hardest person in there to see?"

"Probably," Clonts answered.

"All right. So, if he were . . . hiding himself casually to appear to be playing games, that would be the best game to play, wouldn't it, Frogger?"

"I guess so."

"And that was the game he selected, wasn't it?"

"Right."

"Now, she came over and approached you. Did you find anything strange about her?"

"Well, most . . . people don't come and start drilling you with questions."

"So, you did find something strange about her?"

"Yes."

"Did she appear to try to be friendly with you and didn't know how?"

"She appeared to be friendly," Clonts said. "I never thought that she didn't know how."

"Did she appear to be unsure of herself while she was talking to you?"

"No."

"Did she appear to just talk in a monotone?"

"Not that I noticed."

"You told us there was something strange about her, that she didn't talk like a normal person, right?"

"I said that?"

"I understood you to say that she just came over and started drilling you with questions."

"But her voice wasn't strange."

"The conversation was strange," French said.

"The conversation was strange," Clonts repeated.

"Suzanne, after you had had this conversation with the woman you've identified to be Judy—which I'm not taking issue with you—it probably was. Did you, with your eyes, follow her and the big man out of the arcade?"

"No."

"Did you say anything to your new husband about it as you were leaving?"

"We're Christians," Clonts said. "And I started to witness to her, because I thought she looked like she needed Jesus, and I was telling him that I, you know, was asking him if he thought I should have witnessed to her."

In his redirect, Igou was not interested in Clonts's ideas about Christian witness. He asked only one question, but its answer was meant to go directly to the heart of the issue French had already raised in his opening statement. In that statement French had talked of split lips and broken heads, of eyes reduced to slits. If this were true, he reasoned, then Suzanne Clonts would have seen it.

"Mrs. Clonts," Igou began. "This woman whom you have identified as the defendant, did she appear to you to have been beaten up?"

Clonts's answer was brief and unequivocal, and Igou could only hope that the jury had heard it as deeply and profoundly as he had heard it. "No," she said.

It was not an answer French intended to accept, and in his re-cross examination, he pursued the point relentlessly.

"Did she have anything on her arms other than the T-shirt?" he asked.

"No."

"Did you notice anything strange about her right wrist on the inside of her arm?"

"No, sir."

"Did you notice any bite marks on her body as you were talking to her?"

"No, sir."

"Did you notice any bruises?"

"No."

"Did you notice any splotches around her face?"

"Just acne."

"Did she appear to be ill?"

To be "ill" in Southern usage can mean either physically ailing or angry, irritable, bad-tempered. Clonts needed a clarification. "You mean sick?" she asked.

"Yeah," French replied.

"No."

"Pale?"

"She wasn't wearing any makeup, so she wasn't—"

"Suzanne," French interrupted, "did she appear to you to be a healthy, normal person . . . that you're generally acquainted with and talk to in the malls?"

"No."

At the end of Clonts's testimony, as he rose to call his next witness, Igou breathed a small sigh of relief. In all the places French had wanted her to say yes, she had replied with a quick, determined no. "The state calls Diane Bobo," he said.

Diane Bobo took the stand and, under Igou's questioning, related the details of late afternoon, Sunday, October 3, 1982, when she'd unexpectedly run out of gas on Shorter Avenue, then gotten a ride to a phone booth at the Alto Shopping Center and called her husband. She went through the conversation she'd had with a woman in a brown Dodge whom she positively identified as Judith Ann Neelley.

At the end of his direct examination, Igou made a

mocking reference to the nature of the defense before dismissing Bobo from the stand.

"One other thing, Diane," he said. "You were twenty-two at that time?"

"Yes, sir."

"Were you wearing makeup that day?"

"No, sir."

Igou smiled. "Mr. French will ask you," he said, by way of turning her over for cross-examination.

French approached the witness box, but this time pursued a slightly different tack, hoping to show that Alvin Neelley had orchestrated the attempt to abduct Mrs. Bobo.

"Did you happen to notice a red Ford with a CB antenna on it in the vicinity go by real slow?" he asked.

"No, sir, I didn't."

"At any time during this transaction did you ever hear anyone talk over the CB in her car?"

"No, sir."

"Did you ever hear any CB noises come from her car?"

"No, sir."

"Do you remember seeing any other car go by?"

"Outside of the normal traffic, no, sir. None pulled into the shopping center."

"I'm asking if you saw a red car go by immediately before this car turned in."

"Not to my recollection."

Getting nowhere with this line of questioning, French shifted back to Judith Neelley. "Did she appear to be dirty?" he asked.

"Just like she had gone without taking a bath for several days," Bobo replied. "But not where she had dirt on her face or nothing like that."

A few other questions established the fact that Neelley had looked more or less nondescript, and so French shifted once again, turning his attention to Neelley's psychological demeanor.

"Did she appear to be almost desperate to get you to go riding with her?" he asked.

"Not desperate," Bobo replied, "but anxious."

"She needed you to go riding with her, is that it?"

"Not where she needed me to, but where she wanted me to real bad."

Once again he returned to Neelley's physical appearance. "And as you looked at her, did you see any marks or scratches or bruises on her?" French asked.

"No, sir, not that I recall."

"How did her eyes look? Do you remember?"

"Seems to me that they were sunken in and dark circles, like she had been, you know, awake for quite a while."

"She looked haggard, is that it?"

"I would say."

"She didn't happen to have a black eye, did she?"

"I couldn't say as far as that, no, sir."

"Did she appear to be getting over a black eye?"

"She had dark circles around her eyes to where I noticed that, but as to say where she had a black eye or not, I couldn't say."

After Bobo's testimony Igou called Debbie Smith, the third of Neelley's would-be victims. In answer to a few, brief questions, she related the events of the afternoon of October 4 when she had been walking home from school, dressed in her eighth-grade cheerleader's outfit. She positively identified Judith Neelley as the woman who'd attempted to abduct her on that Monday afternoon.

Once again, French's cross-examination centered on how Neelley had looked as she spoke to Smith from behind the wheel of the brown Dodge.

"You said she looked like she had just gotten up," he said.

"Yes, sir."

"So, that would be before a girl puts on her makeup and gets all put together. That would be sort of haggard, wouldn't it, Debbie?"

"Yes."

"Sort of tired looking?"

"Well, she didn't really look tired. She just looked like, you know, like she didn't have time to put on her makeup."

"She wasn't fixed up."

"Yes."

French then went on to the photographic lineup that Kines had presented to her in the Rome Police Department and from which she had immediately and without hesitation picked out Judith Neelley.

"Were there any men in the pictures?" French asked.

"No, sir."

"Were they all women?"

"Yes, sir."

"Were there any black women in the pictures?"

"No, sir."

"Any Asian women?"

"No, sir."

"Did they all look pretty much alike?"

"Yes, sir."

"Did you have any trouble picking out the woman that you said was the woman?"

"No, sir."

"Did you pick out the one that's been identified here today as Judith Neelley?"

"Yes, sir."

So far in this testimony, Igou and French had questioned only those who had never been victimized by the Neelleys, and who therefore could not testify to their actions and behavior once they'd fallen into their hands. They had been the ones who got away.

Now it was time to engage another kind of witness, one who had actually gotten into the fatal car and miraculously survived.

CHAPTER
24

"She Did"

TALL AND SLENDER, with a gentle, unassuming manner, John Hancock made a convincing witness. His tone was soft, as if he bore no particular grudge against the woman who'd picked him up on the night of October 3 and, a few hours later, marched him into a remote wooded area and shot him in the back. As he would later explain, he had only recently become a Christian, and although he'd been apprehensive about getting in the car with Judith Neelley, his newfound religion had argued for him to act against his fear in order to come to the aid of a stranger.

"She said she was lonely," he said in answer to one of Igou's questions, "that she was from out of town, that she wanted to ride around and talk to someone for a while."

He and Chatman had gotten into the car, and later, after Judy Neelley had contacted her husband by CB, they had met near a bridge and introduced themselves by their respective CB handles.

A few minutes later, Hancock said, he had needed to use the bathroom. The two cars had pulled onto a deserted road, and while he relieved himself, the Neelleys had stepped away and talked together. The next thing he knew, Judith Neelley was walking toward him with a gun in her hand, one he described as having "a long barrel, black, with a dark-looking handle."

With the next few questions Igou tried to establish that what had happened during the critical moments of that evening had been guided by the free will and malicious purpose of Judith Neelley, acting not as the whipped, will-less slave of her husband, but as her own person, free to choose or not to choose the harm that she might do.

"What, if anything, did she say to you?" Igou asked.

"She told me to walk down the road, not to say anything or do anything or try anything funny, so I did. I walked on down the road. And then I was talking to her, trying to—I really couldn't figure out what was going on. I told her that me and my wife wasn't doing them no harm, wouldn't cause no trouble for them or anything like that."

"What did she say to you at that point?"

"Nothing really, just 'Keep walking and keep your back toward me.' And then we came up to this little creeklike stream, and I had told her that there was some water up ahead, that surely she didn't want to walk in it and get wet, and she had told me to turn to my left and walk into the woods. So I did, and then she told me she didn't want to go in there, to come back out. So I came back out and she pointed to my immediate right and told me to walk over to a clearing place. So I did that, and we walked into some hedge bushes, and she told me to stop. At that time I heard him holler down and tell her to hurry up and get it over with, that we had to go. And she hollered back and said, 'Okay, just a minute.' And then I turned and asked her if I could ask her one more question, and she told me, 'Hell, no. Just keep your back to me and don't say anything.' I turned with my back to her, and then she told me not to worry about my girlfriend, that she would take care of her."

Suddenly something struck Igou, a small point, but worth pursuing at a later time. "Did you ask anything about your girlfriend?"

"No. I never got a chance."

"She volunteered that statement?" Igou asked pointedly.

"Yes, sir."

"What happened then, John?"

"I heard the man holler once again for her to hurry, and then she said, 'Okay,' and then shot me. I fell on my face. I laid there."

French began his cross-examination with a discussion of the CB radio communications that had occurred between Judith Neelley and her husband.

"When the woman picked you up and you got in the car and she began to talk on the CB radio, what channel was it on, John?" he asked.

"Channel 40."

"Would you classify yourself as a CBer?"

"Yes, sir."

"All right . . . did you find it unusual, from your experience as a CBer, that the Cobra radio was on Channel 40?"

"No, sir."

"Is Channel 40 used very much?"

"No, sir, not too much," Hancock admitted.

French then took Hancock back through the initial conversation between the two Neelleys, the 10-36 code she had transmitted, a request to know the time.

"All right, and did the man come right back with the time?" he asked.

"Yes, sir."

"Immediately?"

"Yes, sir."

"As if he were waiting to hear from the woman?"

"Yes, sir."

"Did you know how far behind her he was?" French asked.

"He was right behind her," Hancock replied.

"And did they discuss anything other than meeting while you were going toward the Coosa post office?"

"No, sir."

"When you got to the Coosa post office, what happened, in that vicinity?"

"He told her to make a left-hand turn like going back toward Cave Springs, and she did."

"At this point in time he was giving the directions, right?"

"Yes, sir."

"And throughout the evening did he continue to give the directions?"

"Yes, sir."

On the road to Cave Springs the Neelleys pretended to meet for the first time, Hancock said, then the four people introduced themselves.

"Did you form a judgment that there was some type of maybe romantic or girl-boy interest between the two?" French asked.

"Yes, sir."

"She was still doing what she was told to do, was she not?"

"Yes, sir."

French went on to establish that Alvin Neelley was in far better physical condition than his wife.

"What did he look like?" French asked.

"He was heavy built, dark-headed, not real tall, about your height."

"Much bigger than I am?"

"Oh yeah, real husky-built."

"How about his hair? Was he well groomed?"

"Yes, sir."

"Did he appear to be very neat?"

"Yes, sir."

"The woman—the Lady Sundown . . . she did not match the dress or the appearance of the Nightrider, did she?"

"No, sir."

"She had on wrinkled clothes, did she?"

"She had on a jogging suit."

"Was it wrinkled?"

"I didn't pay no attention."

"Was her hair sort of long and stringy?"

"Yes, sir."

"Her hair was not neatly trimmed, was it?"

"No, sir."

"Did he appear to smile and be friendly with you?"

"He never smiled."

"He did not smile?"

"No, sir."

French then moved from the physical differences between the Neelleys to the differences in their automobiles, establishing that while Alvin's car was well kept, his wife's was dirty and disordered.

The key point remained domination, however, and French returned to it shortly. "Who drove away first?" he asked.

"He did."

"And who followed who?"

"She followed him."

"Did she ever allow him to get out of the range of her headlights?"

"No, sir."

French led Hancock back through the long search for the bootlegger, the zigzag, seemingly random drive through the three nightbound counties of northern Georgia, to the final decision to turn off the road so that the men could urinate.

"And so he pulled off about three car lengths off of the highway," French said.

"Yes, sir."

"And she pulled in behind him with her lights off."

"Yes, sir."

While Hancock urinated, the Neelleys talked quietly at some distance.

"Okay, so they were talking confidential between the two cars, right?" French asked.

"Yes, sir."

"And he was doing most of the talking, or could you tell?"

"I couldn't tell."

"Did you ever hear her voice whispering to him?"

"I never did hear her voice."

"Okay, so the only voice you heard in the conversation was his, right?"

"Yes."

"He was doing the communicating, right, and she was receiving, right?"

"Yes, sir."

The conversation between the two continued, Hancock went on, then suddenly it stopped, and he heard Alvin Neelley say, "If we're gonna do it, let's get it over with."

"And what did she say?" French asked.

"She said, 'Okay.' "

Under French's continuing cross-examination, Hancock once again went over the details of the next few minutes. French was interested primarily in establishing Alvin's role, his command of the situation, the way Judith Neelley merely carried out his orders.

"Where were you when you first heard the man yell out to you?" he asked.

"In the bushes."

"And you heard him yell out what, John?"

" 'If you're gonna . . . let's get it over with,' he said 'Hurry up and get it over with. We gotta go.' "

"All right, she didn't do anything, though, did she?"

"She hollered back at him, 'Okay, just a minute.' "

"All right, and then what happened?"

"That's when I turned and asked her if I could ask her a question."

"And what happened then?"

"She told me, 'Hell, no. Just turn and keep your back to me and don't say a damn thing.' "

"All right, and then what happened?"

"Then I heard him holler 'Hurry up' again."

"This time he just hollered 'Hurry up'?"

"Right."

"But he never came down there, did he?"

"No, sir."

"He never—at any time, John, did he ever show you a gun?"

"No, sir."

"Did he ever tell you where to walk?"

"No, sir."

"Did he ever tell you what to do?"

"No, sir."

"But he told her everything you ever heard there, didn't he?"

"Yes, sir."

"And he told her exactly what to do, didn't he?"

"I imagine so. I don't know."

"And he wasn't satisfied with the speed in which she was doing it, was he?"

"No, sir."

"And he urged her to do it again, didn't he?"

"Yes, sir."

"And the second time, when he urged her on the second time, she did it, didn't she?"

"After she told me she would take care of my girlfriend, too."

"Okay. John, throughout this entire transaction you've described to us and discussed, the man always gave the directions, didn't he?"

"Yes, sir."

"He was in charge of that evening's transactions from the time she said, 'What time is it,' wasn't he?"

"Yes, sir."

Igou knew that French had elicited some damaging testimony as to Judith Neelley's unwilling responsibility for the shooting of John Hancock, and he acted quickly to bring that responsibility back upon her.

"John, did it appear to you that this woman was afraid or scared to death of this man?" he asked.

"No, sir."

"Did she seem like she was upset or scared or nervous?"

"No, sir."

"How would you describe her?"

"A very calm person, a person that was aware of everything going on around them."

"Who was giving you directions down into the bushes?"

"She was."

"Who was ordering you around?"

"She was."

"When you got there in the bushes, were you in sight of the car, the man?"

"No, sir."

"John, did she ever tell you that she was awful sorry about having to shoot you?"

"No, sir."

"Did she ever tell you, John, that you could run away and she would just shoot up in the air?"

"No, sir."

"John, who said, 'Don't worry about your girlfriend, I'll take care of her'?"

"She did."

"Was the man down there telling her to say that?"

"No, sir."

"Was he even present when she said it?"

"No, sir."

"Who shot you, John?"

"She did."

At the end of his redirect, Igou felt he had reestablished Neelley's willful culpability in the shooting of John Hancock. And so, supremely confident at the end of only three days, the prosecution rested.

Now they had only to counter the crucial argument

of the defense. Based on the nature of French's opening statement, and the general lines of his cross-examination, Igou knew exactly what that argument would be, but he could not have imagined the hideous detail with which it would be made, or the hurricane of rage it would cause to sweep the town.

PART
FOUR
JUDGMENT

CHAPTER
25

"The Main Part of a Woman"

ON THE MORNING of March 15, Igou sat at the prosecution table, once again eyeing Judith Neelley from his position a few feet away. At any moment she might take the stand, and he wanted to sense her feelings before then, get some idea of how to reach her. She appeared calm, as always, except for her eyes. They were round and slightly bulged, and sudden darting movements sometimes overtook them, as if they were following an argument in the air. Today, however, they were entirely still, and after a while, Igou simply shook his head, giving up again. Unfathomable.

Judge Cole entered, and after a few preliminary exchanges, French began his defense not by calling Judith Neelley or anyone else Igou could have anticipated. Instead, he focused the jury's attention on a large sandy-haired woman who currently lived in Dalton, Georgia. She was twenty-seven years old, and for three of those years she had been married to Alvin Neelley. Her name was Jo Ann Browning.

At the time of her testimony Browning was the mother of three of Neelley's six children, though she had lost custody of them some years before in a dispute with Alvin.

As the questioning began, Browning told the jury that at the age of fifteen, she'd met Benny Farrington at a local market in Dalton, Georgia. Farrington's half brother, Alvin Neelley, often visited the market, and toward the latter part of 1973 she met him.

According to Browning, Neelley displayed a "charm-like attitude," and early in 1974 she moved in with him.

In response to testimony to which Igou continually objected as leading the witness, Browning went on to detail in the most graphic terms imaginable the deterioration of her relationship with Alvin Neelley, its continually escalating cruelty and violence.

She began by describing her first beating at Neelley's hands, during which he had beaten her on the breasts and arms and had stretched the corners of her mouth with his fingers.

But, according to Browning, this beating was only the beginning of a life in which she was beaten "every time he got mad about something."

As time passed, she said, Neelley began to fabricate stories of infidelity and then beat her in a jealous rage. He would sometimes lead her on wild-goose chases as the two of them searched for her imagined partners in adultery. "I would make up addresses just to get him to go to these places, and then when he would go to these addresses and we'd go down the street, I would just tell him, 'Well, they must not be at home.' "

The beatings occurred within a framework of abject servitude in which Browning bathed Neelley, combed his hair, and even put on his shoes and trousers. Far worse, however, was the prevailing mood of random violence, a world of sudden kicks and jabs. "He would sometimes hit me with his fist, sometimes just hit me with his whole arm, and of course I would run from him, trying to protect myself by hiding in other rooms."

"What would he do when you did that?"

"Well, he would bust the door down."

"Then what would he do when he got in there after he had busted the door down?"

"Well, he would try to hit me," Browning replied. "I've been bruised all over my body, and I've been hit in my head and my breast area and my legs and my arms, and he would just beat me all over really."

"While you were pregnant with your first baby, did you take beatings?"

"Yes, sir . . . just about every day."

"And what would he do when he got angry?"

"He would haul off and hit me in the face with his hand. . . . It wasn't a light slap. It was a hard hit."

"Where would he hit you?"

"He would hit me in the face."

"Would it bloody your nose or black your eye?"

"Yes, sir."

"While you were driving, did he ever hit you with any object other than his fist?"

"Well, just things that's laying around that's got something to do with a car, like one of these ice scrapers and screwdrivers, and Al would keep a gun on him, and he would keep it up under his seat, and he would sometimes use that on me."

"Were there visible marks on you, Jo Ann?" French asked.

"Yes, sir."

According to Browning, the beatings continued as Neelley restlessly wandered from town to town, job to job. She continued to serve his needs, she said, and when he began to demand that she expand those services into illegal acts, she complied because she was afraid to do otherwise. Thus, Browning testified, she began to help Neelley rob the convenience stores where he worked in Dalton and Calhoun, Georgia.

His sexual demands also changed, Browning said. Neelley began to demand oral sex, an act that he forced upon her.

"How often did he force you to have sex with him

up until, say, after the children were born?" French asked.

"About every night."

"But even after you were beaten, did you have to perform?"

"Yes, sir."

"Did you enjoy it?"

"No, sir."

In the end, according to Browning, she could endure life with Neelley no longer.

"How did you get away," French asked, "or did you get away?"

"Well, the kids were asleep, and there was a big embankment in front of the trailer, and I went—it's a ditch like, and I went down and I stayed there in sight of the trailer. And I waited until he got back . . . and started hollering for me, that's when I took off down 41 Highway."

"So you got away from him?"

"Yes, sir."

French wanted to make it clear to the jury that Browning had had no choice but to leave her children in order to get away from Neelley. In the following testimony, Browning told the jury that Neelley was a light sleeper and that he always slept with a gun under his pillow. She added that he had threatened to harm the children if she did not do everything he wanted her to do.

French also needed an explanation for why, once away, Browning had returned to Neelley only a week later.

"He told me that if I left and went back over to my mother's and didn't live with him that he would whip Little Al," Browning said, "and that's . . . how he kept me as long as he did is my kids, because I knew that they would be mistreated."

"You finally lost all three of your children to get away from him, didn't you?"

"Yes, sir."

Browning returned to her husband, taking her thirteen-year-old sister, Lisa, with her, and Neelley's outrages resumed the very night of her return.

"Well, that night he produced some little white pills," Browning told the jury. "He told me they were caffeine pills and they would make me feel funny, you know, happy. And so I went ahead and took 'em, and then during the night I started feeling drowsy . . . The next thing I knew my sister was in bed, and he was trying to make out with her, and I couldn't do much because these pills made me so droggy."

According to Browning, her sister managed to fight Neelley off, then went to another bedroom. The next morning, however, "she was screaming, and he had went and put a sheet up over the window, and he was trying to rape her, and she was hollering my name, and I got to the door, and he was over her, and I told him that he better leave her alone, that I would kill him, and so he went on into the kitchen, and he got mad at me for stopping it, and he started beating me."

"All right," French said, "let me ask you this, Jo Ann. Did he rape that child that night or that morning?"

"No, sir. I stopped him before he did."

"Did he do her any damage that you know of?"

"I just—I believe that he left some kind of mental blockage on her."

After the attempted rape of her sister, Browning said that she returned to her mother's house. She remained there until Neelley called her sometime later and told her that he'd been arrested for theft, and that he would implicate her in the robberies if she did not return to him.

Once again, Browning returned to Alvin. By that time he was out on bond, and the two of them moved into his mother's trailer, where another beating took place, one in which both she and Alvin had ended up running naked around the trailer, Neelley chasing her with a broomstick.

Shortly after this beating Neelley jumped bond and he and Browning fled to Albany.

French now switched directions briefly by going into Neelley's eating habits. According to Browning, Neelley liked his food highly seasoned with Tabasco sauce and would not allow her to prepare separate dishes either for herself or the children. "He would throw the food out of the dishes, he would throw it at me, and he would start saying that I could never do anything right, and I was a bitch and a whore and a lot of things that he called me."

From food, French then moved on to other forms of deprivation that Browning said Alvin Neelley had forced her and her children to endure.

"What about medical attention, Jo Ann?" he asked. "Did you get medical attention for you and the children while you lived with him in those days?"

"No, sir."

"Did you or the children need medical attention?"

"I had some bad teeth at that time, and I needed some dental work, but he would always just go out and buy me a big bottle of Listerine and a big bottle of Tylenol, but they wouldn't do any good, because my teeth was usually abscessed."

She had finally separated from Alvin in 1977, Browning said, and during that time the children had remained with him. Neelley would sometimes call her at work, inform her that one of her children was ill, and ask her to drop by. Once she had done so, however, Neelley would simply want to have sex with her. One such incident stood out vividly in her mind, and she related it graphically to the jury.

"Well, that night," Browning said, "that was when he was doing what I said a few minutes ago. . . . He would bite me down there, and I would try to get him to stop, because I knew I was swelling because it was hurting."

"You told us he was biting you on your private parts, was he?"

"Yes, sir."

"Did he ever hit you there, Jo Ann?"

"Yes, sir. He beat me there one day so bad that I was black and blue . . . He told me that he was going to make sure that there wasn't no other men ever want me."

"Where else did he hit you while he was beating you down there, Jo Ann?"

"Well, he mostly hit me down there around, ah, the main part of a woman."

French returned to other activities in Albany, and Browning testified that they "just drifted" for two or three weeks, staying in various cheap motels, places that cost no more than ten or twelve dollars a night. Soon, however, Neelley had become afraid that the authorities were closing in on him, and they had headed north toward home. For a time they stayed in Lanett, Alabama, where Neelley took a job as a cashier for Matt's, a local convenience store. After a short time, Browning said, Neelley robbed the store's safe. He was given a polygraph by the store's owner and passed it.

Thus Browning and her husband remained in Lanett for what she estimated as "four or five months." After that they began to drift again, this time through Opelika, Alabama, and La Grange, Georgia, where there were two other robberies before they finally left town, again heading north, this time toward Murfreesboro, Tennessee.

"All right, now, Jo Ann, how many years at the time you went to Murfreesboro had you been with Alvin Neelley off and on?"

"About three years."

"You had borne him two children?"

"Yes, sir."

"So, most of the time during these beatings you have been describing you were pregnant; is that right?"

"Yes, sir."

"Now, while working at these convenience stores and you did not have a job, did he require you to come down and work at the stores?"

"Well, I would have to . . . mop floors, sweep the floor, stock the cooler. That's what I would do."

"So, what did he do all day, just sit at the cash register?"

"Yes."

"When were the slowest hours in the convenience stores?"

"The slowest hours was the third shift . . . from eleven to seven."

"During that shift did he ever take you into the back room?"

"Yes, sir."

"Did he ever make you commit sex acts there, Jo Ann?"

"Yes, sir."

"Did he make you do anything that you considered unnatural?"

"Yes."

"Where would he commit the act with you?"

"Most of the time in the office."

"Did he ever make you do it standing up?"

"Yes, sir."

"How would he make you act when he did it standing up?"

"Well, I was usually sitting down, and he was usually standing up. He was always wanting oral sex."

After a few additional questions, Browning broke down and was removed from the court. She returned five minutes later and French returned to his direct examination. "I notice that you have a missing tooth," he said. "How did you happen to lose that tooth?"

"Well, I didn't fix something right, and he hit me with his fist and knocked half of it off, and it bothered me so bad, I had to go and have the rest of it pulled out."

"Okay," French said. "Now I'm going to move on rapidly. . . . I'd like for you to tell the jury about the incident of him shooting you."

It had happened in Dalton, Browning told the jury, during a time they had been separated. She had been staying at her mother's house and had just received a November paycheck from the place where she'd been working. Her husband had her driver's license, and she needed it to cash the check. Neelley had been working at Calfee's and he told Browning that he would pick her up and take her there so that she could cash it. Not long after that, according to Browning, Neelley did as he promised, but instead of returning her to her mother's house, he told her that he had no money and that he would like for her to buy him a hamburger. Browning refused, went home, and then sometime later returned to Calfee's with her brother and sister. Neelley subsequently pulled into the market as well. Neelley told Browning that she was not "going to get away with doing him this way, and the next thing I knew I heard a loud noise, and I didn't even know I was shot until I got in the store, and he shot me in the back right down below . . . really in the behind end."

French then turned to the last days Browning had lived with her husband.

"While you were with him in Murfreesboro, did you ever see Judith Neelley?"

"Yes, sir," Browning said. "He brought her to the store where I was working at . . . and he would come in the store, and he would try to rub my hair or put his hands on my breasts or try to kiss me to try to make her jealous of me."

"Were you jealous of Judy at all?"

"No. I just wanted to be left alone."

"When did he last beat you?"

"That's when he jumped up on the bed and started jumping up and down," Browning said. She began to cry. "And I was pregnant at that time, and I was already hurting from being beat, and I told him to stop, and—but he wouldn't stop it. And the springs would hit me in the stomach, and it just was painful."

"What got him away from you?" French asked in his final question of direct examination. "Taking up with Judy?"

Igou objected to the question as leading and Judge Cole sustained the objection.

French then turned to Igou. "I'll let you ask her," he said.

Richard Igou had plenty of questions for Jo Ann Browning. He had not believed her testimony, and it was his task now to make sure the jury did not believe it either. Browning had portrayed herself as an upright, suffering Christian woman, and she had portrayed her husband as a brute who had systematically reduced her to a near-subhuman level of will-lessness and servitude. Igou now had to show that much of her testimony was either false or outrageously exaggerated.

"All right," he began. "You say you are married now?"

"Yes, sir."

"And to whom are you married?"

"Chauncey William Browning."

"When did you and Mr. Browning get married?"

"August 9, 1979."

"Where did you get married, please, ma'am?"

"It was somewhere in Tennessee."

Igou was stunned by the vagueness of her answer. "You can't tell us any better than that?" he asked unbelievingly.

"Everything is going blank to me."

Incredulous, Igou eyed her pointedly. "You say you're blanking out now when I start asking you questions?"

"No, it's just . . ."

"When did you and Alvin get married?"

"We got married in Cleveland, Tennessee, and I think it was in January of '75."

"Where did you and Alvin get divorced?"

"We never got divorced."

Igou could hardly believe his ears. "Didn't you tell me that you had married someone else?"

"Yes, I was married to my first husband."

Igou stared at her in utter consternation. "Didn't you tell me you married Chauncey William Browning on April 16?"

"August 9."

"You married him while you were still married to Alvin?"

"Yes."

"When was it you married Alvin?"

"I married him in '75."

"But you didn't get your divorce . . . until 1978 . . . three years after you married Alvin?"

"Right."

Browning's marital entanglements were highly unusual, and as Igou continued questioning her, he wanted the jury to begin to see this "Christian woman" as one who had twice committed both adultery and bigamy.

After that had been established, Igou moved to the more crucial element of her testimony for the defense.

"When did you say all these beatings started, Mrs. Browning?" he asked.

"That was in '74."

"And where were you living at that time?"

"We was living with his mother."

"He beat you when he was living with his mother?"

"Right."

"And that was within a month or so after you first took up with him?"

"Yes."

"You didn't leave him then, did you?"

"No."

"You did help him put on his shoes and his pants; is that right?"

"Right."

"What was the reason for that?"

"Well, he had a bad leg. He's got a steel plate in one of his legs."

"Did he beat you to make him tie his shoes and help him with his pants?"

"No."

"You said he took his fist and hit you in the head; is that right?"

"Yes."

Igou handed her a picture of Neelley. "He has a pretty good-sized fist?"

"Yes."

"Did it knock you unconscious?"

"No."

"Did he hit you as hard as he could?"

"Yes."

"That man in that picture would hit you in your head and all over your body as hard as he could . . . and it didn't make you unconscious?"

"No."

"How many bones did he break?"

"He didn't break any of my bones."

"You told Mr. French that he beat you with a tire tool, a jack handle, a piece of iron about a foot and a half long?"

"Yes."

"And didn't break any bones?" Igou asked doubtfully.

"No, sir."

"And he didn't knock you unconscious?"

"No."

"How many pregnancies did you have by him?"

"Three."

"You told Mr. French that he beat you all throughout those pregnancies; is that right?"

"Yes."

"That would be, if I calculated right, about twenty-seven months, wouldn't it?"

"Yes, sir."

"Did I understand you to tell Mr. French that he beat you every day while you were pregnant?"

"He beat me every other day."

"I understood you to tell Mr. French that he beat you every day through the whole time. I wrote this note down, and I may be wrong, but I thought you told him that he beat you every day while you were pregnant. You're saying that's not right?"

Browning began to cry and Igou went on to other matters despite the fact that he believed the crying to be diversionary, a way to avoid a more intense probe of the accuracy of her statements for the defense.

"Were all those pregnancies," he began again, "did they terminate in a child being born?"

"Yes."

"Born alive?"

"Yes."

Igou continued to look at her unbelievingly. "You sustained over eight hundred beatings during this time, Mrs. Browning, and you are in the condition today that you are in physically."

Browning did not answer. She began to cry again.

Igou believed that the jury was slowly coming to doubt Browning's earlier testimony. She had appeared almost too eager to give it, anticipating French's questions with obvious relish, her hatred of Alvin Neelley leaking from every pore. Rather than continuing along the same line, however, he shifted slightly and looked at Browning icily. "You said that you had never, until you got on this stand today, told anybody about these things," he said.

"About what?"

"About all these things that Mr. French led you through."

"No."

"You had, in fact, discussed it with other people, hadn't you?"

"No."

"Mr. French?"

"No."

"Mr. French just guessed at all those questions he was asking?"

Browning did not answer, and Igou let her blank stare linger in the courtroom for an instant, then made his final assault upon the credibility of her story. "Mrs. Browning, is the only physical result of that beating that we can see now the chipped tooth, from all those eight hundred beatings?"

"No; I've got scars on my head."

"How many?"

"I've got about four," Browning said, "and a knife mark where he threw a knife at me."

"That's the result of these over eight hundred beatings?"

"No, I had bruises but they went away."

Igou now moved on to complete his cross-examination. "Did he ever force you to shoot anybody?"

"No."

"Did he ever force you to pick up a thirteen-year-old girl?"

"No."

"Did he ever force you to shoot a thirteen-year-old girl?"

"No."

Igou gave Browning a final, withering look. "You don't like Alvin very much, do you?"

Browning's answer could hardly have been more predictable. "No," she said.

At the end of the day's testimony, Igou returned to his office, sat quietly behind his desk for a moment, and thought about Jo Ann Browning. He considered her testimony wildly exaggerated, and the way she'd leaped to answer French's questions suggested a high degree of vengefulness toward Alvin. Even if every word of her testimony had been true, however, it seemed irrelevant not only to the facts of the case, but to Alvin's later relationship with Judith Neelley, a woman very different from Browning—larger, vastly more intelligent, and certainly more deadly. As district attorney, Igou had seen his share of wife beating, and it was doubtless possible that Alvin had, indeed, battered his first wife. But it seemed to him that Judith Neelley's mind and character were a world away from Browning's. He had seen her eyes, heard her voice, read her letters. Nobody could beat Judith Ann Neelley and expect to walk away unharmed.

CHAPTER
26

"He Was Always Smiling"

ON THE AFTERNOON following Jo Ann Browning's testimony, French called his only remaining witness, the defendant herself, Judith Ann Neelley.

Igou drew in a quick, anticipatory breath as his eyes swept toward her.

The woman who walked boldly to the stand had changed a great deal since her arrest in October, and the pictures that had surfaced continually on the front page of the *Fort Payne Times Journal* had methodically recorded that transformation.

At first the photographs had shown a large, bedraggled, unattractive young woman. Pregnant at the time of her arrest, she had been clothed in sloppy, loose-fitting clothes that only added to her overall image as a poor, somewhat pitiable young girl.

But from the time of her arrest, the public perception of Judith Neelley as a forsaken youth began to change, first with reports that French was pampering her, sending her flowers, and arranging for a television in her cell, still later as the outlines of his defense emerged, and finally and most powerfully, as Neelley herself became the object of the town's full concentration during the two weeks of her trial.

As the newspaper photos now made clear, Judith

Neelley was not the frail, broken, perhaps weak-minded young girl she'd appeared to be in earlier pictures. Rather, she was a tall, self-assured, and relatively attractive woman. With her hair professionally styled, and wearing expensive designer clothes and high-heeled shoes borrowed from one of the women in French's office, she was a striking figure as she strode down the corridors of the courthouse or sat proudly at the defense table.

But the transformation in Neelley's appearance alone would not have been enough to inspire the whirlwind of hatred and revulsion that began to swirl around her after the first days of her trial. Other, more important factors were needed to explain that, and one such factor was Neelley's own presentation of herself as an individual personality. For instead of a lost, wayward young girl, reporters and spectators saw an animated, engaging woman who often laughed as she consulted with her lawyers and who did not seem in the least intimidated by them. This was a far cry from the mute, pregnant girl who'd been brought to Fort Payne five months before.

But even more than her animated presence in the courtroom, Neelley's own testimony and the cold methodical voice with which she offered it served to incite the local population against her. In a world where the depravity of human nature had never been seriously questioned, where notions of guilt and retribution held their ancient force, where custom dictated that mercy be extended only in the presence of repentance, Neelley appeared as the frightening, remorseless embodiment of a cruel and degenerate nature, one whose show of sympathy for her victims struck observers as little more than the courtroom theatrics of a monstrous spirit.

Neelley took the stand in a town where church spires lined every thoroughfare, towered over every other building, a town that saw evil and wickedness in language and actions that city dwellers might regard as commonplace, a town that had maintained a sturdy prohibitionist stance from its very origins—throughout its entire history, an alcoholic beverage had never been legally sold or consumed in Dekalb County—a town in which local police had even raided the private bar of the country club.

This absence of alcoholic beverages was mirrored in the absence of pornographic bookstores, movie theaters, or video shops. Thus, despite the onslaught of a more permissive culture, the city fathers and mothers had labored to keep their city clean in ways that extended very far beyond the bounds of punishing litterers. Nor had any serious doubt ever been cast on the appropriateness or necessity of such efforts. It was a given that man's eternal tendency was to go astray, to fall into temptation, and that the work of keeping him to the straight and narrow was both worthy and unceasing. The task of each individual was to keep to that path, a moral achievement that could only be gained by the powerful and determined exercise of personal will. No one had ever taught the people of Fort Payne that it was easy to be good, or that goodness should prevail only under favorable conditions. Fair-weather goodness, honesty, and integrity were as worthless and disreputable as fair-weather friendship. The point of life, most local residents would agree, was to build a ship that would sail sturdily through the darkest circumstances.

In such a place, "sociological" explanations for Judith Neelley's actions could hardly be expected to hold sway against the conventional wisdom of Protestantism's old-time religion and the political conservatism that would mark the following decade. By the time she went to trial, the hollowness of such explanations had been echoing for years in the minds of the people of Fort Payne. The idea that there were no "bad people," only "bad conditions," struck them as not only obviously absurd, but pragmatically unworkable, the quivering foundation of a world that had lost its nerve and thus forfeited its right to bring even the most nefarious to judgment. In such a world, they wondered, where could anyone find justice?

It was within this general ideological atmosphere that Judith Neelley took the stand. She was only eighteen years old, and the first thing French wanted to make clear about her was that she had an odd mannerism, one that might prove disastrous were it not properly explained. The problem with Judy was that she had a tendency to smile inappropriately, an alarming practice that might give the jury the unfortunate idea that they had before them a human being deeply in need of moral correction. Under the influence of such unfavorable impressions, juries had often demonstrated a penchant for severity, and French had to make sure that this would not be the case with Judith Neelley.

"How do you feel before we start?" French asked her gently.

"I'm scared," Judy replied very softly.

"All right, Judy, when you're afraid or nervous, how do you handle that fear or nervousness?"

"I smile a lot."

"Is that what you're doing right now?"

"Yes, sir."

Igou looked at that smiling face and shook his head slightly. He could not help but wonder if the same smile had been on her face when she marched Lisa Millican to the canyon's edge.

"Judy, your face sort of sticks out there around your mouth, doesn't it?" French asked.

"Yes, sir."

"So if you smile, it doesn't necessarily mean you're laughing, does it?"

Igou shifted restlessly. He'd already had enough of French's attempt to give a physiological explanation for what he considered a sociopathic response. It was not buckteeth that caused Neelley's smile, he thought as he rose to object, but the perversity in her heart.

Judge Cole sustained the objection.

Then French asked Neelley who her husband was, and she replied with the name of the man upon whose shoulders she would place the enormous weight of her crimes.

"Alvin Howard Neelley," she said.

For the next hour French led Neelley through her early life, the death of her father, her relations with her family and at school, even the fact that she'd joined the Franklin Road Baptist Church at age twelve. When she declared that she'd been "saved," Igou shifted once again.

French, however, moved forward resolutely, tracing the rowdiness within the Neelley family, the faithfulness with which she'd done her household chores, her achievements at school, the grades she'd attained, clubs she'd joined, until finally she'd arrived at her teenage years and become an eighth-grade cheerleader. "And this is the last year of school you finished," French said, "before Alvin Neelley came into your life."

"Yes."

"And when you saw Alvin Neelley, did you recognize that he was a grown man?"

"No."

"On that night you met Alvin Neelley, did you have any idea that he had a wife?"

"No, sir."

"Did you know that he was the father of three children?"

"No, sir."

"That first night, how did Al treat you?"

"He didn't treat me like a fifteen-year-old," Neelley said. "He made me feel grown up. He was very nice and very charming."

"Was he smiling?"

"Yes, sir; he was always smiling. . . . He was a real smooth talker. He could get anything he wanted. He could make anybody believe anything."

As he watched her, Igou could not help but wonder if Judith herself might have the same talent.

"You've seen him on television since he's been in jail in Chattooga County, haven't you?" French asked.

"Yes, sir."

"Have you seen him walking with that meek, mild way that he does it?"

"Yes, sir."

"Is that just another act?"

"Yes, sir."

"That night did he put any moves on you or flirt with you or do anything unbecoming a gentleman?"

"No, sir. He was a perfect gentleman that night . . . He seemed to respect me. He was very nice, very gentlemanly."

For the next few minutes Neelley detailed the early days of their courtship, emphasizing Alvin's flawless attentiveness, his generosity toward both Judy and the members of her family. "He talked a lot about us and told me about some dreams he had had about us and stuff like that," Neelley told the jury.

"Pretty romantic stuff, huh?" French asked.

"Yes, sir."

"Did he ever discuss your mother with you?"

"He told me that my mother was just using me to take care of the house while she was whoring around."

"How often did he tell you critical things about your mother?"

"Every time we went out."

"How did you feel about your mother?"

"Well, I always knew it was true, but I always thought it was because she couldn't handle my father's death."

"You still loved her very much when you met Alvin Neelley, didn't you?"

"Yes, sir. We were close."

But she was moving steadily toward Alvin, Neelley added. "I didn't think there was anyone like that left in the world," she said.

"He was your knight in shining armor?"

"Yes, sir."

As the summer came to an end, Neelley went to Alvin's small, three-room apartment for the first time. It was in great disarray, Neelley told the jury, and as she began to clean it, she came upon a macabre and chilling sight.

"I found a bloody bra," Neelley said.

"What did he tell you about that bloody bra?" French asked.

"He told me that she [Jo Ann Browning] had been over there trying to get him to go to bed with her, and that he refused, and she kept asking, and he got mad and hit her in the mouth and bloodied her mouth."

He also told her about his children, Neelley testified, that two of them, Amy and Mikie, were with his mother. Jo Ann had lost custody because she had abandoned them. Sometime later, Alvin took her to meet his mother and the children.

By that time, Neelley added, she'd had sexual relations with Alvin.

"He was the first man you ever had sexual relations with, right?" French asked.

"Yes, sir."

"Is he the last man?"

"Yes, sir."

"Is he the only man?"

"Yes, sir."

This first sexual episode, like all the others that followed, was utterly unsatisfying. As Judith described it, Neelley was hardly the solicitous lover. He sought only his own satisfaction, and lost all interest once it had been achieved. He also liked his sex laced with a little pain. Added to these deficiencies was the final one of insatiability. Alvin Neelley was that nightmare lover, a poor performer performing all the time.

"How often did you have sex with him a day?" French asked.

Neelley began to cry, then attempted to hide her face.

From his seat only a few feet away, Igou leveled his

eyes on Neelley. After so much smiling, he wondered where the tears had suddenly come from. He considered all he'd come to know about her since the case began, then, rising from his seat, took a fateful chance. "Your honor," he said. "We ask that she lift her face."

French stepped in immediately. "Judy, you're self-conscious about your face, aren't you?"

"Yes, sir."

"Is that why you're dropping your head?"

"I don't like for people to see me cry," Neelley said.

Cole ordered Neelley to lift her head, and as she did so, Igou looked her straight in the eyes. He would never forget what he saw. "There were no tears at all," he remembered long after the trial. "Nothing, nothing, nothing, except that cold stare. It was all an act."

French resumed his questioning immediately. "How many pregnancies did you have with him?" he asked.

"Three."

"During all that time did you ever receive any satisfaction whatsoever from any sex acts with Alvin Neelley?"

"No, sir."

"Do you even know what an orgasm is?"

"Personally, no."

But it was not just the uninspired sex that plagued her relationship with Alvin, Neelley told the jury, it was the servitude that increasingly became a part of their life together after they began to wander from town to town.

"I cooked for him," Neelley said, "I cleaned his house and helped him dress. I bathed him, tied his shoes."

"How did you bathe him?"

"As you would a child."

"Did you dry him off?"

"Yes, sir."

261

"What about his hair?"

"Well, he was very particular about his hair. I would dry it sometimes and I would comb it sometimes, but if it wasn't just right, then he would get upset and do it hisself."

"When he got upset, did he indicate to you at all that he was going to be cruel to you later on?"

"No. He just—he would have a strange look on his face, in his eyes."

"What was that strange look?"

"Well, he had blue eyes, and when he would get mad, his eyes would turn gray, and they would sparkle and glisten, and he would get a set look in his mouth. . . . It was like his whole face would change."

The beatings had not started yet, Neelley told the jury, but the servitude had already begun to extend beyond her domestic duties to attending him at the various convenience stores where he worked.

"I stocked the shelves," Neelley testified, "stocked the cooler, swept, mopped and kept it dusted, cleaned off the parking lot. I did everything but the register."

"What did Al do all day?"

"Sat there and ran the register is all," Neelley said, "and told me what to do."

As time passed, Neelley said, Alvin began to accuse her of seeing other men. He even declared that she was getting pregnant by them. None of these infidelities served to dampen his sexual desire, however.

"Describe to the jury his sexual appetite," French said.

"I could never satisfy him enough," Neelley answered. "Sometimes he wouldn't wait until he got off work. He just had to have it then, right in the store, anywhere he wanted to, four or five times a day." They had sex in the back room of the convenience store, Neelley added, where she was forced to lie down on the concrete floor. There was also the bathroom, she went on, where "he used to make me bend over, and he would be standing up."

"Which way did he make you bend over, Judy?"

"I bent over forward."

"Where would you put your hands?"

"Either on the floor or on the toilet."

"What did you feel like, Judy?"

"I felt like a piece of meat."

Even at night, Neelley said, there was no relief. Alvin had begun to grow insanely jealous. He could not bear to let her get out of his sight. He followed her everywhere, even to the bathroom, where he stood over her while she relieved herself. When he had to go, Neelley added, the practice was the same, only in reverse.

In the meantime, the aimless drifting from town to town continued, the two of them accumulating crimes and children on the way, but never settling down. Week after week they lived on the run. As for escape, Neelley told the jury, that had never been possible. Not only had Alvin constantly surveilled her, he had also begun to "drill" into her mind the notion that he had friends in high places, that no matter where she might run, he would be able to find her, punish her, kill the members of her family, even their own children "one by one" until she finally returned to him.

The only relief, Neelley went on, occurred when she got a job at Petro's Pizza Parlor in Rome. On her first day at work she stayed at the Parlor for approximately three hours before Alvin picked her up. On the way to the Holden Motel, where they were living, she had begun to talk about the other people who worked at the restaurant, some of whom were male, and Alvin suddenly "started yelling that I had set up a date with a cook named Mike."

"He said that the only reason I wanted to work there was to flirt and screw around," Neelley added. "And he got real mad, and he grabbed me by the hair and he slung me down against the bed, and he kicked me when I fell on the floor, and then he pulled my hair again and made me stand up, and he pushed me on the bed, and he started hitting me in the head with his fist . . . and then—that was the first time he made me give him oral sex."

After the beating, Neelley told the jury, her husband had lain on the bed and watched television, ignoring her for a time before he suddenly demanded that she take off her clothes. Once she had done so, Neelley said, Alvin "took some pictures."

"He had an instant camera," Neelley said. "And he laid down on the bed, and he made me stand up above him, and he was taking pictures of me without any clothes on."

"During the sexual go-around did he kiss you?" French asked.

"No. He hardly ever kissed me."

"Did he ever kiss you during sex?"

"Sometimes," Neelley said. "He didn't mean it. There was no feeling in it."

According to Neelley, this became a recurrent pattern, accusations and beatings followed by sexual demands.

"After he would beat on me," Neelley said, "then he would have sex with me, and it was usually that I had to give him oral sex."

"Did he seem to want that after a beating?"

"Yes, and if I didn't do it right then, he would beat me until I did."

"While you were doing it?"

"While I would be doing it."

They stayed in Rome for only a short time, Neelley told the jury, then they hit the road again, this time stopping in Albany, where she became ill during her first pregnancy. Alvin had gotten a job at a Zippy Mart, and while he worked there, he demanded that his wife stay with him, stocking the shelves and the coolers, just as she always had.

The beatings also continued, only with a new twist, according to Neelley. Her husband had begun to hit her in the stomach.

"Was he hitting you right where the baby was?"

"Yes."

"What were you saying while he was doing that?"

"I was begging him to leave me alone," Neelley said. "I thought he was going to kill me. I told him it hurt, and it seemed like every time I told him it hurt, he hit me that much harder."

"Did he finally take you to the hospital?"

"Yes, sir."

The result was a miscarriage, Neelley testified, at two o'clock in the morning on February 14.

"I had my miscarriage," Neelley said, "and I was in the hospital for, I think, three days. He beat me real bad after I had the miscarriage. He said I had done it on purpose so he wouldn't know that that wasn't his baby. . . . He was real mad at me, full of rage, and he was insane, just started hitting me. He picked up a broom and was hitting me with it."

"You had just come from the hospital?" French asked. "Were you still bleeding?"

"Yes, sir."

"Was there any sex acts involved after that beating the first day you were back from the hospital?"

"Yes," Neelley answered. "He had sex with me, and it hurt real bad . . . and I was hollering, and the more I hollered the faster he went and the harder he went until he was satisfied."

Another beating had occurred the following day, Neelley added, one during which he pummeled her head, stomach, and breasts while she lay on her back in the bed.

"Did he have sex with you that day, Judy?" French asked.

"Yes, sir," Neelley said. "It was like he was trying to ruin me or something. He was violent with it. It was more like abuse."

Under French's questions Neelley continued through the following months of her life with her husband, stopping here and there to detail how Alvin had taught her to write like a computer in order to forge money orders, and to talk of the various robberies that were committed by the couple as they roamed from town to town. But the beatings were the focal point of the questions and answers, and each description was more horrendous than the last.

"After he got tired of hitting me he threw me on the bed, and he had sex with me again," Judy said.

"When he had sex with you, were you still crying and teary from the beating?"

"Yes, sir. I was still bleeding. He had busted my nose and my head."

"You had blood in your hair?"

"Yes."

"Could he pick you up off the floor by the hair of the head with one hand?"

"Yes, sir . . . My feet wouldn't even be touching the floor, and he would sling me across the room like a rag doll."

"Where would he kick you? What part of your body?"

"In the legs, in the stomach, in the side and the ribs."

"When he kicked you, would it move you along the floor?"

"Yes, sir . . . usually about two or three foot."

French then moved on to other, equally grim aspects of what Neelley had described as her husband's character.

"Did he have anything against blacks?"

"Yes, sir. He hates them all. . . . He was telling me about how him and this guy used to go into the black section of town and shoot it up with guns, black out windows in the house, and set cars on fire, and shoot up the cars, and shoot the black people."

But the excursion into Alvin's alleged racism was brief, and after only a few questions French returned once again to the subject of sex and violence.

"Go ahead and tell me how you spent your nights,"

French said of a time when the Neelleys had stayed for a while at a particular motel in Rome.

"They had on the TV one channel that had nothing but pornographic movies," Neelley said. "And we would rent a room in that motel, and Al would watch that station, and then he would have sex with me like they did on the TV."

"You had to do for him what the girls in the porno flick did?"

"Yes, sir."

"Some of those things get pretty gross, don't they?"

"Yes, sir."

Still, despite it all, Neelley agreed to marry Alvin and helped him procure a doctor's statement declaring that she was pregnant in order to do so. The marriage had occurred in Ringold, Georgia, on July 14, 1980, Neelley told the jury, and shortly after that she and Alvin had had their honeymoon in a small motel in Phenix City, Alabama.

Then they had moved on again, this time into Texas.

"We went almost to Dallas," Neelley said, "and turned around and came back."

During that brief interval, Neelley testified, Alvin had been "nice," but on the way back toward Georgia "it was real hot during the day, and he was real grumpy. He had trouble breathing because he was so fat, and he was easily angered, and he was quicker to hit me, and he was always hitting me when he was driving, and in the motels he would mostly rest and take it easy in front of the air conditioner."

After the trip to Texas, the two had gone to Florida, Neelley continued, and "it was just the same thing over and over."

"Just the run-of-the-mill beatings?" French asked.

"Yes, sir."

They lingered for a time in Florida, Neelley said, then drifted north again, toward Rome. Soon they ran out of money, and Alvin began to talk about armed robbery.

"We had been spending all day in the Riverbend Mall in the arcade," Neelley said, "and we had been arguing a lot because we didn't have any money, and Al was mad. . . . He would tell me about taking his gun and robbing a woman of her purse and then us leaving. And Halloween night he was real harsh with me and saying if I don't do it, that he was going to beat me, and I was scared of him leaving me where I didn't know where I was at or how to get home without any money or anything."

"Judy, were you big and pregnant?" French asked.

"Yes, sir."

"It was just thirteen days before you delivered the twins?"

"Yes, sir. I weighed one hundred and ninety-six pounds."

"Did he give you a gun that night?"

"Yes, sir. It was a .25 automatic. He told me to pick out a woman, a young one that I would be able to handle, that looked like had a lot of money, and he told me how to rob her, you know, how to scare somebody talking, with what you say."

"How is that?"

"By sounding calm, but your words are harsh," Neelley said. "Your words seem threatening though your voice is quiet."

"Did you walk up to a woman and rob her?"

"Yes, sir. I said, 'Bitch, don't you say a word and you don't get hurt.' She was scared, and she didn't say anything."

They were both arrested shortly after the robbery, Neelley went on, and she was sent to the Rome and later to the Macon Youth Development Center. She then went on to discuss her experience at the YDC in Rome, the kindnesses that had been extended to her there, particularly by two of its staff, Ken Dooley and Linda Adair.

"How long did you stay in the YDC in Macon?" French asked.

"Six months."

"Judy, how did the people treat you at the YDC in Macon?"

"They were nice to me. They tried to help me. It was mostly blacks, and Al knew that, and his letters were real bad there."

"Did you have any trouble there?"

"No, sir."

"Did you get along well with the black people?"

"Yes, sir."

"Did you ever have any trouble at any YDC, Rome or Macon, either one?"

"No, sir."

"Did you ever have any fights with any of the girls?"

"No, sir," Neelley answered. "I got along with everybody, especially the staff."

"How did these people treat you, and how did you do?"

"Well, they treated me real good. I got pretty close to the social worker over at my cottage, Albertine Green. She was a black lady. Every day we had group for an hour, and she helped me a lot."

It was now late in the afternoon, and as Judith Neelley finished the last few remarks of her testimony, Detective Sergeant Elaine Snow sat only a few feet away. All day she had listened as Neelley related her story about the armed robbery at the Riverbend Mall, her subsequent arrest and confinement in the Rome and Macon YDCs. At times their eyes had met, but Neelley's face had not registered the slightest recognition, although Snow could not imagine that she had not instantly recognized her. "It was amazing the way she told her story," she recalled later. "I might have believed it myself if I hadn't known Judy before, hadn't seen her in the same room with Alvin and noticed how she was the driving force of the two, the one in charge. She was very meek on the stand, a real sweet girl. I'd look at the jury and think, 'My God, she's going to get away with it.'"

Danny Smith also sat in the packed, at times restless, courtroom. He had rarely seen a better performance. But the Judith Neelley on the stand was entirely different from the Judith Neelley of her letters. What had happened to the girl who hated "niggers" and considered the staff of the YDC as little more than vicious meddlers? On the stand was a woman who'd never enjoyed sex or experienced an orgasm. Where was the one who'd spoken constantly of it in her letters, addressed her husband as "Horney," and written teasingly of those times when the back of Alvin's Gremlin had shuddered with their love?

CHAPTER
27

"Al Did"

FAY FREEMAN HAD worked for nearly twenty years in
Robert French's law office by the time he was ap-
pointed to defend Judith Neelley, but she had never
experienced anything like the hatred that poured into
that office after the first day of Neelley's testimony.

It had been building overtly for several weeks, and
already she had noticed a dwindling of clients, along
with the fact that members of the local bar association
no longer dropped by French's office or called in to
say hello. All of which added to the siege mentality
that had begun to develop in the office even before
the trial, a sense of being separated from the surrounding community.

But what had been little more than an intimation
became a firestorm after the defense began, one that
hit its peak during the four days Judith Neelley was on
the stand.

The telephone calls varied from genuine expressions
of concern and wonderment to threats and reproaches.
Some people called to ask why French was making
such a passionate defense of a woman who clearly
failed to deserve it. Other calls were considerably more
offensive. While Freeman listened, astonished by the
vitriol, anonymous voices declared that Neelley "should

be fried," that they would be willing "to pull the switch" themselves or at least "pay the electric bill" when it was done.

Many of the calls, Freeman noticed, centered on Neelley's looks, her fancy lipstick, the cut of her hair, the style of her dresses, the price of her shoes. Others demanded that Neelley wear "jailhouse clothes" rather than those which, they said, had been purchased for her at Black's Department Store, where "the doctors' wives go to buy their stuff." Callers claimed that French had bought the clothes for that "bitch" he was defending because he'd fallen in love with her. Some of the callers went even further. "Anybody who would defend that Neelley girl," one of them told Freeman coldly, "ought to be fried with her."

The mail was similar, and after a while Freeman deposited it in the nearest waste can without bothering to show it to French.

"Even at the beginning, I never liked that case," Freeman said long after the trial. As it progressed, she would have cause to like it even less.

Judith Neelley resumed her testimony at 9:00 A.M. on March 16, 1983. French opened the questioning by reading excerpts from a number of letters Neelley had made available to him and that presumably were written to her by Alvin. He wanted to know what certain phrases within the letters meant, and he enumerated them one by one.

"Some of the words that I see appear in there over and over again," he said. " 'If you prove your love to me.' What does he mean by that phrase?"

"That's his way of saying that if I didn't do what he asked me or told me, that I knew what was coming," Neelley told the jury.

French read another line from the letter: "I wanted also to say you're a very special lady. You always will be, no matter what." He then asked Neelley the meaning of the phrase "no matter what."

"The 'no matter what' was his way of always trying to get me to tell him that I had been with other men," Neelley said, "and when I told him that I hadn't, he kept trying to get me to say that I had."

French plucked another letter from the pile on his desk, this one dated June 29, 1981, and asked Neelley what her husband had meant by his references to "bad dreams."

"He was always telling me about bad dreams he had," Neelley explained, "because people wrote him and told me that I was messing with people in Macon, the guards and some people."

"When you were living with him and he had a bad dream, what would he do?"

"Sometimes he would punch me while we were laying there and wake me up, and sometimes we'd just get up in the morning, and he would be in a bad mood."

The next letter had been written on June 30, 1981. One passage was of particular interest to French: " 'There's a lot of people I'm going to talk to when I get out,' " he said, quoting the letter. " 'Some of them don't even know I know their names. Smile.' "

"What does that mean?" French asked.

"I told him the names of some of the men that were nice to me down there," Neelley said.

"What is he going to do to them, anything serious?"

"He had said that he was going to get them," Neelley answered, "but he never gave any details at that time."

French went on to a letter dated July 8, 1981. It was the postscript that interested him: " 'PS: Think about what I wrote in my last letter,' " he read. " 'It could happen. I really want it to happen unless—I really don't want it to happen unless you ask for it.' What does that 'PS' mean to you?" he asked.

"He was talking about how he had gotten Jo Ann back," Neelley said, "and . . . he was saying that he would kill me."

French next offered an assortment of letters, written between August 1981 and February 1982, in which

Alvin accused Judith of various deceits and acts of adultery. They were tormented letters that maddeningly alternated between protestations of passionate love and monstrous threats.

"Do you have any knowledge of the reason he appears to be so hard on the YDC?" French asked.

"He told me in the YDC that they sexually abused me, and he didn't like it."

"Well, did they?"

"No, sir."

"These people that he continually refers to with these vile threats in the letters, do you know who they are?"

"Yes, sir . . . It was some of the security people in Macon. The security guards were male. The rest of the staff was female, and it was some of the teachers in the YDC and some of the people, the Christians, that had helped me with the Bible."

French moved from the letters to the time when Alvin's appeal for a reduced sentence had first been denied, then inexplicably granted, although with two full pages of provisions, none of which, Neelley testified, her husband had ever met.

According to Neelley, the night of Alvin's return was nothing more than an occasion first for painful sex, then another beating, one which included kicking and punching, pulling her hair, and finally, beating her with the wooden handle of a bathroom plunger.

"When he got that plunger handle and brought it back in there, what did he do?" French asked.

"He started hitting me with it, because he said he was tired of hurting his hands on me."

"At the time of that beating, Judy, did you notice anything strange as far as he was concerned?"

"Yes, sir. I saw that he had an erection while he was hitting me."

A second beating followed the next day, Neelley told the jury, one that ended with a new sexual demand.

"He was beating me real bad," she said. "Then he

wanted to have sex with me in an odd way, a different way. It wasn't normal. It was in my bottom. He would make me lay face down on the bed, and every time I would holler he would hit me in the back of the head."

"How much did he weigh then, Judy?"

"Almost two hundred pounds then."

"Had you ever had anything stuck up your anus before?"

"No, sir."

"Was it painful?"

"It was very painful. . . . I was bleeding, but that didn't stop him."

Neelley then told the jury that Alvin had become upset with notions that she had been sexually abused at the YDC. Until then, she had denied such abuse, but under the pressure of the beatings, she'd finally confessed to it. "I told him that what he had said about me being with other men—I told him it was true." Later, her story became more elaborate, Neelley said, in that she gave him all the details about her sexual activity at the YDC that he demanded. She told him she'd had sexual relations with security guards and other staff, both black and white. The beating that followed, Neelley said, was unimaginably severe.

"He grabbed both my ears, trying to pull my ears off, and he took his thumbs and dug them into my eyes, trying to pull them out. He started beating me in the breasts and trying to pull my breasts off. . . . And he kept hitting me and he slung me off the bed, and he backed me up in the corner and took his mother's gun, and he started hitting me in the head with it, and then he grabbed my hand, and he bit me real bad. . . . Then he took the stick from the plunger and made me lay down on the bed, and he told me that if I was going to screw niggers, he was going to screw me with that, and he was sticking it up as hard as he could. . . . I was bleeding and he finally stopped, and he got up. He said he had to go to the bathroom. He told me to kneel down on the floor. He told me not to move, that he was going to piss on me, and he did a little, and then he told me to open my mouth. He told me he was gonna pee in my mouth and I better not spit it out. Then he did."

Throughout the rest of the afternoon Neelley continued her account of life with her husband after his release from prison in March of 1982. She described the criminal acts she had committed, the robberies and forgeries, before they headed toward Macon the following August. It was her husband's obsession with her life in the YDC that drove them there, she said, his vengeful determination to make certain people pay. Under his terrible instructions, she had done everything he asked, firebombed Linda Adair's house and shot into Ken Dooley's, then journeyed to Macon where she'd bought Liquid Plumber, Liquid Drano, and a few diabetic needles and syringes. In every phase of her testimony the central feature remained her utter helplessness in the face of Alvin's violent assaults, the scores of beatings and humiliations she'd endured, the various foreign objects with which she had been assaulted—guns, sticks, a leather strap, a hacksaw, a hard piece of plastic, finally a baseball bat, which, Neelley said, Alvin forced up her vagina after telling her that since she had "fucked niggers he was going to show me how big my hole was." Sexual intercourse, Neelley added, had become a permanent part of the beatings. "Whenever I was able to look when he was beating me," she told the jury, "he would have an erection."

As evidence for the truth of Neelley's testimony about her physical abuse, French offered a series of startling Polaroid photographs.

"I'll show you defendant's exhibit number 61," he said as he handed the photograph to his witness. "Can you identify that picture, Judy?"

"It's a picture that Al took when he was having sex with me."

"Now, Judy, these big black spots that are on the inside of your legs and on your arms, are those still on you from that beating the third day he was home?"

"Yes, sir."

"Those black spots around your breasts, did he put those on you?"

"Yes, sir."

"Judy, those long marks on top of your breasts, is that where he tried to pull your breasts off of you?"

"Yes, sir."

During the next few minutes French offered a number of photographs into evidence, pictures of Judy and Alvin having sex, or of her various parts, pictures that could only have been taken by someone who had stationed himself directly beneath her widely parted legs.

"Did you ever consent to any of these pictures?" French asked.

"No, sir."

"Who took the pictures, Judy?"

Neelley's answer came without hesitation, an answer that during the next days of her testimony, would be repeated so often that it took on the quality of a chant.

"Al did," she said.

The last day of Judith Neelley's testimony began at 9:00 A.M. on March 17, 1983. Slowly, methodically, for three days, French had taken Neelley through her life as a child and a teenager, to her steady victimization by Alvin Neelley. For years she had been the only victim of his psychopathic wrath. But toward the end, one victim had not been enough to satisfy him, and he had demanded that Judith procure others for him to victimize, and then, under his instructions, that she victimize them herself.

"He talked about how he was tired of me in bed," Neelley told the jury, "and he wanted me to find him somebody."

But he had not only given the order, Neelley said, he had instructed her on how to accomplish it. They were to use different cars, and she was to pick girls up and bring them to him, "and then he was supposed to have them as long as he wanted them, and then I was supposed to get rid of them."

"How were you supposed to get rid of them?"

"I was supposed to kill them, ah, with the Drano."

Neelley said she didn't know exactly how many girls she'd tried to pick up in Rome. She was looking for a type, however, the kind Alvin wanted. "He said he was trying to get a virgin," Neelley said. "And he wanted one that was small, if she wasn't a virgin, because he knew she would at least be tight, and that was what he wanted . . . a tight hole."

"Is that the phrase he used all the time?"

"Yes, sir. That one and . . . 'a tight pussy.' "

During the last week of September, Neelley said, they had hunted every day, tirelessly cruising the streets of Rome, and after each unsuccessful foray she had been beaten.

At last, however, early on the evening of Saturday, September 25, 1982, they had gotten lucky.

"The cars were parked about four car lengths apart," Neelley said, "and Lisa Millican was standing out in front of the mall, looking around like she had lost her ride . . . I offered to take her where she wanted to go. She hesitated for a minute, and then she decided she would get in the car and go with me. So she got in and I headed out of the parking lot. I swung around where I could go in front of Al—where he would see Lisa in the car on the passenger side, and he followed me out."

They drove south, Neelley said, and as they drove, she began to talk to Alvin on the CB. Later, she told Lisa what a nice man he was, how he'd bought her the brown Dodge she was driving, about how good he was.

"Where did you get that line to give her?" French asked.

"From Al."

Not long after that, Neelley said, the three of them met, shared some junk food, and continued south to the Chattahoochee Motel in Franklin, Georgia.

Once in the motel, Alvin had gotten impatient and had wanted Lisa immediately. Judith had tried to get her to go along with what Alvin wanted. In that effort, she said, she had taken her into the bathroom and told her once again how good Alvin was and how it was better to learn about sex from an experienced man. But Lisa was still unwilling to go along, and later, outside the motel, when she'd reported Lisa's refusal to Alvin, he responded by hitting her.

"So I took her [Lisa] back into the bathroom," Neelley said, "and I told her she didn't have a choice. So she went out there and she was very quiet. I didn't hear much. She was very quiet. She was crying and told Al that she was scared; she didn't want to, and Al told her that if she didn't, that I would kill her, and finally she agreed."

"Where were you?"

"In the bathroom."

"Could you hear Lisa making any noises?"

"She was crying."

Later Al had called her out of the bathroom and she had seen Lisa and her husband having sex. Her husband was nude, she told the jury, but Lisa had refused to take off her blouse and was only naked from the waist down.

"Then what did you do, Judy?"

"I went back to the bathroom."

She came out later to do laundry. Once back in the room, she had followed Alvin's instructions and handcuffed Lisa to the bed. Lisa had slept there all night, completely nude as she huddled on the floor.

The next morning they had gone to pick up the

twins, then journeyed to Scottsboro, Alabama, where they had stayed at the Five Points Motel.

"How did Lisa get along with the kids?" French asked.

"She liked them a lot," Neelley answered. "She was playing with them, looking after them."

The next night, acting on her husband's instructions, Neelley told the jury she had physically attacked another human being for the first time.

"We had a flapjack," she said. "Rubbery like. It's leather, and it has, I think, a piece of steel in the end of it. They use it to knock somebody out . . . and he told me to take the flapjack and hit her in the head with it and knock her out, and when she fell, for me to pick her up and put her on the bed and to call him. He told me when I called him in there that we would undress her, and when she come back to that he would be having sex with her. So . . . I hit her in the head, and she turned around and asked me what I was doing, and I hit her several times, trying to knock her out, and it didn't do it. I couldn't hit her hard enough . . . Al come in the door, and he told me, 'Never mind' . . . and he told me to tell Lisa to get undressed . . . and to tell her he was gonna make love to her again."

Neelley did as she was told, she said, adding that her husband had demanded she watch while he had sex with Lisa. She had done this, too, watching television with her children while Alvin raped Lisa.

The next morning Alvin raped Lisa again, this time brutally. "It wasn't like he had done it before," she said. "This time he raised her legs up, which raised her hips up, and it hurt her more. She was crying again."

"How big was she?"

"She was small."

"And what did he do with that child's legs?"

"He put her legs across his shoulders. It was like doubling her over . . . She was crying and asking him to please stop, that he was hurting her. He was doing it real hard. When she said it hurt her, he did it harder."

"Tell us what he did to hurt Lisa Ann Millican."

"Whenever he raised her legs up like that, it put her into a position where he would go further up in her . . . when he did it real hard, it hurt very bad."

"Well, would he pull himself all the way out each time?"

"Yes, and then go back in harder."

"I believe you said he weighed how much?"

"About two hundred and fifty," Neelley said. "She was asking him to stop, and he just kept on. Then he told me to undress and come over there where he was at. . . . I did, and he was on one side of the bed with Lisa. While he was having sex with Lisa . . . he was sucking on my breasts. He told me he was making believe that Lisa was me."

"Was Lisa doing anything?"

"She was crying."

"What were you doing?"

"I was crying."

After the rape, Neelley went on, Alvin instructed her to bathe Lisa and she had done so. The two of them had then returned to the room and watched television with the twins while Alvin slept.

When Alvin awoke, Neelley said, he was obsessed with a man in a green car whom he'd seen at the Dairy Bar the day before. He told Neelley that he was convinced that the man was a hit man who worked for a prostitution ring in Macon and that Lisa knew him. He instructed Neelley to find out who the man was. Neelley described what happened next.

"I took her in the bathroom, and I handcuffed her . . . and I started asking her," she said. "I sounded like Al. Very accusing. When she said she didn't know him, I wouldn't listen to her. I kept telling her she was lying and that I wanted to know who it was."

In the end Lisa had confessed that she knew the

man, Neelley said, but her husband had done nothing about it, save have sex with her once again that same afternoon.

French now began to direct Judith Neelley's attention to the fatal moments on the canyon, first going through the details of the early-morning departure from Scottsboro, how she and Lisa had dutifully packed the car while Alvin stood by, huge and ponderous, watching silently.

In this, as in everything else, Neelley said, it was her husband's work, from the original plan to its execution.

"He was telling me that morning we were going to drive out to some deserted place," Neelley said. "I was supposed to give Lisa that shot and leave her."

The two cars, with Alvin alone in the Granada and Judy in the Dodge with Lisa and the twins, headed north out of Scottsboro. Over the CB Alvin talked to her about looking for a place to have breakfast, while talking in code about a place to murder Lisa. Finally, Alvin told her that he had found such a place.

"We turned in over at Little River Canyon," she said. Then they moved on up the road until they found a place beneath a span of power lines. Lisa was handcuffed in the Dodge, Neelley said, while she and Alvin paced about the area, trying to find the best place to murder her. By that time, she added, Alvin had become suspicious of her, walking with her in such a way as to make sure she could not push him off the canyon.

Finally, Alvin approved of an area. It was time for Lisa Ann Millican to die.

"I took Lisa and told her to lay facedown and put her arms around the bottom of the tree," Neelley testified. "I went back to the car and got out the syringe out of my pocketbook. . . . I squatted down beside her. I was just looking at her and Al hollered at me and told me, 'Do it.' So I gave her the shot in the neck, and she was talking about it was hurting her."

But the shot was not fatal, and so her husband told her to give a second injection. He showed her where to give it, she said, by pointing to the position in her own neck.

The second shot did not work either, and Alvin became furious, calling her a host of obscene names—"bitch," "whore," "nigger lover," and "nigger fucker"—and threatening to kill her.

For the next thirty minutes one injection followed another, punctuated by intervals during which Lisa had been forced to walk about so that the Liquid Plumr and Liquid Drano would act more quickly. Once, she had been allowed to urinate in the brush near the tree to which she had been handcuffed, while all the time the layer beneath her skin was being reduced to something like bacon grease.

After six separate injections, Alvin had had enough, Neelley told the jury. He wanted Lisa dead.

"I told Lisa to walk to the edge of the canyon," Neelley told the jury, "and to stand with her back to me and to look out into the canyon. She did."

Alvin yelled to her, Neelley said, screaming, "What's taking so long, bitch," and unable to delay any longer, she had taken the next step. "And I . . . told Lisa to turn around with her back to me." Then Alvin hollered, " 'Do it, bitch,' and I pulled the trigger."

But Lisa's body pitched backward instead of forward, and she lay at the edge of the canyon, faceup, her hands at her chest, blood streaming from between her fingers.

At that point, Neelley said, Alvin had called to her again—"Do it, slut,"—and in response, she had used her knee to push Lisa's body over the side of the canyon.

Within a few minutes after the murder, Neelley went on, she had changed clothes and thrown the jeans, towel, and syringes over the side of the canyon, all at Alvin's command. "Then Al walked over to the edge of the canyon to make sure that Lisa was dead," she added. "He looked over—down at Lisa—and he was smiling, and I heard a sound."

"What sound?" French asked.

"The sound that he—that Al always made whenever he—whenever he satisfied himself."

After Alvin had masturbated to orgasm while staring down at Lisa's body, Neelley said, he returned to the Granada and drove away, heading down the southern mountain slope toward Rome. Following his instructions, she fell in behind him. He was talking to her again, his voice droning incessantly from the speaker of the CB radio.

"He didn't say anything about Lisa," she told the jury. "He started talking about me picking up somebody else for him."

"How far from the canyon were you when he started saying that, Judy?" French asked.

"About a mile," Neelley replied. "We had just left."

Neelley went on to describe the next few days, the series of calls that, she said, Alvin had made her make to various police departments and other places in the Rome/Fort Payne area.

"He knew that the Rome Police Department recorded calls," Neelley said, "and he had told me to call about the shooting and the firebombing, and he knew they had my voice on tape . . . and so he was reasonably sure that they knew who I was."

But she had made the calls anyway, she told the jury, one after the other, until the body was discovered.

The beatings had resumed by then, relentlessly brutal beatings inevitably followed by sexual intercourse.

"Now, after he had beaten you and you'd have blood all over the place, was it then that he would want sex?" French asked.

It was, Neelley answered, and on those occasions he would force her to lie facedown on the bed and take her from behind.

"And he was rougher than he had been before?"

"He was trying to hurt me."

But at the same time, she said, Alvin had renewed his insistence upon finding another victim. Finally, on the evening of October 3, after several fruitless efforts, she had found one.

"So, next we have Janice Chatman and John Hancock, is that right?" French asked.

"Yes, sir."

Again, under her husband's instructions, Neelley said, she had picked the couple up, taken Hancock out to a deserted area, and shot him. After that, she had taken Janice to the Oak Hurst Motel in Rome, where Alvin raped her.

"Was Janice crying or anything?" French asked.

"No, sir," Neelley said, "she seemed to be enjoying it."

Later that night, Neelley showed Chatman newspaper clippings concerning the murder of Lisa Millican in order to terrorize her, but they had little or no effect. "She didn't seem very emotional," Neelley said of Chatman's demeanor during her captivity. "She didn't cry."

The next morning, Neelley said, they all pulled out of the motel and headed north. On the way, following Alvin's detailed directions, she took Chatman to a deserted area in Chattooga County, Georgia. They were going to kill her, but before doing so, Alvin had informed her that "he wanted another piece of pussy."

"The seats of the Granada let completely back," Neelley said, "and he told me to sit in the Dodge with the twins until he was finished. So he satisfied himself in the Granada in the front seat with it let back on the passenger side."

"Did you see them doing it?"

"Yes," Neelley said, "because the cars were parked side by side, and just glancing over there at the car you could see it."

When he finished, Neelley went on, Alvin told her to walk Janice out into the bushes and shoot her, which she did.

"I shot her once in the back," Neelley said, "and she started hollering, and I was scared that somebody was going to hear her, and I shot her. . . . She fell backward on her back, and she was hollering, and I shot her two more times in the chest to shut her up."

The two cars had then driven off, and on the way back to Rome, Neelley said, Alvin "started talking about picking somebody else up already." Only a few hours later, Debbie Smith, an eighth-grade cheerleader had stepped off a school bus, walked a few yards down Leon Street, and seen a woman in a brown Dodge pull up alongside her. *Are you Patricia?*

But the Neelleys had failed in their hunt and returned to Murfreesboro. Not long after that, Neelley added, she told her mother that she and Alvin were leaving and that they would be somewhere on the Nashville Highway. She said that she wanted her mother to call the police and tell them to arrest her there.

She and Alvin had left Mrs. Adams's house not long after that, Neelley said, and began to hunt for another victim, finally picking up a young woman whose street name was Casey. They took her to a motel on the Nashville Highway, and it was there, on October 9, that the nightmare had finally come to an end when the policeman had arrived at her door and asked her the same questions she had asked so many others during the last twenty days, though with different intent. *Are you Judy Neelley?*

CHAPTER
28

"How Would You Draw Hers?"

AT 1:15 P.M. Richard Igou rose to begin his cross-examination. He had not believed a word of Neelley's testimony. Much of the physical evidence, he thought, did not support it. Neelley's letters while in the YDC had not suggested a woman who had been systematically brutalized, and other than a single photograph, there were no pictures of that brutality. French had offered no medical evidence to support Neelley's contentions, despite the fact that she had given birth twice in public hospitals. He had offered no corroboration from her friends or family members, not one witness who had been willing to testify that he or she had seen Judith Neelley in a battered state.

In addition, Igou's office had been contacted by Tommy Blaine, a trusty in the Dekalb County Jail who had often talked with Judith Neelley and to whom she had written a number of letters. Blaine had been arrested for forging medical prescriptions, and while incarcerated in the county jail, he'd come to know Neelley well. She had confided a great deal in him, he said in a statement to Darrell Collins, and he'd been so impressed by the curious nature of her character that he'd begun to think about writing his own book about her.

According to Blaine, Neelley had told him that the motive for picking up Lisa and Janice had been partly sexual, but that it had been more a matter of the enjoyment she took in dominating people, making them fear her. As for the killings, they had been Judy's idea from the beginning. Her husband had had nothing to do with them. According to Blaine, Judith had boasted that she'd made only one mistake, the telephone calls to the Rome and Floyd County police. Had she known they were being taped, she said, she never would have made them and, consequently, never would have been caught. Judith Neelley, Blaine told Collins, was a woman who had killed in cold blood, for pleasure, and who had experienced no remorse.

It was a view of Judith Neelley that Igou shared. His task now, as he began to question her, was to make the jury share it, too.

"Mrs. Neelley," Igou began, "tell us why you asked your mother to call the police."

"I don't know."

"Alvin didn't tell you to do that, did he?"

"No, sir."

"What was your mental operation in this?"

"Well, there's some things I don't know the reason to."

"Tell us those things."

"Ah, well, right offhand I—I don't know just right offhand."

"There are many times when you would leave the various motel rooms, why didn't you go to the police at those times?"

"I don't know."

"You told FBI Agent Burns that you were not intimidated by anybody, didn't you?"

"Yes, sir."

"Why did you make them turn their backs to you?"

"That's what Al told me to do."

"Did he tell you what to say to him?"

"He told me to tell John Hancock not to say anything."

"And he told you in detail to tell him to turn his back?"

"Yes, sir."

"You're smarter than Alvin, aren't you?"

"In some ways."

"In what ways?"

"Al didn't learn a lot in books. He learned more from life and how to manipulate people."

"Your basic level of intelligence is higher than Alvin's, isn't it?"

"Ah, yes, sir."

"In Murfreesboro you cooked for him, cleaned house, helped him dress, bathed him, tied his shoes. He wasn't beating you, was he?"

"Not then, no, sir."

"But you really loved him, didn't you?"

"Yes, sir, I did."

"And you did run away from home, and you left the ugly note to your mother. Did anyone force you to leave?"

"Physically, no, sir."

"It was mental domination, right?"

"Yes, sir."

"You have pretty good insight into yourself, don't you?"

"Now I do."

"When did you suddenly have this insight?"

"When I got away from Al."

"You were away from Al in Murfreesboro when you were talking to the investigators, weren't you?"

"He was contacting me through letters," Neelley said, "and I had talked to him on the phone."

Igou let a hard edge penetrate his voice. "I'll ask you if your insight didn't suddenly begin after you started consulting your attorneys?"

"No, sir."

"Didn't you tell Mr. French that the first thing you asked him was if you could see Alvin?"

"Yes."

"You said that Alvin always bragged to you about how masculine he was, how tough he was."

"Yes, sir."

"How he had beaten up people?"

"Yes, sir."

"And you found that to be a little exciting, didn't you?"

"Intriguing maybe," Neelley admitted.

Having attempted to establish that Neelley had been attracted rather than repulsed by her husband's fanciful tales of violence, Igou went on to call into question the sexual obsessiveness that Neelley had described.

"You said that he forced sex on you four or five times a day, is that right?"

"Sometimes, yes, sir."

"And made you feel like a piece of meat?"

"Yes, sir."

"There were no beatings at that time?"

"No, sir."

"And you stayed with him?"

"Yes, sir."

"Because you wanted to."

"Not as I wanted to," Neelley said, "as he wanted me to."

Igou went on to note that by her own testimony, Neelley had admitted that on many occasions she had been very far away from her husband, miles away, in a car of her own, but that at the same time she had testified that she had not been allowed to go to the bathroom by herself.

Igou then moved on to a time when Neelley said she had been robbed at gunpoint while Alvin was in the store.

"You told us that Alvin was more scared than you were," Igou said.

"Yes, sir."

"That's sort of been consistent with your whole life with Alvin, hasn't it?"

"No, sir."

"You have been the calm and the cool one," Igou said, "and he's been the one who didn't have the nerve?"

"No, sir."

Igou turned to a Valentine card that Neelley had taped to the wall of the Macon YDC, noting the fact that she'd pasted her husband's picture at the center of it.

"You put Alvin's picture on it?" Igou asked.

"Yes, sir."

"You still loved Alvin, didn't you?"

"Yes, sir."

"I'll ask you, Mrs. Neelley, if it's not a fact that what bonded you and what kept you and what tied you to Alvin was just that, love, wasn't it?"

"No, sir."

"It was not fear," Igou declared. "It was love."

Igou also doubted the truth of Neelley's descriptions of the beatings she claimed to have received from Alvin.

"You testified that he hit you in the mouth with a gun," he said. "Did he hit you hard?"

"Yes, sir."

"What damage did that blow do to you?"

"One time he broke my tooth."

"Can we see that again."

Neelley showed a small chip from one of her teeth.

"That huge man hit you in the mouth with a gun and that's the damage that resulted from it?" Igou asked.

"Yes, sir."

Igou asked Neelley how many times her husband had beaten her with a baseball bat, and she replied that he had done it "maybe eight to ten times."

"And he would swing with both hands?"

"Yes, sir."

Igou wanted to know where the bat had struck her, and Neelley answered that she'd been hit in the head, back, arms, ribs, but that her husband had not been trying to kill her with the blows, only to hurt her.

"How many broken bones did you receive from the beatings?" he asked.

"I'll say two fingers."

"Never broke your skull?"

"No, sir."

"Never broke your arms?"

"No, sir."

"Or ribs?"

"No, sir."

Igou then moved Neelley through the crimes she had committed with her husband, concentrating on those moments when, according to Igou, she had acted alone, without direction from her husband, particularly during the last horrifying seconds of Janice Chatman's life.

"She was just hollering," Neelley said, describing Chatman's reaction to the first gunshot, "just screaming."

"You were afraid somebody would hear her, weren't you?" Igou asked.

"Yes, sir."

"And you shot her twice more in the chest, didn't you?"

"Yes, sir."

"Because you were afraid somebody would hear her?"

"Yes, sir."

"And Al wasn't at your side then, was he?"

"No, sir."

"He didn't tell you to shoot her two more times in the chest just to shut her up, did he?"

"No, sir."

"You did that on your own, didn't you?"

"Yes, sir."

Under Igou's assault, Neelley related all the crimes she would have committed had Alvin told her to do so. She denied having sex with either Lisa or Janice, however, and she reiterated that she had never enjoyed her sexual relationship with her husband.

"Not even from the beginning, did you?" Igou asked.

Neelley's answer was unequivocal. "No, sir."

Igou offered the jury a few pictures of his own, pictures that showed Judith Neelley with her husband in what appeared to be a state of joyous companionship, proudly displaying their stock of arms, sometimes leveling them at various family members, Judith's brother and sister. Neelley said that Alvin had orchestrated all the photographs to the point of instructing her on how to smile.

Igou passed from the photographs to the murder of Lisa Millican, and in response to his questions Neelley began what became a kind of chant.

"You injected her again in the neck, didn't you?"

"Yes, sir."

"Why did you do that?"

"Because Al told me to."

"And you injected her in the arm, why?"

"Because Al told me to."

"And you injected her in the other arm, why?"

"Because Al told me to."

"And you injected her in the buttock, why?"

"Because Al told me to."

"You injected her again in the buttock, why?"

"Because Al told me to."

"Did you feel for her?"

"I didn't feel anything."

"Actually, what you felt, Mrs. Neelley, was enjoyment, wasn't it?"

"No, sir."

"You enjoyed being dominant, didn't you?"

"No, I did not."

"And you marched her right up to the edge of the canyon."

"I didn't march her. She walked up to the canyon."

"How close?"

"To the edge."

"Did you tell her how close?"

"Yes."

"Did you say, 'Go a little further?' "

"I told her where to stand," Neelley said. "I marked it with my foot. . . . I walked up beside where she was at and stepped my foot in front of her a little bit and told her to stand right there."

"You didn't want to get too close to the edge, did you?"

"I didn't think about it."

"Because Al told you not to?"

"He didn't tell me not to get too close to the edge."

"What did she say to you when she looked at you?"

"She didn't say anything at first," Neelley said. "When she—when she was standing there at the edge of the canyon, she asked me to take her back either to the Harpst Home or to her mother's and she wouldn't say anything."

"How did she say that, Mrs. Neelley?" Igou asked. "Did she say it just like you said it now, real calm and cool and quiet?"

"She had a pleading tone in her voice."

"Were her feet right up next to the edge of the cliff?"

"They were, I guess maybe—maybe two inches away from the cliff, maybe three."

"She was looking out over into the canyon?"

"She was looking straight out."

"Did she beg you any more or plead with you any more?"

"No, sir. She just stood there and was quiet."

"How long did she have to stand?"

"I don't know. Maybe a minute."

"You were just doing what Alvin told you?"

"Yes, sir."

"When you and Alvin had them," Igou asked, "who fed the children?"

"I did."

"Who diapered the children?"

"I did."

"Who would bathe the children?"

"I did."

"Did Alvin tell you to do those things?"

"He told me when to do them, yes, sir."

"He told you at every point when to wipe the baby's nose?"

"Yes, sir."

"When to change the baby's diaper?"

"Yes, sir."

"When to give the babies something to eat?"

"Yes, sir."

"You just didn't do anything at all without Alvin telling you to, did you?"

"Whenever I went to the bathroom, I went on my own."

"The only thing you ever did on your own was to go to the bathroom?"

"And eat," Neelley added. "If we had something in the motel, I would eat."

Igou shrugged. He could hardly express the contempt he had for testimony that he felt was so utterly preposterous. "That's all I have," he said.

In redirect, French offered a few more photographs that, he told the jury, proved that Neelley had been beaten. He also offered photographs of Alvin in which Neelley pointed out the glistening eyes that she said preceded an attack. Last, French showed the jury a pencil drawing, the product of one of Neelley's special talents, French said, a sketch she had done while living at the Macon YDC. It showed a single hand reaching from behind a wall of bars.

"Judy, were there any bars in Macon where you were?" French asked.

"No, sir," Neelley said. "There were no bars at all."

"So that didn't represent yourself in Macon, did it?"

"No, sir."

"What did it represent?"

"My life," Neelley answered. "How I thought of my life as a prison."

Neelley went on to say that she had not cooperated with French and his co-counsel until after she'd heard Jo Ann Browning's testimony. She had not been aware of the nature of French's opening statement. But Browning's testimony, along with the generosity of her attorneys in their effort to win her trust, had awakened her, she said, from the long nightmare that Alvin Neelley had imposed upon her life.

"Judy, what has changed to now?" French asked. "What is the difference now?"

"Now I'm a person," Neelley answered. "I've got feelings and emotions. I'm not a puppet."

Igou thought Judith Neelley was a person, all right, a criminally sociopathic one, and his re-cross-examination centered on that part of her personality.

"Mrs. Neelley," he began, "the Bonnie and Clyde thing kind of appealed to you, didn't it?"

"No, sir. I wouldn't say that."

"Well, you sort of smiled when Mr. French asked you about that. Did that bring back some pleasant memories?"

"It just brought back some memories of how he used to tell everybody we were Boney and Claude."

"And that appealed to you, didn't it?"

"I think Boney and Claude is funny, just the names, the phrase."

"What about the image of it as Bonnie and Clyde?" Igou asked. "That appealed to you, too, just like it appealed to you when he told you about being a tough guy and beating people up and that kind of thing excited you, didn't it?"

"No, sir. I don't like violence."

Now, in the closing moments of Neelley's testimony,

Igou returned to the reason it had had to be given in the first place.

"Did you ever find out, Mrs. Neelley, if Lisa Millican had any hobbies or if she had any special talent?" he asked.

"I don't know."

"You didn't care about that very much, did you?"

"I didn't think about it."

"How would you draw her life?" Igou asked softly, in the last question he would ever ask Judith Neelley. "You've drawn yours. How would you draw hers?"

"I don't know," Neelley said.

Igou let his eyes rest on her a moment. "That's all," he said finally. "Thank you."

Beyond his cross-examination, and in order further to refute the four days of Judith Neelley's testimony, Igou called one rebuttal witness, Dr. Alexander Salillas, a psychiatrist with the Alabama Department of Mental Health. Responding to a few direct questions, Salillas testified that Neelley had known the difference between right and wrong at the time she had murdered Lisa Millican and that she had made a conscious decision to commit that murder.

In his cross-examination, French went directly to the point.

"In your experience," he asked Salillas, "have you ever come in contact with the term 'coercive persuasion'?"

Salillas replied that he had, then listened as French enumerated the elements that were involved in the term: 1) isolation of the victim and total control over the victim's environment; 2) control of all channels of information and communication; 3) psychological debilitation by means of diet control, insufficient sleep, poor sanitation, or other physical conditions; 4) assignment of repetitive tasks; 5) manipulation of guilt and anxiety; 6) threats of annihilation by the all-powerful persuader who insists that the victim's sole chance for survival lies in identifying with the persuader; 7) degradation of and assaults on the preexisting self; 8) peer pressure, often applied through ritual or struggle sessions; 9) required performance of symbolic acts of self-betrayal, betrayal of group norms, and confession; 10) alternating harshness and leniency.

One by one, Salillas agreed that these were the separate elements of coercive persuasion, a technique, French pointed out, that was known more commonly as "brainwashing."

"I grant that," Salillas said.

"All right. Now, we take the person and we expose the person to those conditions, we get a response that is out of the ordinary, don't we?"

"You might."

It was precisely the answer French needed, and from it he began a point-by-point recitation of Neelley's life with her husband that more or less matched the requirements of the condition of coercive persuasion. According to French, Alvin had subjected Judy to every single element, had isolated her from others by taking her from her family, controlled her channels of information and communication by surveilling her continually, debilitated her through diet and sleeplessness, given her meaningless and repetitive tasks such as bathing him and tying his shoes, manipulated her guilt and anxiety by alternating terror with protestations of love, kept her in a constant state of fear by periodically threatening her life, assaulted her preexistent self by referring to her disparagingly by her maiden name, required symbolic acts of self-betrayal by forcing her to confess to acts that she had not committed or to engage in humiliating sexual practices, and had alternated demonstrations of leniency and severity.

Salillas responded by saying that none of these factors was necessarily present in the case of Judith Neelley, but that even if they were, she still retained the power of choice.

French asked Salillas if he were aware that forty million women were battered in the United States. He then enumerated the various reasons these women did not report their condition or attempt to leave their batterers, everything from the desire for privacy to extreme economic and emotional dependency.

Salillas told French that he had no disagreement with him as to the reality of this situation, but that such women did, in fact, have a choice in such matters, and that for whatever reason, they chose to endure the beatings, rather than to report them.

French went on to ask about kamikaze pilots, the followers of Jim Jones, Moonies—did such people, he asked, in the throes of nationalist or religious frenzy have what could be referred to accurately as choice regarding their behavior?

Salillas's answer was absolute. "Yes," he said.

"Well, when you get down to it, doctor," French said, "the only thing that we can do in the world is make choices, isn't it?"

"Right."

"But the point that we come back to is there are times, would you agree, that our choices are taken away from us by others?"

"Never is."

"But . . . there are times during coercive persuasion that the choices we make are directed for us, aren't they?"

Salillas remained adamant. "Directed, but still a choice, Mr. French."

French continued to stalk Salillas, trying to break through the impenetrable wall of his conviction that in the final analysis, regardless of the level of coercion imposed, a human being, the "hypothetical girl" to whose situation French addressed his remarks, retained the capacity to choose. Under a barrage of references to Lao-tzu, Pavlov, Buddha, and the Marquis de Sade, Salillas continued to deny the ultimate loss of choice.

Still, for Salillas the question did not reside in the

hypothetical woman whose life French was presenting, but in the woman he saw before him, sitting quietly at the defense table, a woman who, had she received the kind of assault French had graphically described, Salillas said, "would probably still be in the hospital, would probably be severely damaged all her life, would probably not be so intellectually capacitated to understand." She would, he concluded, "probably have every bone broken in her body."

Precisely, French said, she was broken in body. He asked Salillas to look at one of the photographs he had offered in evidence. Were the bruises in the picture, he asked, not "consistent with being beaten with a ball bat?"

"Not necessarily," Salillas answered. "A pinch would give you the same result."

"What?" French asked unbelievingly.

"If you take a piece of flesh between your forefinger and your thumb, that would give you the same result."

"Say, a hematoma?"

"Yes."

"That's a real bad bruise, is it?"

"Not necessarily. I've had them all my life."

"In your judgment, this could be caused by twisting skin or pinching?"

Salillas would not give in. "Certainly," he said.

Salillas's assured and unequivocal answers were damaging, and French went after him energetically, accusing him of having been coached by the prosecution during the lunch break that had interrupted his testimony.

"And you are on the state of Alabama payroll here today, aren't you?" French asked finally.

"I am working for the state of Alabama."

"And you're wanting to cooperate with the district attorney in this case, aren't you?"

"We're after the truth, Mr. French," Salillas replied evenly. "We try to be impartial. You could have easily subpoenaed me to come here, and I would have given you the same answers."

"Okay, fine," French told him. "We'll leave it up to the ladies and gentlemen of the jury."

But not quite. For the most critical and dramatic moment of the trial was still ahead, the closing arguments that French and Igou would make before the jury. It was the force and credibility of these arguments upon which Neelley's life now entirely depended.

CHAPTER
29

"Evil, Evil"

THROUGHOUT THE TRIAL, Igou had watched in growing wonder as the nature of the defense had steadily broadened from the more narrow notion of showing that Judith Neelley, because of the nature of her relationship with her husband, had not been able to formulate the intent to murder that the law required on a charge of capital murder, to the larger question of wife battering and "coercive persuasion." But he could hardly have anticipated the sweep of French's closing argument. For the Ninth Judicial District, it was unprecedented in its use of philosophy and social criticism.

Clearly, by the time French rose to make his closing arguments, the case of Judith Neelley had become, as he told the jury, "the most serious case I have ever been involved in."

But it was even more than that, he would say later in the afternoon, much more. It had become a critical event in his personal history, an epiphany, something that had revealed the world to him more fully than any previous experience. "I want you to realize that this is the most important thing I have ever done in my life," he said, "and I'm almost fifty years old."

Animated, pacing restlessly back and forth before the jury, flinging his arms passionately, French told the jury that months before, when he'd first met her, Judith Neelley had been an isolated woman who believed herself the only person who had ever suffered Alvin's barbarity. She had tried to protect him to the very end, and only Jo Ann Browning's testimony had awakened her. Now justice required that the jury awaken, too, in order to understand that Judith Neelley had remained emotionally numbed for months after her arrest. "Let me tell you something about people," he said. "What we don't understand, we're afraid of. You take a praying mantis that eats insects in your garden. Did you ever let one live? You take a snake that eats rats around your house. Did you ever let one live? No. We kill snakes and praying mantises because we don't understand them."

The jury had to understand Judy Neelley, or they would kill her, too. They had to understand that she might handle fear differently than they. She might appear cold, distant, and without remorse, but this physical presentation of herself was merely the way she chose to handle her own fear. "Don't criticize Judy for handling her fear in front of you. Don't criticize Judy Neelley for not shedding the tears that you think ought to be shed. Don't put up a standard like some psalm-singing, two-faced Christians who . . . gossip and lie and backbite and cheat and annihilate character and violate the Ten Commandments and still go to church every Sunday and sing 'Nearer My God to Thee.'

"The murder of Lisa Millican is a tragedy none of us can undo," French continued, but killing Judy Neelley would only serve to compound it. "She breathes and she cries and she hurts and she may not have met your expectations as she handled her fear," he said. "You might have acted differently, but then you were never subjected to Judy Neelley's experience."

At first, French said, he had shared what might be the jury's initial impression of Neelley, that she was a cold-blooded killer, a monster, "the bride of Frankenstein." Finally, however, as he had continued to look at "those dull, lifeless eyes," he had come to realize that "inside there's nobody home."

French offered evidence from the testimony that "there was nobody home" in the mind of Judith Neelley when she had tried to pick up Suzanne Clonts. "You know what hurts me about Suzanne Clonts, and I wouldn't have had the gall to tell it. I would have lived with it and hurt with it the rest of my life. She felt a need to witness to that girl, and didn't. I don't know whether I could handle that. She felt the need. If she had given her Christian witness to that girl, none of us would be sitting here today. Maybe that ray of hope, maybe that glimmer, maybe that light, maybe that pinpoint of light that this zombielike person needed would have come through in a Christian witness. Ah, such a bad indictment on church members. I'm going to tell my Sunday-school class over and over and over until they get so tired of hearing it they'll reduce it to memory. The failure of Christian witness."

This failure of Christian witness should not be compounded by the jury's failure to understand that Neelley was a zombie at the time of the murder. "Don't you hold Judy Neelley to a standard of some healthy robust female whose husband may slap her around now and then or, God forbid, all he does is shake her or puts his hand around her head. You hold her to the standard of a woman that's beaten every day of her life, not enough to kill her, just enough to hurt, just enough to bust her head, just enough to leave teeth marks on her skin."

But Judy had not been Alvin's only victim, French said, calling attention to the testimony of Jo Ann Browning. "I'll compare Jo Ann and Judy for you as to what Alvin Neelley did to them. He made love to both of them in the back rooms of stores and didn't care how dirty it was. He made both of them work inside and outside the store. He accused both women of being unfaithful to him and having sexual relations with blacks . . . Both had three pregnancies. He denied all six children. He never committed violence around either of their families. . . . He had sex with both of them in the rectum and performed oral sex. Both were hit in the mouth with a pistol and lost a tooth. Both say his eyes would always glisten. . . . He called both wives bitches, sluts, and whores. He made them both big and fat and ugly. . . . And Alvin, just as he is today, was always the victim. . . . Let me tell you how strong Alvin Neelley is . . . because on January 3, 1983, Judy Neelley delivered his baby right here at the Baptist Medical Center in Fort Payne, and Steve and I were there within three hours of the birth. We wanted her to name that baby Robert Stephen Neelley or Stephen Robert Neelley. We didn't care. We thought she ought to name him after us, but we hadn't brought her far enough. We hadn't brought her as far as we thought we had. She named the child Jason Alvin Neelley and asked me to please take a photograph and send it to Alvin's mother so she could deliver it to him so he could tell the baby wasn't the child of a black man."

It was Alvin Neelley, "the jolly ole fat man," who had turned Judy Neelley into a robot. He was a modern Svengali. "Svengali is a character out of du Maurier's book *Trilby*," French said. "What Svengali did was he took this peasant French girl, who was just a plain girl, and he took her and he turned her into the world's greatest opera singer, but he did it through mind and thought control. . . . 'And with one wave of his hand over her and with one look of his eye . . . Svengali could make her do whatever he liked . . . and think his thoughts and wish his wishes and love him at his bidding with a strange, unreal, factitious love.' "

Alvin Neelley was a modern Svengali, French said, a practitioner of mind control and brainwashing on the order of Charles Manson and Jim Jones.

Judy Neelley had been Alvin's last victim, French said, and Alvin's letters proved it. He read lengthy excerpts from the letters themselves, emphasizing their love of viciousness and rage, their brutal threats. "Because he is an articulate writer," French said when he had finished reading them, "we have Alvin Neelley right where we want him."

"Then he talks about the female," French said, before reading one of the excerpts. "I want you women, particularly, to hear this. This reflects in all the acts that the man did. It says, 'I'm this way about it and so are most men. Women that easy, that screwed up, are good only for using for a while, and all you have to do is tell them what they want to hear and then dump their dumb ass and laugh. I liked to used to do that when I went with married women. I said just what she wanted to hear to get what I wanted. When I got all I wanted, she got dumped 'cause just like I knew and everyone else knew, if she fucked one man around, she would another. So, all she got was used, suckered, and dumped, she got fucked up and lost her family and everything, and usually a man that really loved her. For what? A few little words and promises that were a lie, a joke? You can believe the guy who used her is the one who's laughing the hardest. Some women never learn. They just keep getting used, suckered, and dumped, because they just keep saying, "This one will work out," and after they've been had by everybody . . . no man, even a punk, is gonna want you for nothing but a fuck, a suck, and a break, and when they're tired of you, they're gonna pass you on to the next poor sucker like a cheap thing.' "

Toward the end of his argument, French began an appeal to the overall humanity of the jurors. Such an appeal, he admitted, could not be expected to succeed, since history provided abundant evidence that "human beings are more cruel than they are bent toward compassion."

"We kill those over and over and over again who tell us to forgive, to love," French said, and he was perfectly aware that some of the jurors "may want to send her to the electric chair . . . where they jerk your body around and give you three thousand volts and let you bounce around and stink and fry."

Others might not be so vengefully motivated, however, French said, people who were "motivated by the desire to love and care and understand," people who were, he added, "primarily females." It was to these people, French said, to whom he was appealing, and had he had it his way, he would have had nothing but women on the jury because of their greater capacity to love. It was to that love that he was making his argument for mercy and understanding. "Let me tell you this: that although we have two sides and two hemispheres to our brain, the right and the left, the male and the female, or if you were Chinese, the ying and the yang, the soft and the hard, the theoretical and the practical, the musical and the mathematical, for want of a better word . . . if we allow the pragmatic to overtake our beings . . . our possibility of being mean and our characteristic toward being cowards, then we're assured of nothing more than human misery . . . and we will do away with Judy.

"We're limited by ignorance and we're limited by physical weakness and by fear, and uncertainty and disease haunts us each day, and we grope through life looking for a helping hand," French went on. "Let me assure you, that Judy Neelley begs you, through me, for a helping hand . . . If you ever had any tenderness and mercy in your being, it is time to bring it to the forefront."

But if women had a greater capacity for love, French told the jury, they also had a greater capacity for pain. "But the tragedy of this situation is because the woman . . . is physically weaker and because everybody comes here by spending nine months inside a female body and because she's incapacitated and because she has menstrual cycles and because she has pain and because she has tremendous feelings inside. . . . I tell you that the woman learns to live with pain." In recompense for the added pain women must endure, French declared in what is surely one of the most extraordinary statements ever made to an American jury, "God gave them the multiple-orgasmic response . . . the added pleasure in the sex act that men will never have." And if any woman had not experienced that pleasure, French stated, she had "only one man to blame, and that's the one that she has as a mate."

As for himself, French said, he was a "mama's boy, a fifty-year-old mama's boy" who had been taught by her to "think somewhat like a woman," more softly, capable of greater mercy.

The jury system was designed to allow that mercy to come forward, French said. America, he added, was "not a nation of Ayatollah Khomeinis," although during the trial he'd seen a few "Dekalb County Ayatollah Khomeinis" who, if they didn't understand something, wanted only to kill it. "And they've told lies about me all over this town for defending her."

But for now, French wanted to appeal to what he called the "feminine side" of human nature, the "love side," that would "never ever, ever convict Judy because Judy has been punished enough."

But not only Judy, French said, but women in general had been punished enough. "You go down through history," he said, "the woman takes the blame." And if the members of the jury continued in that tradition, they, too, would blame Judy Neelley, rather than her husband.

"If Judy Neelley is seen by you as most women are seen," French declared, "she will be seen as a thing and you will destroy her. If she is seen as an it, you will kill her."

The task for the jury, French told them, was to see her simply as a human being, one whom the ravages of Alvin Neelley had reduced to a robot. Sexism might prevent them from doing that, but a woman was "not an it." "Women have brains," French said. "Women know what's happening. Women have rights. Women have abilities and talent."

French then moved on to the final remarks of his argument. "I'm telling you, and I want you to hear me," he said, "Alvin Neelley has killed two women. It was Alvin Neelley who killed them, Alvin Neelley who vented his sexual desires on them." Then, to the jury, he addressed an unforgettable question. "So what does he want from you," he asked, "his final orgasm? He got it off of two of the dead women. Are you going to give him one as he sits in Georgia and laughs at all of us because he's pulled it off again?"

French ended his defense with a tale often told by well-known defense attorney Gary Spence, and which French altered only in order to give it local color.

"I'll close by telling you a story that I heard years and years ago about a town about like Fort Payne," he said. "And there was a mountain right above the town, and there was a wise old man that lived on the mountain. . . . One day a couple of boys thought they would fool the old man . . . and so they caught a bird, and they said, 'Let's take this little baby bird up there . . . and I'll hold the bird in my hand and ask him if it's alive or dead, and if he says, "It's dead," I'll open my hands and let it fly away. If he says it's alive, I'll kill it and hand it to him. . . .' So they caught a little robin and they went up there and they called the old man out. One of the boys said, 'Guess what I've got in my hand?' The old man thought a minute. He said, 'I think you've got a bird in there, boy.' And the other one said, 'That's right, but is it alive or dead?' And the wise old man of the mountain thought for a long, long time, and finally he looked at the little boy holding the bird and he said, 'It is as you will, my son.' "

French paused a moment, then asked the jury his final question. "I leave to you my trust for Judy Neelley," he said. "Is she alive, or is she dead?" He followed with a final plea. "For God's sake, this woman has been punished enough. Do something for the female of the species one time, when you have a chance."

Igou could hardly believe what had just transpired before him. French's performance had been utterly theatrical, he thought, and its attempt to exonerate Neelley on the basis of her undemonstrated abuse struck him as the most specious he'd ever heard in a court of law. Still, its scope inspired him, and the passion that rose from French's voice and gestures was nothing if not admirable. It was utterly opposed to his own style, as defense styles often go, but grand nonetheless. Now, however, it was time to see if he could present the facts in such a way that they spoke more eloquently than French's high-geared rhetoric. "I felt that I had the truth on my side," he would say many years later, "but that is sometimes a weak weapon against an appeal to the emotions. Still, it was all I had."

As he had done throughout the trial, Igou addressed the jury formally, from behind a lectern, and with much greater brevity than French's two-hour argument.

"This case is not about birds," he said. "It is not about Hindu philosophy or ancient Chinese philosophy. This case is about one of the most hideous crimes that ever occurred anywhere in the country. . . . I would like to know if Mr. French has actually been able to make you forget about Lisa Millican. She's not a bird. She's not a goldfish. She is very dead."

French, Igou said, had been trying throughout the entire trial to present Judith Neelley as the most important person in the case. But she was not the most important. Lisa Millican was, and her killer deserved to be punished.

Then, for the first time, Igou personally distinguished himself from Robert French, both as a lawyer and a man. "I'll tell you this," he said. "I haven't lived my whole life for this moment. I wish we hadn't had this case to try. It hasn't fed my ego one smidgen. I haven't gotten any pleasure out of trying this case. It's not something I've looked forward to all my life."

But French was a defense attorney, Igou said, and he had tried to defend Neelley as best he could. He had tried to convince the jury that the case was about women, but it wasn't, it was about murder. He had tried to suggest that Neelley had been brainwashed, but had presented no evidence to that effect. He had presented no scars on Neelley's head, even though he claimed that it had been laid open by a baseball bat swung by a two-hundred-and-seventy-five-pound man. "If there had been any scars," Igou said, "one by one you would have been shown them."

French had even brought the story of Svengali into his defense, Igou went on, the story of an opera singer, a piece of fiction "just like this whole defense is a piece of fiction. We could read science fiction stories to you and they would have as much to do with this trial as that does," Igou declared.

As for French's particular argument to the women of the jury, Igou told them that he found it contemptible. "And then there's the argument to your womanhood, the soft side to find her not guilty," he said. "A woman finds the facts just as a man does. You can't be pushed around and shoved around and have your ideas mangled by some smooth talker."

But if Igou had not liked the appeal to women, neither had he cared for the appeal to Christianity. "Quoting the Bible to you," he said, "he did a lot of that. I really don't—I'm not going to talk much about that. I think you have your own thoughts about that. I don't believe that you think the teachings of the Bible hold that Mrs. Neelley shouldn't be responsible for her acts here on earth."

And who was this Mrs. Neelley? "He kept her on the stand so long so that you could know her," Igou said. "I think he did that, and I think you do know her, and I think now you do know more about what kind of person she is and how she could calmly and coolly kill the people that she did."

In general, Igou added, "You didn't hear much about the facts in his statement to you. You heard an appeal that was based on emotion, based on sentiment, not based upon the facts. There are emotions, certainly, to consider. There are emotions concerning the body of Lisa Millican as it was thrown over the canyon that day. That's an emotion, but that is not what you consider the case on. You consider it on the facts.

"He spoke to you about motherhood," Igou went on. "I would ask you to look at the facts in this case and to see the example of motherhood that we have."

As for the brutality that Neelley had supposedly suffered at the hands of her husband, Igou reiterated that there was practically no evidence of it. Witness after witness—Debbie Smith, Suzanne Clonts, Diane Bobo, John Hancock—all had been asked if they had noticed cuts or bruises or other evidence of injury on Judith Neelley, and all had testified that they had not. "He has insulted battered women in my judgment. No, I can't know what a battered woman thinks or feels like. I see a number of them from time to time, but I think he has insulted them by comparing them to Judith Neelley and what she has done. That's the biggest insult I've heard in this case. . . ."

For the first time Igou gave his own idea as to what was actually being done by Alvin and Judy Neelley. In Georgia, Alvin was blaming everything on Judith. In Alabama, Judith was blaming everything on Alvin. "It's very clever. It's brilliant, because if both those concepts are believed, are bought, then neither one of them is guilty and nobody is responsible for the death of Lisa Millican. Nobody is responsible for putting the bullet through her back and her winding up dead in the bottom of the canyon, and we have the elusive and mythical thing called the perfect crime."

The real story was quite different from this concoction, however, and it could be reduced to a simple truth. "Alvin didn't have the nerve, but she did. I think that's the thread that runs through this whole thing. Alvin didn't have the nerve, but she did. She pulled the gun on John and she took him off into the woods. She was calm, you remember him saying, and she was not nervous. When John wanted to ask a question, she said, 'Hell, no. Shut up.' She told him to turn around, and she also told him, 'Don't worry about your girlfriend. I'll take care of her, too.' That was Judy Neelley, not Svengali.

"You get a more accurate and a more truthful and a more realistic picture of what really happened to Lisa Millican by knowing what happened to John Hancock and Janice Chatman. . . . She put the cuffs on her, she injected her with this stuff that we clean out our drains with, she took her to the edge of the canyon, she lifted her gun up to her back, and she pulled the trigger. . . . Later she did the same thing to John Hancock and Janice Chatman. Her desire to please Alvin in doing it, maybe so, maybe so."

But that was precisely the point. That it was desire, rather than fear. "She has told us that Alvin taught her how to lie and that she was accustomed to rehearsing things. You've seen her in court, and she's admittedly a very intelligent person. She attached herself to Alvin Neelley . . . who was more important to Judith Neelley than the life of a thirteen-year-old girl. That's what it all boils down to. Who was more important? The most important person was Alvin Neelley."

The same characteristics that charmed her in the beginning, Igou declared, had continued to charm her through her life with her husband. "Bonnie and Clyde," he said. "It appeals to her. It appealed to her then, and it still appeals to her. Abnormal? You bet it is. There is nothing normal about this. You remember the tape that was played, the calmness, the coolness, the coldness in that voice, just hours after this crime against Lisa. Monotone? French would try to tell you it was monotone. It was just the voice of a cold-blooded killer. You remember the different episodes of calmness, during the robbery of the woman at the mall, her confessions to Danny Smith and FBI Agent Burns. Calm and cool through the killings, through the investigation, and now in the courtroom."

This coldness was the heart of Judith Neelley, Igou said, but hers was not the only heart in the story, not the only life to be considered. There was, at last, Lisa Millican.

"You cannot know how she felt," Igou said, moving now toward his conclusion. "It's hard for you to imagine that moment at the canyon. You can't do it unless you were Lisa, unless you had been laid down there and injected with Drano, unless you had been marched to the edge of the canyon, unless you had looked like Lisa did out over the canyon. You cannot know how she felt. She stood there and she begged for her life. . . . You can't know how she felt knowing that her life had stopped right there at the edge of Little River Canyon at the age of thirteen years in a way like that. . . . There is not a word strong enough that I can use to tell you what happened to Lisa and to convey to you the things that you feel and know from the testimony what happened to her."

For thirty long minutes on the rim of that canyon, a scene had been acted out that had nothing to do with duress or wife battering or fiction or Chinese philosophy or any of the other things the defense had brought out to justify or explain it. And now, in the closing moments, Igou told the jury what he thought he'd seen in the room with Judith Neelley as she was being interrogated by Smith and Wetzel. "It was evil, evil," Igou said. "And I don't think I've ever used that term before in a criminal case. I've tried murders, rapes, sodomies, but I don't ever remember that coming to my mind, but if it ever applied to a situation—if it ever applied to a couple, it applies here in this case, and you have felt it. It has hung in this courtroom, and you have felt it. It's been more than an atmosphere of evil; it's been a reality."

Judge Cole charged the jury immediately following Igou's final remarks, then released them to their deliberations at approximately 4:30 P.M.

By 10:45 A.M. the following morning, Tuesday, March 22, the jury had reached a verdict. They had found Judith Neelley guilty of murder and kidnapping.

CHAPTER
30

"She's Mine"

THE SENTENCING HEARING to determine whether Judith Neelley would live or die began at 1:15 P.M. on March 22, 1983, only a few hours after the jury had delivered its verdict.

The courtroom was filled with spectators, along with the jurors and court officials who would present, record, or judge the final arguments before the jury.

Assistant District Attorney Michael O'Dell opened for the prosecution. In a statement of fewer than two hundred words, he informed the jurors that they had entered the last phase of their service. He did not see any need, he said, to repeat what they already knew. He wished only that they remember "the last four days of Lisa Ann Millican's life."

French now rose to make his argument. He appeared shaken, emotionally drained, the powerful presence of only a few hours before now curiously shrunken, the voice somewhat gentler, though no less passionate in its appeal. "I don't know whether you can understand what I'm about to tell you or not," he began softly, "but in this trial I have given you all I have. Now I'm going to give you some of my soul and see if you'll take that in exchange for this girl's life."

During the next hour French did precisely that in a

statement that shifted incessantly from personal anec-
dotes to Christian sermonizing and that included extended discussions of his personal philosophy, the nature
of sin, and even the chemical and molecular structure
of biological life.

Toward the end of his address, French returned to
religion, in this case, the parable of the Good Samaritan. "Who is your neighbor right now?" he asked the
jury. "Your neighbor is Judith Neelley."

Once again, French made his case for her abuse,
then pleaded with the jury not to compound their
initial error by sentencing her to death. "You could
have fired a shot heard 'round the world by righting
the wrongs that were committed on Patricia Hearst,"
he said. "You never understood the chance you sat in
to do something for women, and that's okay, because
we never had time to really teach you, and I wasn't
smart enough to show you that you could have all
been heroes for women's rights, but maybe that doesn't
concern you. Maybe you'd rather have a pound of
flesh. Maybe you'd rather have an eye for an eye and
a tooth for a tooth. Maybe you'd rather have polarized
living—living in an abysmal ignorance. Most of us
do."

Now, thoroughly exhausted, in a state his wife would
later describe as utterly worn down, French approached
his final moments before the jury. "Now I want you to
look at this girl because she's a human being. Right
now she breathes. Right now she weeps. Right now
she feels, and right now she's so desolate and alone in
this crowded room and so helpless. If crying would
help, I'll cry. If getting on my knees would help, I'd
get on my knees. If I could bare my bones for you and
save Judy Neelley, I would gladly do it. Don't send
this girl to the electric chair. I beg you. I plead with
you. Don't do it. Don't kill what God has created."

Igou, too, felt the weariness of the trial as he walked
slowly to his usual place behind the lectern. "Before

this case began," he said, "I really hadn't considered seriously what recommendation the state was going to make to you, but the feeling of this case is different from anything I've ever experienced. There are cases in which the death penalty is not only appropriate, but necessary for the defense of society, and we're talking about the very bottom line, the ultimate defense of the ultimate predator on society." Judith Neelley was such a person. He asked that she be put to death.

It was late in the afternoon by the time the arguments were completed, and the jury was taken to a nearby restaurant for dinner. They ate quietly, then prepared to return to the jury room for their final deliberation. They were now in the closing hours of the eleven-day trial they had witnessed together, whose ultimate outcome they were about to decide.

Before leaving, one of the jurors spoke about the ordeal through which they had passed, the terrible story it had been their duty to hear. She suggested that they join hands and sing a hymn before leaving the restaurant. And so they did, singing quietly the words to "God Be with You."

As they sang, Mary MacPherson, the court bailiff, let her eyes drift around the table. "That moment was very moving," she would say later. "So many of them were crying."

Only a few minutes later they returned to the courtroom and delivered their recommendation to Judge Cole. Their choices had been life imprisonment or death. By a vote of ten to two, they had sentenced Judith Neelley to life.

Under Alabama law, the jury's determination of a life or death sentence in a capital-murder case stands as a recommendation only. It was Judge Cole's prerogative either to except or refuse the recommendation. He set April 18, 1983, as the date when he would hear arguments for and against his acceptance of the jury's recommendation of life imprisonment.

On April 3, the *Huntsville Times* published an interview Judith Neelley granted to its reporter Peter Cobun. Neelley told Cobun that she did not want to die and that she could accept life imprisonment since anything would be better than the three years she had spent with Alvin. One of her lawyers told Cobun that Judy wanted Alvin to sit on her lap when the switch was thrown. The lawyer had then thrown his head back and begun to shake wildly in a mock electrocution, after which he and Neelley had "dissolved in laughter."

"If I get the electric chair," Neelley told Cobun jokingly, "I guess I'll take it sitting down."

The sentencing hearing before Judge Cole began at 9:00 A.M. on April 18.

French spoke first in an address that would last nearly an hour and a half and fill almost one hundred transcript pages; in it, he repeated many of his earlier arguments, then added a lengthy discussion of such other matters as America's treatment of the Indians, the "price" of the Industrial Revolution, America's need for "instantaneous gratification of desires," its place in the world as an arms manufacturer, its storehouse of poison gas and weapons for biological warfare, its addiction to violence on television, and finally the "legalized murder" of capital punishment.

As for Judith Neelley, she was "the original damsel in distress," French said. But she was also the human being who had taught him the most in his life. "She's different. She's not like a daughter, because I have two daughters. She's not like a wife, because I have a wife. She's like something else. She's like—she's mine."

To demonstrate the depth of Neelley's transformation, French called her to the stand for a final time. "I want you to tell Judge Cole just exactly who is Judy Neelley," he told her.

After a long pause Neelley began. "Judy Neelley is a caring person, gentle. Ah—I don't hurt anybody. I don't do anything wrong. I like to help people. Ah—I'm very quiet." There was another pause, then Neelley resumed her answer. "I'm very confused about some things, very scared. Ah—ah—I'm very worried about myself and about my children, very lonely."

"How do you feel about the possibility of getting the electric chair?" French asked.

"I don't want to die," Neelley said. "There's so much that I could do to help. I know that. I just want to prove it. I don't believe in the electric chair."

It was now time for Igou to face the judge for the last time in the Neelley case. His remarks were very brief and to the point.

"She doesn't want to die," he told Judge Cole. "She says there is much that she could do. I would submit that there is much that Lisa Millican could have done. Who knows what she could have done? She might not have done anything extraordinary at all. We really would not have expected her to. From her background, and from the opportunities that she had, we would not expect her to, but she deserved the opportunity to be what she wanted to be and to control her destiny and herself."

Judith Neelley, Igou said, had not allowed her to do that.

Judge Cole recessed the court for twenty minutes and returned to his chamber. During the time between the jury's recommendation and this moment, he had thought of very little but the fate of Judith Neelley. He had already written two completely different decisions as to her sentence, and as he sat in his chambers, he could see both of them resting faceup on his desk. For a moment he let all the aspects of the case move through his mind, then he reached for the decision that rested nearest his right hand.

At 12:20 P.M. Cole returned to the courtroom. He

began by thanking the defense for the vigor with which it had presented its case, then went on to his final decision.

In the determination of this sentence, he said, the law required that mitigating circumstances be weighed against aggravating ones. In terms of mitigation, he cited Neelley's youth, the influence of her husband, and the fact that by telling her mother to have her arrested, she had set in motion her own apprehension.

But there were also aggravating circumstances, Cole added, the murder had been committed during the course of a kidnapping, it had been especially heinous, atrocious, and cruel when compared to other capital offenses because the victim had been a child, and had been terrorized, assaulted, sexually violated, and tortured by six separate injections of liquid drain cleaner before her murder.

"The court finds by any standard acceptable to civilized society," Cole said, "this crime was heinous, atrocious, and cruel to a degree beyond that which is common to most capital offenses."

He then told Judith to rise.

"Accordingly," he said, "Mrs. Neelley, the court hereby fixes your punishment at death."

Neelley immediately slumped in her chair, dropped her head, and began to cry.

Only a few feet away, Igou watched as she wept quietly. Once again he remembered the moment in the trial when Neelley had been ordered to lift her head and he had seen no tears. Now, he noticed, they were falling profusely. "They were the only tears I ever saw her shed," he recalled. "And they were only for herself."

CHAPTER
31

"If It Had Been True"

IN MARCH OF 1983, at the conclusion of his wife's trial, Alvin Neelley was still awaiting trial in Chattooga County, Georgia, where he had been arrested for murder and kidnapping.

Assistant District Attorney Ralph Van Pelt handled the case, and during his first meeting with Neelley he had been struck by how utterly unthreatening he appeared. Rather than the typical profile of the serial killer, Van Pelt saw a fat, round-faced man who chattered endlessly about a "YDC prostitution ring" and claimed to be afraid of his wife.

Later, Van Pelt read the arrest records of both Neelleys and something struck him immediately. It was Judith who had committed the armed robbery, rather than her husband, and armed robbery was a crime that even the prison population felt to require so much raw courage that armed robbers had traditionally been considered the kingpins of prison life, the ones with the real guts.

As he continued to evaluate the case, Van Pelt decided that it was Judith Neelley who would need to be tried first, her husband later, because the case against him was so frighteningly weak. Chatman's body was far too decomposed to provide usable evidence as to rape or even assault, and the testimony of John

Hancock could not support charges of either assault or kidnapping.

In the meantime, Superior Court Judge Joseph E. Loggins granted a motion for a psychiatric examination of Neelley, and pursuant to Loggins's order, he was examined at the Northwest Georgia Regional Hospital in Rome for a total of six hours on January 29 and 30. The subsequent report concluded that Neelley was "competent to stand trial and criminally responsible for his actions as related to the charges against him."

In addition, Neelley's examiners found "no evidence of psychosis or thought disorder that would constitute delusional compulsion which overmastered his will to resist committing the crime." Nor did they find "indication of any defect of his mental abilities that would interfere with his capacity to distinguish between right and wrong."

The report noted that Neelley complained of being nervous and sleepless because of the pending charges, and that he was moderately depressed about his circumstances. He denied that he was suicidal, but it was recommended nevertheless that he be seen by a local mental health counselor.

For now, Van Pelt decided, he would wait Judith Neelley out.

Shortly after her conviction in Alabama, Van Pelt's strategy paid off. Already sentenced to death, Neelley was anxious to avoid a second death sentence in Georgia. As a result, she quickly agreed to plead guilty to kidnapping and to testify against her husband if the state of Georgia would not press murder charges against her or ask for the death penalty in the kidnapping case. She was sentenced to life imprisonment and returned to Alabama.

Faced with the prospect of Judith's testimony, Alvin Neelley agreed to plead guilty to charges of kidnapping with bodily harm and murder in Georgia if the state would not ask for the death penalty. The state agreed, and Neelley was sentenced to two life terms, the sentences to run consecutively.

On Tuesday, May 10, 1983, Alvin was indicted in Scottsboro, Alabama, for the rape of Lisa Millican.

In 1984 he filed a habeas corpus action in which he declared that because he was suffering from high blood pressure and other medical problems and not feeling well at the time of his confession, the confession had not been voluntarily and freely given. He also stated that his trial counsel had failed to give him competent representation in that he had been coerced into entering pleas at a time when he was unable, because of medical problems, to resist such coercion. In his petition, Alvin said that he had been under the influence of Darvon and thus had not been fully cognizant of the affects of his waiver of a trial by jury. His lawyer, he added, had failed to interview witnesses, refused to subpoena them, and had misrepresented the law. His lawyer had also refused to request a change of venue, investigate the facts, or otherwise provide adequate counsel.

The habeas corpus motion was denied on July 16, 1984.

Alvin Neelley is currently serving the first of his two life terms at the Jack Rutledge Correctional Institute in Columbus, Georgia.

The investigation of Alvin Neelley's many and assorted charges against both his wife and Georgia's Youth Development Centers was begun immediately after his arrest.

Shortly after his initial statement, Georgia Bureau of Investigation Agent Sam House interviewed Kathryn McKenzie, of the Chattahoochee County Sheriff's Office, about any unsolved murders in her jurisdiction. McKenzie told him that there were two such cases on the books. In June of 1982, a female soldier had disappeared on a motorcycle. When her body had been found, it was determined that she had been shot in the back of the head with a shotgun. A second woman had been found dead in Stewart County, her hands tied with wire.

House talked to Deputy Bill House from the Stewart County Sheriff's Office at 3:05 P.M. on October 19. Bill House told him that there were three unsolved murders in Stewart County. In December of 1981, the badly decomposed body of a fourteen-year-old girl had been found tied with wire to three small oak trees. She had been tied at the wrists, shoulders, and thighs. Due to the extent of the body's decomposition, authorities had not been able to determine whether she had been sexually molested. Two months before, the body of a seventeen-year-old girl had been found burned in her house. It was later determined that a clothes hanger had been tied around her throat. In April of 1982 the body of a sixteen-year-old black female had been found, her hands tied behind her back with a bra. She had been taken from her house on the night of March 28.

After investigating each of these cases thoroughly, Sam House determined that none of the crimes was likely to have been the work of either Alvin or Judith Neelley.

In the meantime, a similar investigation conducted by Lew Brendel, an investigator for the Youth Development Centers, found no basis for criminal charges against any YDC staff members based on accusations made by either Judith or Alvin Neelley.

In April 1983, Judith Neelley was returned to Fort Payne, Alabama, from her cell on death row in the Tutwiller Prison for a hearing on a motion for a new trial. The motion was based on a long list of accusations, particularly against Eileen Hargis, the jury foreman, who, French contended, had not paid attention to the trial, had mouthed words to the spectators, and had even sung to herself quietly as the trial progressed. Other specifications included the court's allowing facts concerning the shootings of Hancock and Chatman to be offered as evidence, as well as the testimony of potential kidnap victims in Georgia, the general behavior of courtroom spectators, the unconstitutionality of the Alabama capital punishment law, and even the age and disrepair of the current electric chair.

That same month, an article on the Neelley case appeared in the *National Examiner* under the headline "LOVE SLAVE MURDERS FOR SADISTIC MASTER." The article claimed that Lisa Millican had been "slaughtered" and was peppered with such sensationalistic phrases as "sadistic torture" and "merciless clutches of her lust-driven husband." It was featured on the same page as a piece about Dracula, who, the story declared, was now living in the United States.

According to a later article in the *Fort Payne Times Journal*, this particular issue of the *Examiner* was "selling at a brisk pace" in Fort Payne.

In May 1983, Judith Neelley granted an interview to the *Birmingham News*. The article described her daily routine on death row at Julia Tutwiller, the two-hundred-and-eighty-four-inmate women's prison in which she was incarcerated. According to the article, Neelley took her meals alone, showered each morning in a stall adjacent to her cell, and was allowed a half hour of outside exercise. At those times when Neelley was allowed to leave the prison, the rest of the prisoners were confined to their cells to prevent her from having any contact with them. Draped in a white cotton prison-issue dress and wearing rubber sandals purchased from the prison canteen, Neelley first stated that she was praying not to be electrocuted, then later said, "I don't ask God . . . for me not to be electrocuted. I only ask that if I'm going to be electrocuted, to give me strength to go through it."

On Tuesday, September 6, 1983, Neelley's motion for a new trial was denied.

*   *   *

After the trial, Fay Freeman continued to work in French's office across the street from the Dekalb County Courthouse. She had always had doubts about the wife-battering defense. Despite the fact that she'd worked tirelessly for French in Neelley's defense, Freeman had never been able to dismiss the aura of hardness Neelley exuded, or the way she reveled in her power to charm and dominate the people around her.

In addition, Freeman had seen scores of pictures of Judith and Alvin together by the time the trial ended, and in all but one of them she had looked free and unharmed, nothing more than a girl in love. Still, that single photograph inevitably rose in her mind to support Neelley's tale of brutality and enslavement. It was the picture French had shown to the jury, in which Neelley was incontestably bruised on her thighs, arms, and breasts.

Many weeks after the trial, Freeman tripped in French's office and went sprawling across the floor. While not seriously injured, her body was black and blue. A few days after the fall, she visited Judy in prison, where Neelley immediately noticed the injuries.

"What happened to you?" she asked. "You look all beat up."

"Oh, nothing much," Freeman said. "Just a fall in the office. I just bruise easily."

Neelley nodded quietly. "Yeah," she said, "I'm like that, too."

On March 25, 1984, the following item appeared in the *Fort Payne Times Journal*:

> *A 1980 Porsche 924 was involved in a chase late last week with Dekalb County deputies and the owner, Fort Payne attorney Bob French, says the vehicle was stolen from a garage in Chattanooga.*
>
> *"It's just one more thing," lamented French, who has filed for bankruptcy, "I'm broke and now my car has been wrecked."*

French said officers recognized his car and tried to stop it early Saturday morning. The lengthy chase ended on Highway 75 in north Dekalb County, and two occupants escaped after the vehicle was driven into a garden. The occupants threw a semiautomatic weapon out of the car during the incident.

French said he was asleep at home when officers called him.

During the chase, which involved several officers in Georgia and Alabama, the vehicle crashed through roadblocks and was eventually wrecked.

According to Harper's Body Shop, the car suffered about $1500 worth of damage. The vehicle was expensive, worth an estimated $25,000 when new.

French says the Porsche was not in a running condition when it was left at the garage, and a new motor was to be installed.

On August 11, 1984, a young woman walked into the Murfreesboro Police Department. She said that two days before, in the *Daily News Journal*, she'd seen a picture of the woman who'd kidnapped her in October of 1982. The picture was of Judith Ann Neelley, and according to the young woman, who said her street name at the time of the kidnapping had been "Casey," Neelley had struck up a conversation with her in a mall, then invited her to go riding. Casey said she'd agreed, and that later, while riding together, Neelley had communicated with a man via the CB radio in her car. Neelley had then driven her to the University Inn, pulled a .38 revolver from the glove compartment of the car, and led her into a motel room where an armed man was already waiting.

According to Casey, Neelley had told her that she'd killed another girl in Chattanooga and that she would also kill her without the slightest hesitation. She then ordered her to strip, climb into the bed, and have sexual intercourse with her husband.

Casey told the officer that she'd done what the

Neelleys demanded, and that after the rape Judith Neelley had handcuffed her to the bed. As for the man, he'd simply turned over and gone to sleep.

Judith Neelley had not slept at all, however. Instead, she'd sat down on the bed and begun a long litany of her crimes. She claimed that she'd killed a great many people and that she had newspaper clippings to prove it. According to Casey, Neelley had talked incessantly through the entire night and into the morning in a monologue that had only ended with her arrest, at which time the man had rushed Casey into the bathroom and held her at gunpoint until Judith had been taken away. During the long night's account, however, Judith Neelley had gone to great pains to depict herself as a hardened criminal, Casey said, one who took pleasure in observing the look on people's faces when she held a gun on them and who felt great delight in their terror.

When asked why she'd come forward after seeing the photograph in the paper, Casey replied unequivocally that since the paper had mentioned the possibility of Neelley's release, she had felt an obligation to come forward, because "if there is anything I can do to keep her from being out on the street killing people, then I want to do it."

At just after midnight on June 27, 1985, a full two years and two months after Neelley's conviction in Fort Payne, Danny Smith sat in his car in Murfreesboro and read the four-and-a-half-page, single-spaced transcript of the interview with Casey. "No one involved in the case other than the defense had ever had any doubts about what Judith Neelley had done and why she'd done it," he would say many years later, "but reading that transcript was something else, because she'd never described herself like that to anyone who'd ever lived to tell about it."

During the years following the trial, Richard Igou reconsidered the Neelley case many times, especially

French's passionate defense and its encyclopedic scope. He remembered the ferocity of his opponent's final remarks before the jury, his uncompromising portrait of a lost and terribly brutalized woman. "It would have been a great defense," he thought at last, in words that seemed to sum up his final feelings about the case, "if it had been true."

Over the last seven years, Judy Neelley has filed several appeals to both the United States and the Alabama Supreme Courts. Her latest appeal was a Motion 20 in which she charged, among other things, that she had not received a fair trial due to the incompetence of her counsel.

Thus far, all appeals have been denied.

Judith Ann Neelley is currently awaiting execution at the Julia Tutwiler Prison for Women in Wetumpka, Alabama.

April and Jeremy Neelley, the twins born of Judy and Alvin two years before the murders, have been legally adopted by Jesse Lee Neelley, Alvin's mother, and live in Murfreesboro, Tennessee. A third child, Jason Alvin, born during Judith Neelley's incarceration in Dekalb County, now lives in Nashville. Judith is continuing her attempt to maintain legal custody.

On Tuesday November 7, 1989, Kenneth Kines, forty-five, died of a massive heart attack at his home outside Rome, the recently published autobiography of Ralph Abernathy still open in his lap. The funeral procession that bore him to his grave on November 9 was three miles long. Watching it pass by, John Hancock, now working for a private cemetery service, regretted that he had not had the honor to dig his grave.

FIRST BLOOD

CHAPTER

1

River Road
Seminole County, Georgia

BY FIVE-THIRTY in the afternoon, the smell of scorched gunpowder was thick in every room. No one knew exactly how many shots had been fired, only that the old man had required more than anyone else, rising determinedly from the bed, one side of his forehead already blown open, but rising anyway, as the bullets rained down upon him until he slumped back finally, still breathing, but only for a few seconds more.

Another body lay beside his, thick and husky, the arms made strong by the rigorous farm labor he'd done all his life.

In the next room, a third body sprawled face down across the small sofa, the legs hung over the side so that the feet touched the floor. In the opposite bedroom, two more men lay on a tiny bed, the blue smoke from the pistols still curling out the half-closed door.

With five men dead, the only question that remained was what to do with the woman.

She lay on her back beneath the kitchen table, whimpering softly, but entirely conscious, her blouse pulled over her breasts, her panties in a crumpled mass beside her.

The four men who moved about the trailer hardly

glanced at her as they rifled through the drawers and cabinets and closets, looking for guns and money.

From her place on the floor, it would have been hard to keep track of the men. The tiny windows of the trailer let in very little light, and that was further constricted by the curtains which hung over them. As for the lights inside the trailer, the men had not turned them on, preferring to skulk through the rooms in a gloomy shadow, muttering to each other about their next move, their eyes averted as if they did not want to remind themselves that she was still there, still alive, that there was one to go.

In the end, it was a topic that could not be avoided, however, and they discussed their options quietly while she continued to lie beneath the kitchen table, her eyes combing its low ceiling, or crawling along the walls and windows, lighting from time to time on some little knickknack she'd bought across the border in Florida or in one of the small shops of nearby Donalsonville.

She'd married her husband, Jerry, only a few years before in a ceremony at the Spring Creek Baptist Church, a small wood-framed sanctuary that sat on a shady hill a few miles from the trailer. All Jerry's relatives had crowded into the church that day, the whole Alday clan. Among them: Ned, Jerry's father, dressed in his Sunday best; Aubrey, Ned's brother, beaming from the front pew; Shuggie and Jimmy, the two brothers who kidded Jerry mercilessly, their faces grinning over their roughly knotted ties. All their bodies were with her now, their feet dangling from the beds or off the sofa, their shoes still encrusted with the rich topsoil of their farm.

The strangers told her to get up, and one of them stepped over and jerked her roughly from the floor. He was a short man, hardly more than a boy, with long dark hair that swept over one eye. Earlier, he'd called her a bitch and slapped her while the others looked on, waiting their turn. Then he'd forced her down, first to her knees, then to her back, ripping at her clothes, his hands all over her, his teeth sinking into her breast, breaking the skin, leaving a jagged purple mark.

"Get dressed," he barked.

She'd worn turquoise pants and a matching sweater to work that day, and she put them back on slowly, already exhausted, standing completely still, except for the trembling, while the blindfold was pulled tightly over her eyes, then another cloth stuffed into her mouth.

A few seconds later she was outside, the last light of afternoon pouring over the undulating rows of freshly planted corn and beans and peanuts as they pushed her toward the waiting car.

Once in the car, she crouched down in the back seat floorboard, moaning softly, her knees against her chest, while the one black man among the three white ones held the gun on her, staring silently from over the barrel, his brown eyes wide and bulging behind the thick black-framed glasses.

The car moved in a zigzag pattern for a time, then turned off the road entirely and headed into the woods, its wheels bumping across the rutted ground, weeds and branches slapping noisily at its sides until it finally came to a halt.

In a moment she was outside again, first perched on the hood of the car, like an ornament for the men to gaze at, then on her knees, dragged to them by her hair, and finally on her back again, with the dark-haired man on top of her, the black man watching from above, while the other two moved quickly around and inside a second car, wiping it with brightly colored bits of cloth.

Soon the other two returned to the car, one of them sucking at a bottle of whisky. The other one, blond and lanky, the youngest of them all, stood away, slumped against the back of the car, as if keeping his distance from the others.

She felt the dark-haired man pull himself off her, his eyes now trained on the others. He laughed and nodded toward her, his gaze still fixed upon the other men. "Any of you want some more of this?" he asked casually, as if offering his companions one last sip from the nearly empty glass.

About the Author

THOMAS H. COOK, a native of Fort Payne, Alabama, has won extensive critical acclaim for his ten novels, including two Edgar Award nominations for *Blood Innocents* and *Sacrificial Ground*, and for his true-crime book, *Blood Echoes*. He lives in New York.

Save up to **$400** on **TWA**® flights with
The Great Summer Getaway
Ⓩ from Signet and Onyx! Ⓔ
Look for these titles this summer!

JUNE

EVERLASTING
Nancy Thayer
EARLY GRAVES
Thomas H. Cook

JULY

INTENSIVE CARE
Francis Roe
SILK AND SECRETS
Mary Jo Putney

AUGUST

AGAINST THE WIND
J.F. Freedman
CEREMONY OF INNOCENCE
Daranna Gidel

SEPTEMBER

LA TOYA
La Toya Jackson
DOUBLE DOWN
Tom Kakonis

THE GREAT SUMMER GETAWAY

Save the coupons in the back of these books and redeem them
for TWA discount certificates
(Up to a maximum of four certicates per household).

• **Send in two 2 coupons** and receive: 1 discount certificate
for **$50**, **$75**, or **$100** savings on TWA flights
(amount of savings based on airfare used)
• **4 coupons: 2 certificates**
• **6 coupons: 3 certificates**
• **8 coupons: 4 certificates**

***TWA®*/SIGNET/ONYX BOOKS**
"GREAT SUMMER GETAWAY"

TERMS AND CONDITIONS

This certificate is valid for $50 to $100 off the price of a qualifying TWA® published fare to any TWA destination excluding Las Vegas, Cairo and Tel Aviv. Travel is valid one-way or roundtrip provided the minimum fare is met. Ticket issued in conjunction with this certificate is valid for travel through October 31, 1993. See the chart below for amount of discount.

Purchase a one-way or roundtrip ticket for at least:	Receive the following discount:
$200	$50
$300	$75
$500	$100

Discount cannot be applied to V or T class fares anytime. Discount applies to fares BEFORE application of any departure taxes, customs and security charges, other governmental fees or surcharges not part of the published fare. Travel is valid one-way or roundtrip provided applicable rules and fare minimums are met before discount. Applicable discount will be applied only once to the total fare of the ticket. Only one certificate may be used per ticket issued.

Additional blackouts:

Domestic:	1992:	Nov 24-25	Nov 28-Dec 1	Dec 18-31
	1993:	Jan 1-5		Apr 2-4/8-9/16-19
Additional:	Florida/Caribbean Southbound:		Feb 11-13	
	Northbound:		Feb 20-22	
Super Bowl	To Los Angeles/Ontario/Santa Ana:		Jan 28-31	
	From Los Angeles/Ontario/Santa Ana:		Jan 31-Feb 2	
Mardi Gras	To New Orleans:		Feb 18-19	Mar 26-27
	From New Orleans:		Feb 24-28	
Kentucky Derby	To Louisville: Apr 28-May 1		From Louisville: May 2-4	
Indy 500	To Indianapolis: May 26-28		From Indianapolis: May 31-Jun 1	
International:	1992:	Jul 1-Aug 31		Dec 18-31
	1993:	Jan 1-5	Apr 2-4/8-9/16-19	Jul 1-Aug 31

1. When making reservations advise the TWA agent that you're holding a TWA/Signet $50-$100 discount certificate and provide the source code located on the front of this certificate.

2. Open jaw itineraries and/or additional stopovers may be taken only when permitted by the fare type purchased.

3. This certificate is valid for tickets issued on TWA stock for travel on TWA and/or Trans World Express flights 7000-7999. Travel is not permitted on TWA-designated flights operated by another carrier. Any travel on another airline must be ticketed and paid for separately.

4. Consumer is responsible for transportation to nearest airport served by TWA and/or TWE.

5. Tickets may be issued by TWA or your travel agent. All certificate travel must originate and be paid for in the U.S. Certificates must be presented when ticket is purchased and will not be honored retroactively.

6. Once redeemed for tickets, certificates may not be reissued. Certificates will not be replaced if lost or stolen. No copies or facsimiles will be accepted.

7. Certificate cannot be redeemed for cash or applied against a credit card balance. Certificates are void if sold, bartered or purchased in bulk.

8. Ticket refunds/itinerary changes are permitted only in accordance with the fare type paid. Ticket refunds will be issued only for the dollar amount actually paid TWA for the ticket, less any applicable penalties. When the ticket is wholly or partially refunded, the certificate will not be replaced, and further discounts or upgrades will not apply.

9. Tickets issued against this certificate may not be combined with any other coupon, Certificate, Frequent Flight Bonus award ticket or other promotional offer or upgrade program. This certificate is not valid with travel industry employee discounts, or with special travel programs, such as the TWA Travel Club℠, Senior Travel Pak℠, or Business Flyer Award℠ Program.

10. Use of this certificate for international travel is subject at all times to the applicable laws and regulations of foreign governments and is invalid where prohibited by local law.

Agency Commission: Travel agents receive standard commission on funds actually collected.
The check or money order is to be made out to TWA/Signet Offer for $2.50 postage and handling fee for each certificate ordered (maximum four per household).

Certificate requests must be postmarked no later than December 31, 1992.

Mail to: TWA/Signet Offer
      Box 4000, Dept. P
      Plymouth Meeting, PA 19462